Archival Fictions

A Volume in the Series **Page and Screen**

Edited by Kate Eichhorn

Archival Fictions

Materiality,

Form,

and

Media History

in Contemporary

Literature

Paul Benzon

University of Massachusetts Press

Amherst and Boston

ISBN 978-1-62534-599-8 (paper); 598-1 (hardcover)

Designed by Deste Roosa
Set in Fira Sans and Cormorant Garamond
Printed and bound by Books International, Inc.

Cover design by Deste Roosa
Cover art by ralwel, *Modern Interior Room,* 3D render. Adobe Stock.

Library of Congress Cataloging-in-Publication Data
A catalog record for this book is available from the Library of
Congress.

British Library Cataloguing-in-Publication Data
A catalog record for this book is available from the British Library.

Portions of chapter one originally appeared as "Lost in Translation:
Postwar Typewriting Culture, Andy Warhol's Bad Book, and the
Standardization of Error," in *PMLA* 125, no. 1 (Jan 2010): 96–106,
published by the Modern Language Association (www.mla.org).

For

Sarah,

who

has always

been

there

Contents

Preface

Like many literary scholars, I can chart my personal and intellectual growth through the books I encountered at various stages of life: the first "grown-up" literature I discovered in my parents' living room bookshelves in grade school; the contemporary novels I wandered across in bookstore aisles as a young adult, which mirrored my world back to me in ways I could not have imagined without them; the theoretical texts I discovered in college, which opened up lines of thinking and reading that seemed at once both impossible and necessary. This project builds on all of those texts and moments, yet its true origin point lies in an earlier, less canonical text, Thomas Rockwell's 1973 middle-grade comedy novel *How to Eat Fried Worms*.

How to Eat Fried Worms tells the story of Billy Forrester, who bets his friend and rival Alan fifty dollars that he can eat fifteen worms in fifteen days. Once the bet is set in place at the outset of the novel, the characters proceed through a linear narrative of gross-out meals, family dramas, and petty conflicts typical of the genre. Nearly all of its chapters, some only a page or two in length, cover a single scene, often focusing on Billy's eating his daily worm, with many of the chapters titled as such: "The First Worm," "The Second Worm," and so on. After making my way through the early sections of the novel, I remember becoming uneasy with its middle stretch, not only for the way the tension escalated between Billy and the duplicitous, conniving Alan, but also—and far more so—for the way the novel's paratextual apparatus (although at age eight or nine I hardly knew to call it that) registered that tension. Chapter 23 was titled "Admirals Naumo and Kusaka on the Bridge of the *Akaiga*, December 6, 1941," and subsequent chapters followed the suit of this strangely weighty, Orientalist parallel between the Pacific theater of World War II and elementary school rivalry: Chapter 25 was "Pearl Harbor," and Chapter 26 was "Guadalcanal."

Chapter 29, in which Billy and Alan finally come to blows, was marked in the book's table of contents by what looked to my untrained eyes like a blotch of black and white, an inkblot, a printer's error of some sort on the cheap, pulpy paper of the school library paperback. I briefly considered finding another copy to compare it against—in hopes of finding the "real, actual" title of this pivotal chapter in the narrative—but page ninety-three of the novel, where this title appeared in situ, was larger, more detailed, and clearer in its implications. While I didn't at the time know all of the historical particulars the previous chapter titles invoked, I knew that this one was an image of a mushroom cloud, the atomic bomb detonating over Hiroshima. How was I supposed to read this? The metaphor of explosive conflict was clear enough, if overburdened with geopolitical and racial insensitivity. But how was I supposed to read the image itself amid words— how did it resonate against those words, not only thematically but visually, spatially, materially, textually? What did it mean for a chapter title, a paratextual element that I implicitly understood to be a transparently explanatory label, to swerve so diametrically from conventional protocols of narrative, of typography, of textuality, of codex form? While I didn't have anything like the vocabulary to fully articulate these questions at the time, they took hold in my mind as the first seed of the reckoning with textual experimentation that I pursue in this book.

The media theory I encountered during and after graduate school some two decades later is another. Reading the work of scholars—many of whom appear in this book—who were thinking through the materialities of media formats, from the phonograph to the hard drive, revealed to me the outline of a material poetics in those formats that resonated with how I had by then begun to see literary form. But that poetics was nowhere to be found in critical writing on contemporary literature in relation to media technology. Scholars in this domain largely treated technology at the level of culture—of what it meant in a generalized sense within the imagined world of a given novel or poem—without attention to how it worked or how the text itself might work in relation or response to it. What might a closer, more syncretic attention to those workings reveal—about literary form, about media format, about the relation between the two? Where might we find a media poetics of and in literary experimentation?

Archival Fictions seeks to explore these questions. Bringing the domains of literary form and media theory into contact, I aim to understand what is at stake in moments where literature engages with media technology not in discursive or narrative terms but rather in formal ones, and to suggest how we might read those moments in ways that are sensitive to both literary form and media format. Turning to a series of formally innovative print literary texts from roughly the last fifty years, I focus on instances of experimentation and rupture, where mimesis breaks down and literature as conventionally understood fails and refuses to transparently represent its technological others. My intent in focusing on these moments is not to emphasize literature's shortcomings or limitations in comparison with other media but rather precisely the opposite—to locate a point of departure from conventional critical conceptions of the literary that allows us to turn to type, paratextuality, layout, blank space, and other elements that lie outside of language, narrative, and discourse.

These moments become productively redoubled and overdetermined when the question of literary representation comes to bear on other media forms: when text on the print page not only has to describe or narrate celluloid, vinyl, or silicon but also somehow figure the materiality of those forms through ruptures in its own materiality. The codex book is perhaps the most stable media format in human history—so much so, in fact, that we often see it as transparent to the point of invisibility. Thinking about the materiality of literary form through media theory, we might see that form anew, as being entangled with other technologies in ways that are both more microscopic and more capacious than we might first imagine. In this sense, *Archival Fictions* picks up on a tradition of print formal experimentation that dates back at least to Stéphane Mallarmé's 1897 innovation with typography and layout in *Un coup de dés jamais n'abolira le hasard*, tracing how the contours of that tradition transform within the context of the contemporary media landscape. Looking for ways in which moments of formal experimentation might help us to map that landscape in new ways, I aim to imagine literary textuality itself as its own kind of media format, one that is capable of tracing other technologies across history in ways that are as intimate as they are uneven.

Acknowledgments

This project has been a long time in the making, unmaking, and remaking; I'm grateful to everyone who has been with me along the way and played a role in its development, and mine.

While *How to Eat Fried Worms* might have produced the first sparks of *Archival Fictions*, I took a massive leap into reading the way I do in this book in middle and high school Latin class at Trinity School. Allen Schroeter, Charles Fornara III, Maureen Rayhill, Doug Tobin, and Donald Connor taught me about graphic word order, chiasmus, and synchysis; tracing my pen back and forth across Latin words, I began to see language as material—as having shape and weight, taking up space on the surface of the page. Even though the content of this project is millennia away from the lines of Catullus and Virgil, the methods are, in many ways, nowhere near as distant. My time at Williams College laid further foundations for my work in this project and beyond: I learned how to close read from Bob Bell, how to think the contemporary and the paracanonical from Nico Israel, how to conceptualize the poetics of technology from Tom Murtaugh, and how to read the popular for the political from Kristin Carter-Sanborn.

The first true inklings of what would become this book appeared during my time at Rutgers University, thanks to the support of a group of dedicated, generous teachers, each of whom championed my work in different ways. Richard Dienst was there from day one: with a few comments on my work in his seminar on Deleuze and cinema, he set the course for much of my thinking since about media, form, and format, and always believed—even when I did not—that attending to the preposterous in a text or a problem could uncover what was exciting about it. Brent Hayes Edwards somehow managed to simultaneously meet me where I was in my thinking and be miles ahead, and modeled an approach to treating texts capaciously, generously, and sensitively that I still aspire to. John McClure respected my interests when they seemed eccentric, and challenged me to rein in my thinking when it seemed—and was—outlandish. Marianne DeKoven opened the door for me by encouraging me to write my first-ever seminar paper on graffiti and to submit it to a conference on text and image, and will hopefully be pleased to see that this book turns to Bob Dylan in its closing pages. Cornelius Collins, Rachel Greenwald Smith, Megan Ward, and honorary Rutgers student Sean Grattan kept me as smiling and sane as possible, whether in the seminar room, at Au Bon Pain, on Listserv back channels, or on NJ Transit.

At Temple University, Eli Goldblatt, Keith Gumery, Rachael Groner, and Christine Palumbo-DeSimone welcomed me as part of a community of thinkers and teachers, and I'm grateful for their support, for the collegiality of everyone in the Temple Writing Program, and for the thinking and learning I did with my students there—special thanks also go to Richie's for the late-afternoon/early evening coffee and to all the conductors on Septa and Amtrak who scanned my ticket and left me alone to keep on writing.

I feel lucky to have found a home at Skidmore College; many thanks to Mason Stokes, Susannah Mintz, Beck Krefting, Beau Breslin, and Crystal Dea Moore for helping me find it, and to Katie Hauser and Jeff Segrave for their support and mentorship along the way. I'm doubly lucky to have a wonderful cohort of colleagues in the English Department, the Media and Film Studies Program, and across the college, and to have the chance to talk and think with creative, intrepid students every day. I also thank the Skidmore Faculty Development Committee for granting a sabbatical leave that facilitated the completion of this project, and for their financial support of it.

Over the years I've been working on this project, I've presented various elements of it (as well as a few that didn't make it in) at venues including the Media in Transition Conference, the American Comparative Literature Association Annual Meeting, the International Conference on Narrative, the annual meeting of the American Studies Association, the annual meeting of the Modern Language Association, and the conference of the Society for Textual Scholarship. I'm thankful to the organizers, moderators, copanelists, interlocutors, and audience members at these and other venues for helpful feedback and discussion. I completed crucial work on chapter 5 as a Researcher in Residence at Signal Culture in Owego, New York; thanks to Jason and Debora Bernagozzi for the support, hospitality, and conversation. Portions of chapter 1 originally appeared in the January 2010 volume of *PMLA*; I'm grateful for the journal's permission to include them here.

The academic community of media studies Twitter came along for me just when I needed it most, and gave me an intellectual home that has been invaluable to my development as a scholar, teacher, and academic, both online and offline. I'm grateful to have engaged with and learned from Brian Croxall, Mark Sample, Erin Templeton, Zach Whalen, Kathleen Fitzpatrick, Kathi Inman Berens, Amanda French, Lauren Klein, Matt Kirschenbaum, Jentery Sayers, Jussi Parikka, Lev Manovich, Mark C. Marino, Jeremy Douglass, Jessica Pressman, Shannon Mattern, Lori Emerson, Ben Robertson, Andrew Ferguson, Matt Schneider, Roger Whitson, Leonardo Flores, Amaranth Borsuk, Whitney Trettien, Élika Ortega Guzmán, Andrew Pilsch, and Shawna Ross, to name a few among many. I've gotten to know other colleagues in other ways; I consider myself particularly lucky to have been in conversation with Jim Hodge, Danny Snelson, Rita Raley, Annette Gilbert, and Tyler Bradway over the years I've been working on this project.

Brian Halley at University of Massachusetts Press has been an ideal editor for this project. From our first conversation about the Page and Screen series, he has been enthusiastic, supportive, and patient. He and series editor Kate Eichhorn have both championed and challenged this book, and it is by far the better for it, as it is for the thoughtful feedback that I received from two anonymous readers of the manuscript. I'm also grateful to Rachael DeShano for helping to bring it into the world—from screen to page, as it were—and to Ivo Fravashi for making it cleaner, clearer, and more correct.

My parents gave me my love for reading, and always supported it, even and especially when it took strange detours of the kind that have ended up in this book, and I hope that seeing this in print can pay even a little of that back. My mother never minded too much—or maybe at all—when I had my nose in a book to the exclusion of something else, and my father took me to the New York Public Library on 96th Street to smell the smell of books when I was only an infant; perhaps those moments are the true origin of this project. Ellie and Jack have sat through many books' worth of "Dad Lectures" in good spirit, and it has been one of my greatest joys to see them grow up and become people in the world.

But mostly this is for Sarah, my biggest champion and best friend always, for always talking with me, listening, believing, and walking beside me. So often we have remarked on how these times—this work, this place, these students—are the good years. And that is true; we are lucky in so many ways. But that is not the half of it—with you it is always the good years.

Archival Fictions

INTRODUCTION
On the Undeath of the Book

The endless stream of letters,

the naked factuality of writing as the autoreferentiality of letters,

instead points to a realm beyond letters:

to their Other,

the reality of the technical media.

—Bernhard Siegert, *Relays: Literature as an Epoch of the Postal System*

Those objects that are casually referred to as "media," accordingly,

are perhaps better considered as nodes of articulation along a signifying chain:

the points at which one type of analysis must stop and another can begin;

the thresholds between languages;

the limns of perception.

—Craig Dworkin, *No Medium*

The Kindling of Literature

If the Kindle didn't make it clear enough, the Fire certainly did. Amazon's first e-reader device, released on November 19, 2007, bears a name with a complex constellation of resonances. To "kindle" means to arouse interest, or to excite—a fitting, if perhaps fittingly nondescript, connotation for a new product. Yet of course it also has a more materially urgent connotation as well: the *Oxford English Dictionary*'s first definition for the word, dating to circa 1200, is "to start or light (a fire); to set fire to, ignite (something flammable)."[1] The naming of the Kindle, then, originally promised to ignite not only the interest of potential buyers and readers but also the very object and totem of reading itself—the book, a flammable, vulnerable, persistent mass of paper and ink. And in the unlikely case this first name was too subtle, Amazon's 2011 introduction of the Kindle Fire, a multimedia tablet known since 2015 simply as the Fire, made it all too glaringly clear: if Amazon named digital culture's first major e-reader in order to imagine the initial kindling of the book, it named the second in order to suggest the book's wholesale incineration.

Abstraction and materiality intertwine here in complex ways. The Kindle and the Fire are technologies whose cultural resonance is inseparable from the metaphors that give them their names. Yet these metaphors paradoxically demand to be taken seriously—in their apocalyptic, incendiary resonances, conjuring the smoldering, ashen end of the book in the shadow of the digital, they speak to the material imaginary of the literary object, and thus also to how the book and other storage formats, both analog and digital, might imagine their shifting relationships with one another across time.

In this sense, then, these appellations are part of a longer history of speculative imagination in which thinkers from a range of cultural vantage points have envisioned cultural and technological change around the book in extreme terms—if not in outright incineration, at least in death. Whether as tragedy or as triumph, the death of the book in the face of digital media has been a recurrent literary and cultural concern since at least Robert Coover's 1992 essay "The End of Books." Coover's reflection on the place of print-based literature in an increasingly electronic landscape articulates a concern about the obsolescence of the print object in the face of new media that in turn dates at least back to Thomas Edison's 1878 list of potential uses for the phonograph, a document that imagines the replacement of various print forms—dictations, family records, and indeed books themselves—with recorded sound and voice.[2] As Leah Price puts it, "Every generation rewrites the book's epitaph; all that changes is the whodunit."[3]

These recurrent cultural anxieties that the book is dying imagine technocultural change in overly binary terms, taking on more than a little of Amazon's incendiary rhetoric, and a number of recent engagements with the intermedia history of the book have worked to complicate this narrative.[4] Indeed, it is worth noting that across nearly a century and a half, these prophesied deaths have all been partial, irregular, uneven—closer to undeaths, as I suggest in the sections and chapters to come. Most digital literary reading happens not within the nonlinearity, multimodality, and interactivity of hypertext that Coover imagined would render the print codex obsolete, but rather on the surface of e-readers such as the Kindle and its competitors, devices that largely constitute something closer to a print book onscreen than to widespread, wholesale textual interactivity.[5] Literature in the digital age has then become, in many cases, print literature onscreen—the codex, at once both burnt and resurrected in the handheld space of the Kindle. If the Kindle interweaves obsolescence, persistence, and renovation in complex, uncanny ways, what then becomes of the print book, the codex form of bound paper? How might we see it, too, as productively and critically intertwined in these strands of temporality and technology? If the Kindle captures one moment of technological and textual transition on the surface of its screen, what moments might the print book capture on the surface of its paper? How might this material structure serve as a testing ground for representing and responding to the emergence of digital technology, or indeed to any other moment of technological change?

This study explores how the print book reckons with these questions, sifting through its own figurative ashes across the late twentieth and early twenty-first centuries in an attempt to reimagine contemporary media ecology and its place within it. The technological imaginary made visible by the metaphors of the Kindle and the Fire suggests a rich speculative landscape in the space where metaphor verges on the material. There is more at stake in this imaginary than simply the fate of the book: beyond the stakes for any single medium, it provides a space for the destabilization of historicity around media technology more broadly. In *Archival Fictions*, I study how literary authors represent and respond to this destabilization as a means of coming to terms with the larger sweep of media history. Tracing literary reckonings with new technology, I argue that literary authors who experiment with form and materiality imagine a larger history of nonlinear, discontinuous media change; attending to the media poetics of literary form, then, allows us to see modern and contemporary media history—and the place of the book within it—in new creative and speculative ways.

On the (Un)Bookish Book and the Archive as Fiction

The argument I make on behalf of literary form and formal reading in relation to media technology in *Archival Fictions* opens up a series of questions at the intersection of literary and media studies: How do cultural and material forces such as obsolescence, ephemerality, and distortion shape our understanding of media history? How do literary authors situate their works and practices in relation to these forces? What does it mean for contemporary authors to reflect on literary texts as devices of mediation, and what role does literary form play in this treatment? In attending to these questions by placing a series of experiments in form alongside the material protocols of different media technologies, *Archival Fictions* diverges from many earlier studies of literature and media, which focus on media technology as a generalized cultural condition manifesting largely at the level of narrative. I turn instead to the question of how literature engages with materiality through form, an approach that provides new insight into the historical and historiographic dynamics of literature and technology across a crucial period of media change. Considering charged moments of textual experimentation alongside material histories of technological phenomena ranging from protocinematic toys, vinyl records, and midcentury typewriters to the circulatory mechanisms of the Internet, I offer a methodology for reading contemporary print texts as media artifacts that self-consciously model a new history of media change defined by partiality, ephemerality, recursion, and uneven development. Most significantly, then, *Archival Fictions* contributes to the fields of literary studies and media studies by arguing that their approaches might interweave and function together in intimate, microscopic ways: reading the poetics of literary and technological objects through one another, this book locates a new critical approach to media history within the uncanny material imaginary of print literary production.

The literary texts I consider here largely resemble—at least in their external surface materiality—any conventional codex from the modern era of mass printing. They are rectangular, bound collections of physically intact pages. While my stating this might seem to be dwelling on the obvious, I maintain that it is crucial to distinguish these texts from those that experiment physically with the book as an object: Marc Saporta's "book in a box" *Composition No. 1*, for example, with its 155 unbound pages that can be read in any sequence; or Jonathan Safran Foer's *Tree of Codes*, an appropriation of Bruno Schulz's *Street of Crocodiles* whose pages are punctuated with holes, creating a new narrative through material absence; or Mark Z. Danielewski's *House of Leaves*, an encyclopedic novel whose complex, proliferating narrative threads are interwoven with a dizzying array of experimentations in layout, type, color, and space on the page.[6] Jessica Pressman characterizes texts such as these as "bookish," bodying forth a "fetishized focus on textuality and the book-bound reading object." For Pressman, bookish books "exploit the power of the print page in ways that draw attention to the book as a multimedia format, one informed by and connected to digital technologies. They define the book as an aesthetic form whose power has been purposefully employed by literature for centuries and will continue to be far into the digital age. . . . [C]ontemporary works that employ an aesthetic of bookishness present a serious reflection on the book—and the literary book in particular—through experimentation with the media-specific properties of print illuminated by the light of the digital."[7] While my critical approach shares much with Pressman's concerns here, the books I examine in *Archival Fictions* are not bookish. Their reflection on the medium specificity of print and of other technologies is, for the most part, more oblique than in bookish texts such as those Pressman considers or those that I have enumerated as examples above, an approach befitting their longer media-historical outlook (indeed, only one of the print texts I discuss bears directly on the digital).

Each chapter of *Archival Fictions* situates its analysis of a literary artifact within a theoretical and material framework informed by the technological objects, affordances, and infrastructures that characterize a specific moment in media history. In chapter 2, for example, I read the imagined phonographic materiality of Kevin Young's book-length poetic text *To Repel Ghosts: Five Sides in B Minor* against the history and materiality of phonographic inscription. Contextualizing Young's work within the histories of the phonograph and the book, I read his formal strategy as a reflection on the relations between different modes of storage—analog and digital, codex, disc, and drive—across a complex, nonlinear history of media. Similarly, chapter 4 considers what the book might reveal about the history of the Internet through form. Situating the formal breaks and disruptions in Hari Kunzru's novel *Transmission* alongside the global history of undersea data cables, I show how Kunzru raises the question of digital history through the breakdown of the Web on paper. Tracing how these texts render media objects, technologies, and protocols through text on the surface of the page, I argue that they reflect on the book not only in order to think about its place within the media landscape but also to think about that landscape itself across time, subversively turning the material and formal trappings of the codex against themselves in order to imagine other technologies. As in the claim by Bernhard Siegert that serves as an epigraph to this introduction, in the texts I discuss "the autoreferentiality of letters . . . points to a realm beyond letters: to their Other, the reality of the technical media."[8] Thus literary experimentation provides a means for thinking speculatively and theoretically in relation to media technology and media history: imagining the materiality, protocols, products, and other elements of other technologies through formal experimentation on the surface of the page, the authors I consider in *Archival Fictions* trace an uneven history of media change through formal and technological discontinuity. In this sense, they imagine what it might mean for books not to be bookish, but rather to be vinylish, filmish, cabelish, and so on. These terms are admittedly unwieldy neologisms; they lack the preexisting connotations of the bookish. Yet that is precisely their value—the unwieldiness of these terms bodies forth the disjuncture, incompatibility, and discontinuity on which these texts, and *Archival Fictions* itself, hinge. Just as the text of a print book on a Kindle both is and is not the same as the print book itself, the literary texts I explore in *Archival Fictions* do the uncanny work of testing and probing how literature both can and cannot represent and render the workings of other media forms. In terms of Amazon's incendiary textual devices, the condition of literary and technological materiality that these print texts imagine is not a question of burning or ignition, life or death, nor is it a burning and then a reignition—rather, it is both at the same time, inseparable, a duality that imagines a third possibility.

This dynamic, ambivalent, deeply unstable imagination is central to my labeling of these texts as archival fictions. I use this term to signal something different from and more complex than the literal fact that these texts largely consist of narrative prose that takes up questions of the archive. While some of the texts I discuss, such as Don DeLillo's *Running Dog* or Kunzru's *Transmission*, can indeed be classified as fiction, others cannot—Young's text, for example, which might be better described as a serial poetic collection, or Andy Warhol's documentary novel *a*.[9] Yet over and above the taxonomic question of whether any single text here can be generically categorized as fiction or not, archival fictions collectively take up questions of the archive *as* fiction. This is not to say that archives and their bearings on history and knowledge are themselves fictions—indeed, quite the opposite—but rather that the texts I consider here approach the idea of the archive as a site for speculative, imaginative work. In this sense, archival fictions as I define them engage with questions of media and the archive—questions of mediation, of inscription and transcription, of format, storage, erasure, and circulation—through the work of literary form, imagining a media poetics through text on the page.

In foregrounding the literary in this distinction, I acknowledge that I am situating myself within a group of scholars in the humanities who have focused critical and theoretical attention on "the archive" as a concept rather than on archives themselves as concrete entities as understood by practicing archivists and scholars of archival studies. Archivists and archival studies scholars understand archives as "collections of records, material and immaterial, analog and digital . . . the institutions that steward them, the places where they are physically located, and the processes that designated them 'archival.'"[10] Humanities scholars, by contrast, approach the archive as a theoretical concept, a touchpoint for a constellation of questions and issues around mediation, inscription, and memory that has its origins in Jacques Derrida's 1995 *Archive Fever: A Freudian Impression.*[11] These two strains of scholarship are largely parallel and distinct: as Michelle Caswell succinctly puts it, "'The archive' is not an archives"—that is, the concept is different and distinct from the physical entity—and the theoretical work of Derrida and those writing in his wake, myself here included, is thus not archival studies, but rather an intervention in relation to the humanistic questions I invoke above and discuss in depth within the chapters that follow. Kate Eichhorn notes that such humanistic consideration of "the archive" has addressed questions of "politics, desire, longing, death, memory, history, and [the] list goes on . . . in lieu of grappling with the material questions that archival practices invariably raise."[12] While *Archival Fictions* grapples with the materiality of various media formats and technologies—things that are characterized by their capacity to record, and that might be included in archives as records—it ultimately does so along lines that are still grounded in the domain of humanistic inquiry rather than in the province of archival scholarship and practice proper; the materiality that these literary texts traffic in is largely speculative, or at least confined to the surface of the printed page. Thus *Archival Fictions* offers an exploration of how literary texts might engage questions of medium, inscription, and record through a materially inflected attention to form.

In this sense, archival fictions engage the theory-fiction of the archive along the lines of Matthew Kirschenbaum's use of the term. Kirschenbaum writes that "Derrida's 'archive' (granted the force of that definite article) was [not any archive that actually existed but] instead what we might see as a theory-fiction, that is an imaginary, a projection, a trope that made the 'question' of the archive usable—consumable—for theory work."[13] Just as Derrida creates the theory-fiction of the archive in order to make certain abstract questions legible, usable, and consumable, the texts in *Archival Fictions* hinge on smaller-scale theory-fictions: their literary workings model theories of recording, storage, inscription, erasure, and other technological processes, projecting those processes onto print text as a way of rendering them at least partially consumable. At times, certain of them engage specific media records and documents, whether real or fictional—the imagined LPs that constitute the paratextual structure of Young's *To Repel Ghosts*, for example, or the clerical output of the postwar typing pool in Warhol's *a*. Yet more frequently and pervasively, they engage the theory-fiction of the archive more broadly, reckoning with the archive fever of particular media texts and technologies—including but not limited to that of the book—and attempting to make the material contours of information and its storage and transmission visible, even if they never make it materially graspable. Indeed, the texts I consider hinge on this intangibility, this status of the archive as a fiction within a fiction. As much as they insist on material specificity as a way of reimagining media materiality, they also render that specificity fugitive, slipping and sliding through the filter of the paper page and the discursive, alphabetic forms that it stores. In doing so, they seek to redefine and redirect how we imagine that materiality: their underlying project is a historiographic one, using formal experimentation not only to write new fictions around media but also to sketch new ways altogether of writing those fictions.

Form, Affordance, Format: How the Book Writes Media Poetics

As suggested by the impressionistic and experimental approach to media history and the theory-fiction of the archive that I sketch here, I take it as axiomatic in my selection of texts for this study that it is impossible to think the materiality of media fully and effectively through solely narrative, thematic means. Previous waves of scholarship have explored the relations between literature and media in narrative terms: texts such as Joseph Tabbi's *Postmodern Sublime: Technology and American Writing from Mailer to Cyberpunk* and John Johnston's *Information Multiplicity: American Fiction in the Age of Media Saturation* situate contemporary literature about technology within a rich historical and, in some cases, technological context, treating a range of key authors such as Thomas Pynchon, Joseph McElroy, Don DeLillo, William Gibson, Philip K. Dick, and Neal Stephenson.[14] While critical works such as these provide a necessary foundation for the study of contemporary literature and media, they largely focus on media technology as an abstract, generalized cultural condition manifesting at the level of narrative—in this sense, they frame the field in terms of fictions *about* the archive, but not in terms of fictions *of* the archive.

In order to confront more fully how the poetics of the archive bears on literature, literary scholars need to reckon more fully with the materiality of literary form. Thus in *Archival Fictions* I turn to a set of literary texts that utilize form as a speculative tool. My approach to form as a literary means for imagining media technology and writing media history builds on the new formalist turn in literary studies exemplified by the recent work of Caroline Levine. For Levine, form is "much broader than its ordinary usage in literary studies," encompassing "all shapes and configurations, all ordering principles, all patterns of repetition and difference," everything from literature to architecture to social structure.[15] Just as literary categories such as the sonnet or the realist novel have formal characteristics, so does a skyscraper, or a political system—or, more to the point for the concerns of this study, a vinyl record, or a transoceanic cable, or a codex book. Levine adopts this broad definition of form because it offers scholars access to form's highest stakes. "Forms," Levine writes, "are the stuff of politics"—and also, as I will suggest, the stuff of history and historiography, an often untapped language for both writing history and reflecting on that writing.[16] This political valence arises in large part from her consideration of affordances, a concept she borrows from design theory to "describe the potential uses or actions latent in materials and designs[:] . . . both the particular constraints and possibilities that different forms afford, and the fact that those patterns and arrangements carry their affordances with them as they move across time and space."[17] Attending to affordances, Levine suggests, allows us to turn from the direct and literal efficacies of a text to the underlying discursive possibilities of its structure: "Rather than asking what artists intend or even what forms *do*, we can ask instead what potentialities lie latent—though not always obvious—in aesthetic and social arrangements."[18] She offers the issue of gender in Thomas Hughes's Victorian novel *Tom Brown's Schooldays* as an example of how affordances shape the form of a literary text, focusing not simply on the text's representation of questions of gender, but rather on how the form of the novel itself serves as a tool for thinking gender, its own affordances working in conversation with the affordances of gender as a form.

This interchange exemplifies her understanding of "fictional narratives as productive thought experiments that allow us to imagine the subtle unfolding activity of multiple social forms."[19] As Kirschenbaum demonstrates, the concept of affordances also speaks in particularly illuminating ways to media technologies, both digital and otherwise: "Like the vertical filing cabinets of a previous era, contemporary information storage devices have distinct affordances that contribute to their implementation and reception. . . . Attention to the affordances of various kinds of storage media can reveal much about computing in different contexts, allowing us to reconstruct salient aspects of now-obsolete systems and the human practices that attended them."[20] Thus just as the novel has specific affordances, so do storage media, both the digital ones that Kirschenbaum studies (the CD-ROM, the hard drive, the floppy disk) and their analog antecedents (the vertical filing cabinet he mentions here, but also the record, the celluloid film reel, the precinematic flip-book, and a range of others across history). Attending to the affordances of different media technologies, as he suggests, whether they be from the present or the past, offers us a thicker vision of their historicity, of their working operations and the protocols and infrastructures surrounding them. These visions, in turn, serve as hinge points for imagining a new history of media technology.

Archival Fictions expands and deepens the implications of form and affordance as conceived by Levine and Kirschenbaum by treating the print book itself as a thought experiment, putting it in conversation with a range of other modern and contemporary media technologies with their own material forms and affordances. Indeed, Levine's expansion of the category of form provides a particularly useful foundation from which to consider form in relation to materiality: we might logically extend her argument to suggest that thinking media form (whether through literature or otherwise) is inseparable from thinking media materiality. Thus *Archival Fictions* situates print literary textuality at the juncture of Levine's and Kirschenbaum's thinking, asking how the formal affordances of print literary inscription (rather than of narrative, poetry, the novel, or another literary genre) shed new light on the affordances and historicity of media technology. This self-referential friction around form challenges us to look beyond print literature's linguistic and generic affordances (as in the "fictional narratives" Levine focuses on in *Tom Brown's Schooldays*) to ask questions of its material and technological ones: How does the storage medium of codex-based print writing think the form of another storage medium through its own form? How can the affordances of the book—its paper, the way its pages marshal ink and blank space, its pagination, indices, and so on—imagine the affordances of drastically different storage media? Each of the texts I discuss in *Archival Fictions* uses form to unpack the working operations of its own print textuality in dialogue and intersection with other media operations: transcription, distortion, playback, deletion, circulation, and so on. Lisa Gitelman writes, "The histories of genres and the histories of media don't so much overlap as they intersect, constituting partial and mutual conditions for one another."[21] Along these lines, *Archival Fictions* treats the genre of the archival fiction as imaginatively constitutive of and constituted by a range of differing media technologies, and thus also as simultaneously constitutive of and constituted by a multithreaded, nonlinear media history.

Jonathan Sterne's concepts of format and format theory provide a means for tracing the intersection Gitelman describes and situating the formal and historiological work of archival fictions within it. As Sterne writes, format exists as a kind of subcategory within a given medium, the term denoting "a whole range of decisions that affect the look, feel, experience, and workings of a medium. It also names a set of rules according to which a technology can operate. . . . The format is what specifies the protocols by which a medium will operate." For example, a vinyl record player might play a range of formats—the 33 1/3 rpm LP, the 45, the 78—"while a tape deck might only take [the single format of] compact cassettes," whereas the medium of digital audio encompasses formats such as the MP3 (the titular focus of Sterne's analysis), the .wav, .rm, .wma, and so on.[22] Sterne's call for format theory invites us to map the media landscape with a more granular, microscopic specificity, an invitation that *Archival Fictions* takes up in turning from literature's narrative engagements with media to its formal representations and responses to media—from one format of the literary page to another, as it were.

Indeed, just as media studies needs to map the theories, histories, and poetics of different media formats in the way that Sterne suggests, *Archival Fictions* sets out to map the literary format that gives it its name, and thus to argue for it as a specialized subset of print literary writing. Because the rules and operating protocols of a given format "are not publicly discussed or even apparent to end-users," Sterne writes, "they often take on a sheen of ontology when they are more precisely the product of contingency."[23] If, as Sterne suggests, we often see media formats as opaque, might we say this about the literary codex or page as well? Perhaps literary writing is both a genre—a set of discursive conventions and contracts with the reader— and a format, a set of protocols for the physical and spatial deployment of text on the printed page. If we imagine as much, it becomes possible to see that the texts I categorize in this project as archival fictions engage in a kind of textual and formal experimentation that imagines other modes of contingency, other operating protocols for the format of the book and the page in relation to other technologies.

Imagining the page in terms of format thus opens onto a complex play of materiality, signification, and dialogue among media forms. As Bonnie Mak argues, "[T]he page . . . is not always what we may think it is."[24] *Archival Fictions* works in the spirit of this provocation in order to consider literary format in relation to other storage technologies, tracing how "the page transmits ideas, of course, but more significantly influences meaning by its distinctive embodiment of those ideas. . . . The architecture of the page is thus a complex and responsive entanglement of platform, text, image, graphic markings, and blank space. The page hosts a changing interplay of form and content, of message and medium, of the conceptual and physical."[25] The authors I discuss in *Archival Fictions* work to destabilize that interplay and expand its scope around other technologies, seeking new ways in which the page can embody meaning, new ways of formulating the conceptual through the physical, and new ways in which one medium might speak to and of another through its own protocols.[26] Writing of the MP3, Sterne describes this last quality—the interplay of message and medium—as "*mediality* (and *mediatic* in adjectival form) . . . *a quality of or pertaining to media* and the complex ways in which communication technologies refer to one another in form or content."[27] *Archival Fictions*, then, explores the mediality of the literary page and its related formats (the codex, the line, the paratext, etc.) within the contemporary media ecology: the complex ways in which their form, content, and format are in dialogue with those of other technologies.[28] In the context of mediality, format takes on a doubled connotation. It invokes both the formatting of page design (itself a term derived from digital layout workflows) and the form factor of hardware design, referring to the physical specifications of objects ranging from hard drives to portable computers to mobile phones. Thus the format of the mediatic page signifies for a contingent relation among materiality, design, and inscription, a figurative protocol for how the spaces of the page and the book might be managed and marked.

In order to explore the relations between print literary forms and formats and media-technological ones seriously and deeply, I attend to radical, experimental manifestations of form in the literary texts I consider in *Archival Fictions*. My approach to the relations between form and medium here takes its cues from the work of Craig Dworkin, particularly his focus on "the politics of the poem." In contrast to the politics through the poem and the politics in the poem, the politics of the poem inheres not (or at least not only) in discourse, content, or thematics, but rather in "what is signified by [the poem's] form, enacted by its structures, implicit in its philosophy of language, how it positions its reader, and a range of questions relating to the poem as a material object." For Dworkin, attention to the politics of the poem serves as the basis for the radical formalism he sees as necessary to thinking the political in meaningful ways: "[T]he closest of close readings *in the service of* political questions, rather than to their exclusion."[29] While Dworkin's use of the term focuses primarily on poetry as a genre (albeit in his terms a capaciously and radically defined one), here I expand his thinking as a means of examining the politics of form in any work or moment of literary experimentation—a politics of the text *as* text, so to speak. Here again the distinction I draw from earlier literary and literary-critical engagements with media technology and politics is crucial:

while those texts engage media on the level of narrative content—the media and politics in the text, as it were—archival fictions engage the media and politics of the text. Indeed, in the case of the texts I discuss in this project, this engagement of the text is redoubled: archival fictions not only think media politics through literary form but also think media form through literary form as a way to think media politics.

Viewed in the context of technologies beyond writing, the formal-material politics of the poem that Dworkin describes also sets the stage for an extreme poetics of mediation at the moment where signification becomes material. Writing of such a poetics in the context of blank media in *No Medium*, he imagines words as material: "If words, conventionally, are thought to clothe thought, they also . . . cover the page." Here Dworkin traces the duality of words as language and as inscription; on the surface of the page, textual signification becomes visible as material, layered, and dimensional. Likewise, the marking of the page through text reveals "the substrate as a formal device."[30] Here the surface and space of the page provide a ground of convergence between form and format, where the materialities of language, paper, and text reverberate against one another, illuminating a textual imaginary that bears on other media as well. Diverging from the linguistic focus of Derrida's work, Dworkin writes of this imaginary, "The point then is not so much the play of presence and absence that has animated studies of inscription, but rather the recursive realization that every signifier is also itself a sign."[31] The textual and formal play of archival fictions, then, both depends on and refigures the surface of the page as a material format and a media object—within these texts, form serves as a lens for imaginatively interrogating format, mediality, and media history.

These interrogations are significant both in spite and because of their seemingly minor condition. Indeed, rather than the directly physical manipulations enacted by many of the authors Pressman categorizes as bookish, the authors I discuss deform and experiment with the book more microscopically, at the level of the word, or the space of the page, or even the alphanumeric character. As Dworkin's attention to form suggests, authors destabilize and reimagine these inscriptive traces as material on paper in order to present alternate conceptions of media technology and media history. On one hand these manipulations are nothing more (yet also nothing less) than speculative, largely imaginary in their relation to materiality, print or otherwise—another dimension of the fictionality of archival fiction. Yet on the other they are, in this speculative condition, radically mediatic: engaging media technology and media history neither through narrative representation nor through wholesale reimagination of the book as object, they instead inhere within the liminal space of the document, where discourse becomes formalized and materialized, and where literary inscription operates both with and as technology.[32] Thus *Archival Fictions* inquires into how literary form, which in its most extreme conception we might consider the materiality (both imagined and otherwise) of writing itself, represents the mediality and materiality of media technology. As alphabetic marks gloss the working protocols of the typing pool, or undersea fiber optic networks, or the LP record, veering asymptotically close to these other storage formats but never able to become them fully, those marks sketch new ways of thinking about writing, about media technology, and about writing the history of media technology. The question of form, then, appears in *Archival Fictions* not as a question of generic character but rather at other levels of scale and scope—as the connective thread of a media poetics that entwines inscription, materiality, format, affordance, technology, and historicity.

Nonlinear History and the Undead Book

Through formal experimentation, the authors I discuss in *Archival Fictions* position print writing as a means for understanding contemporary media technologies in terms of radical material effects such as error, erasure, distortion, disintegration, and disappearance. My framing of media poetics across this project in terms of inexactitude and loss is deliberate, and crucial to how I conceptualize both mediality and media history through these texts. After all, a literary text can never fully represent, say, a vinyl record or a frame of film, much less "be" those things, even discursively—hence the uneven concepts of these books as vinylish, filmish, and cableish mentioned above. Yet this, I argue, is precisely the goal of these works: rather than a transparent representation, the authors I discuss imagine technology through the formal and material friction between the discursive and the nondiscursive, the moments where the textual verges on the nontextual. In keeping with this friction, the texts I discuss here imagine media history speculatively and elusively, along indirect lines, and the trajectories of technological change they sketch through formal experimentation are uneven, nonlinear, and recursive, taking shape in the image of the technological materiality and mediality they foreground. Cracking open these moments in order to reveal glimpses into an alternate constellation of media history, my approach in *Archival Fictions* is multidirectional: I read experimental literary texts through the lens of recent critical work in media theory and media poetics, and at the same time show how experimental literature itself engages in media-theoretical inquiry through its self-conscious interrogation of literary form. In doing so, I show how media theory and media poetics illuminate literary texts—indeed, how we might read those texts as imaginary media artifacts themselves—and also how those texts themselves offer a kind of media theory, poetics, and history through form. As a structure for this multidirectional analysis, each chapter of *Archival Fictions* situates its analysis of a literary artifact alongside the objects, affordances, and infrastructures that characterize a specific moment in media history. The book opens with three chapters that pose questions of analog media materiality to print literature, while the final two chapters pivot to examine how literary experimentation engages the formal, material, and historiographic relations between print and digital media. Each of these five chapters concludes with a coda that reconsiders the central questions of the chapter through a work of media art or media culture connected to the central text of the chapter.

In keeping with the material extremities I note above, the uneven, recursive trajectory of technological change is a key dimension of how the texts I discuss in *Archival Fictions* model media history. Many of the technologies I discuss here, such as the vinyl record, the typewriter, and celluloid film, are technically obsolete, and the most temporally contemporary technology, the undersea cable, is effectively largely unseen. Yet with the exception of the protocinematic toys I discuss in chapter 5, it would be hard to label any of these as fully forgotten or unrealized. On the contrary, they continually appear and reappear in uncanny, partial ways, whether via nostalgic reclamation, remediation, residuality, or some other process. Fitting this temporality, the authors I consider imagine technology in moments of transition and instability: film as an imminently obsolescent format in the late 1970s culture of DeLillo's *Running Dog*, for example, or the office typewriter at the peak of its 1960s popularity, just before its precipitous decline, in Warhol's *a*. The literary texts of *Archival Fictions* register these macrohistorical moments of change through microscopic moments of technological dysfunction manifested in literary form: the typewriter's embedding of error within text, for example, or the combustible vulnerability of nitrate film. Thus form becomes the ground on which these authors chart a media poetics shaped by the breakdown of technology, but also of teleology. These texts place material categories such as inscription and storage under pressure; their formal breaks reveal not only technology's material instability and indeterminacy but also a profound dysfunction at the heart of linear historiography.

This dysfunction is not unique to the case of media history by any means, but it becomes particularly charged and overdetermined in that case. As Gitelman notes, "[M]odes of inscription are complicated within the meaning and practice of history, the subjects, items, instruments, and workings of public memory. Inquiring into the history of a medium that helped to construct that inquiring itself is sort of like attempting to stand in the same river twice: impossible, but it is important to try, at least so the (historicity of the) grounds of inquiry become clear."[33] The problem Gitelman outlines is not only one of existing and persisting within history but also one of simultaneously struggling to record that same history. As technologies of inscriptive storage speculatively historicizing other technologies of inscriptive storage, the codex books I discuss in *Archival Fictions* keep one foot in this river and one on a riverbank that is itself always already unstable. Their authors, in looking so microscopically at the instruments and artifacts of modern and contemporary media technology—consciously attempting the futile task of representing these objects rather than narrating them—self-consciously foreground the impossibility of that representation. The lack produced by this impossibility serves as a productive catalyst, as literature's capacities for recording and inscription become distorted in friction against other technologies of recording and inscription. Seizing on this lack rather than resisting it, bending and torqueing their text under the pressure of other technologies, the authors I discuss imagine new media-historiographic possibilities for the book, and thus new modes of critiquing, reinventing, and otherwise mobilizing media technology through the book.

What, then, does the formal redrawing of technological history that these literary authors imagine mean more broadly? As I traced at the beginning of this introduction, the book has been labeled dead many times across its history at the hands of many successors, seemingly "killed" not just by electronic textuality or digitally networked communication but also by earlier technologies such as the phonograph, film, and its technological precursors that I discuss in chapter 5. It remains in circulation and relatively unchanged in material terms in comparison to the media landscape around it, yet this persistence does not mean we should think of it as "not (yet) dead" or as "still alive." Rather, my argument in attending to the uncanny historiographic work of literary experimentation is not that the book remains culturally relevant—not, as Pressman suggests, that "literature retains a central role in our emergent technoculture as a space for aesthetic expression and cultural critique," although the texts I consider do engage in that expression and critique.[34]

On the contrary, *Archival Fictions* argues that the book is neither still alive, as Pressman argues, nor dead yet, as Coover suggests, but rather somewhere both in between those two poles and also wholly elsewhere—that it is, and has long been, undead. To exist as undead is to remain perpetually interstitial and untimely, at once both suspended and unstable, troubling the most fundamental binaries through which we understand temporality, mortality, materiality, and history. Media theory has long concerned itself with specters and supernatural entities of various sorts as metaphors for understanding and historicizing technology.[35] The book is no different as a technology: it retains the importance Pressman attributes to it precisely because of its undeadness, rather than in spite of it. In its untimely condition, undeadness has a great deal to tell us about media history and about how we imagine that history. It is, for a media form such as the book, inseparable from the capacity to think technological and historical change in critical ways; the undeadness of print materiality exists interdependently and recursively with historiographic experimentation of the sort I discuss in *Archival Fictions*, both producing and produced by it. Rather than arguing for the book's continued relevance within a new media landscape—whether that landscape be one of the 1890s, the 1960s, the 1970s, or the 2000s—the authors I study here work to dismantle and reorder the history of that landscape on the surface of the page, remaking it through the irregular, uneven image of the book.

CHAPTER ONE
Lost in Transcription

Postwar Typewriting Culture, Andy Warhol's Bad Book,
and the Standardization of Error

With pens and typewriters you think you know *how* it works,
how "it responds."
Whereas with computers,
even if people know how to use them up to a point,
they rarely know, intuitively and without thinking . . .
how the internal demon of the apparatus operates.
—Jacques Derrida, "The Word Processor"

To understand the typewriter as a freestanding, independent technology of textual production, as the alpha and the omega of a certain kind of quintessentially modern writing, is at the same time to reconceptualize the material, technological, and textual dimensions of that writing. The typewriter is, of course, the ancestor of the personal computer; it is the first technology designed for individual engagement in what contemporary culture commonly understands as word processing. Early adopters of the technology understood the pivotal importance of this self-contained capacity. Mark Twain, writing in 1874 about one of the first widely available commercial models, compared the machine's capabilities to manual typesetting, the practice of arranging individual type characters in order to produce a body of printed text. Typewriting's production of text on the fly, as it were, reminded Twain of a typesetter who "used to set up articles at the case without previously putting them in the form of a manuscript."[1] This self-contained spontaneity meant that a person using the typewriter could, like the typesetter before him, "compos[e] as he composed ([setting] type as he thought up his article.)"[2]

Lisa Gitelman's pun on composition in describing the innovations brought on by the typewriter succinctly captures how it reconfigured what Bonnie Mak terms the "architectures of the page," shaping in new ways the page's complex material meaning "constituted of both—and more than— form and content."[3] This individualized writing machine placed the writing body into immediate contact with the means of producing a standardized, seemingly "finished," type-based text. In doing so, it radically compressed the process of textual production from its previously protracted form under the technological regime of the printing press, effectively allowing the initial aesthetic practice of creation and the final material practice of inscription to take place within a single event of composition, to use Gitelman's language. At the same time, by lending a greater air of material permanence and finality to spontaneously produced text, the typewriter also rendered writing subject to the possibility of error in a newly redundant fashion. Transpositions of letters, stray characters, accidental repetitions, and other textual anomalies were at once both easier to produce and harder to remove. Equally importantly, in the corporate and clerical environments in which it would eventually take hold in greater numbers than in any other context, the typewriter brought the writing body into contact with other bodies and other machines in complex configurations that intermingled chaos and control. By the mid-twentieth century, the corporate office had become a distributed network of textual production intended for the dictation, recording, replay, and transcription of information. Within this recombinant textual ecosystem, bureaucratic, technological efficiency and dispersive textual uncertainty swirled together as two co-constitutive forces.

This chapter pays close attention to media history and literary experimentation in order to develop a material media poetics of typewritten error. Like vinyl records and celluloid film, the technologies I discuss in the subsequent two chapters of *Archival Fictions*, the typewriter was a dominant technology for much of the first half of the twentieth century and then disappeared or obsolesced relatively recently and suddenly; its position within media history is uncanny and unstable. Thus my attention in chapter 1 to the relation between standardization and error that the typewriter sponsored at the microscopic textual level is also an attempt to engage the more macroscopic cultural and historical tensions that gather around its inscriptive mechanics: How does the typewriter embed error in the practice of writing, and how does that embeddedness shape clerical and literary practice? Conversely, what might it mean to imagine those practices as defined through their relationship to error? Most broadly, what can textual error tell us about technological history?

Two dominant narratives of the typewriter as a writing machine persist within the contemporary cultural imaginary. The first of these is the popular fantasy of the machine as an ornament and tool of authorial subjectivity. This narrative is visible in literary urban legends such as the claim often attributed to Ernest Hemingway that "there is nothing to writing. All you do is sit down at a typewriter and bleed"; the free-flowing improvisation mythologically associated with Jack Kerouac's infamous typescript for *On the Road*; or the aura collected around William Gibson's use of a manual typewriter to write the science fiction novel *Neuromancer* and, allegedly, all of his subsequent novels. Each of these stories is only partly true at best: the aphorism attributed to Hemingway is actually a corruption of a line by sportswriter Walter Wellesley "Red" Smith; Kerouac's unbroken, spontaneous 120-foot scroll of type was actually the product of seven years of planning and organization; and while Gibson did indeed write *Neuromancer* on a manual typewriter, he has not used such a machine in over thirty years.[4] Yet the veracity of these legends matters far less than the way in which they function to instantiate a popular narrative of the Great Man wedded to his Great Machine as a means of self-expression within—and distinction against—the dominant technoculture of his moment: the tortured avatar of the Lost Generation cryptically plumbing the depths of mankind's self-destruction, the King of the Beats tapping rhythmically in search of freedom in the shadow of postwar conformity and the Bomb, the father of cyberpunk prefiguring the future of digital technology from an emphatically exterior position.

The work of the German media theorist Friedrich Kittler poses the strongest and most critically prominent counterthrust to the romantic nostalgia for the author present in this popular narrative of the typewriter. For Kittler, who opens *Gramophone, Film, Typewriter* with the totalizing announcement that "media determine our situation," information technologies shape not only the parameters of aesthetic representation but also the very conditions of human subjectivity, ultimately profoundly distorting and evacuating both dimensions: "Once the technological differentiation of optics, acoustics, and writing exploded Gutenberg's writing monopoly around 1880, the fabrication of so-called Man became possible. His essence escapes into apparatuses."[5] In more specific terms, writing via the typewriter similarly constitutes for Kittler the end of writing as such. In moving writing out of the (allegedly) organic individual literary space of the study and into the mechanized public multiplicity of the modern office, typewriting precipitated what Kittler views as the inexorable rise of the computer and the subsequent digitization of all meaning: "For mechanized writing to be optimized, one can no longer dream of writing as the expression of individuals or the trace of bodies. The very forms, differences, and frequencies of its letters have to be reduced to formulas. So-called Man is split up into physiology and information technology. . . . World history comes to a close as a global typewriters' association. Digital signal processing (DSP) can set in."[6] Kittler sees handwritten text as a sensuous trace produced by the body's close contact with paper, a tissue woven by the hand and the stylus. By removing the individual hand from paper and replacing this bodily trace with discrete, standardized characters produced by machines—and, frequently, by complex networks or strings of machines—typewriting effectively eliminates the writing subject in Kittler's mind. Once writing is merely "a new and elegant tautology of technicians," those technicians in turn become inseparable from the machines they use to produce text. Thus Kittler compiles "a register of the literary desk couples of the century," groupings of textual laborers ranging from Henry James and his typist Theodora Bosanquet to Adolf Hitler and his staff of stenographers.[7] He sees these collaborations as constituting data processing rather than aesthetic production: "Mechanized and materially specific," he claims, "modern literature disappears in a type of anonymity."[8] In his dramatic rereading of modern literature, Kittler seeks to make a strategic claim on our conception of the literary under the sign of modern information technology. In his estimation, much as we still exist within living bodies but are no longer human, books continue to be produced and consumed through media technology but no longer consist of the "philosophical dreams of infinity" that characterize literary language.[9]

Kittler's critique of the rise of information technology paints a picture of a deeply deterministic posthumanism, one that has been productively countered by a range of critics.[10] Yet in its totalizing stance, it paradoxically raises a provocative question that strikes at the heart of modern inscription:

What would a literature written wholly by the modern office look like? What would it mean for the typewriter—not the unique, solitary typewriter of the heroic author, but rather the multiplied, networked typewriter of the office transcription system—to be an integral, palpably present factor in the production of the textual content of literary writing? What would it mean, in other words, for the physicality, interpersonal distribution, and transcriptive error that are intrinsic to the typewriter as a writing system to be similarly intrinsic to the writing of literary text?

Taking these questions as points of departure, the poetics of typewritten error I develop below is intended (among other things) as a rejoinder to the Kittlerian narrative of epistemic technological foreclosure at both the micro- and macroscopic levels. If Kittler sees the typewriter as the first writing technology to operate as an opaque, dehumanized black box, preceding and prefiguring the computer, while Derrida, in the epigram that begins this chapter, sees it as perhaps the last "knowable" technology before digitization, I argue that a better understanding unfolds its chronological position toward something more epistemologically and historically complex than either of those approaches. Indeed, the mechanization and standardization of writing through the typewriter are forces that are as internally disruptive, fragmentary, and recombinant as they are reductive, if not considerably more so; moreover, in tracing these effects at the level of individual textual characters, we see their reverberations across how we understand the history of writing technology. Writing on the typewriter in the postwar period was undoubtedly marked by some of the standardization noted by Kittler. Yet this seeming predictability of the act of writing, visible in both the predetermined flatness of the typewriter's textual landscape and the highly structured institutional systems of mediation that surround it, produced undecidability and aesthetic tension rather than negating it, opening the way for a complexly discontinuous textual poetics.

Typewriting produces text in a manner that is historically and technologically distinct from both the writing systems that preceded it—stone tablets, manuscript writing, moveable type—and those that followed it— word processor, smartphone, digital tablet. Allowing not only printers and typesetters but also novelists, poets, and secretaries to compose while they composed, the typewriter was arguably the first technology to produce finished text in real time through fixed spaces on the surface of inscription rather than through manually written characters or electronically coded binary information. In doing so, it also dramatically transformed the shape and scope of the textual output produced in American culture. By allowing for both the relatively easy production of finished text and the relatively easy duplication of that text, the typewriter sponsored an exponential proliferation in textual production, described by Richard N. Current, a midcentury historian of the typewriter, as "swell[ing] tremendously the output of recorded words." According to Current, "Duplicating in earlier days, except of course on the printing press, was tedious, slow, and altogether unsatisfactory. . . . Meanwhile duplicates of typewritten material were being made by means of the old letterpress, or a gelatin pad, a lithographic stone, or carbon paper. The carbon paper was sometimes coated on both sides . . . and in that way as many as thirty copies could be produced at once."[11] The contrast Current draws between the information landscapes of American media culture before and after the rise of the typewriter is perhaps most illuminating in terms of the light it sheds on the emergence of a new kind of institutional textuality. Indeed, whatever textual explosion took place as a result of the typewriter occurred not within the kind of readerly public sphere made possible by the early modern emergence of the book and print culture or the kind of massively networked public sphere of the Web but in business and bureaucracy, precisely the kinds of social domains that would require thirty copies of the same individual loose document.

Thus while the sociocultural change instigated by the typewriter was smaller in scale than that instigated by the printing press or the Internet, the context of this change was itself crucially new and different. While the typewriter was certainly usable for personal letters and literary pursuits, its technology was particularly suited to forms, tables, and official correspondence, mechanical documents whose proliferation produced an uncanny new form of information overload by way of replicability. Current notes of this replicability that "[t]he ready multiplication of documents saved time and labor, but it also added to labor and wasted time. . . . Before [the introduction of the typewriter], records were relatively scarce. After, they piled up by the thousands of tons." While Current's overtone of an epistemic, almost quantum break in the scale of textual production is probably an exaggeration, the strange, null-set feeling of time and work gained and lost through the typewriter's proliferation of documents in duplicate, triplicate, and beyond speaks volumes (pun intended) to its implications for inscription more broadly. As Current himself notes, this shift in scope was a historiographic issue as much as one of daily lived experience: after those thousands of tons, "the historian's problem became not how to find [records] but how to find his way through them."[12]

Error provides a back-door entry into this question of mechanized inscription. It complicates how we read the textual output of modern writing technologies, and at the same time places pressure on how we understand the historical and cultural conditions of possibility that shape the emergence, dominance, and obsolescence of those technologies. Archival problematics such as the one Current describes above are always simultaneously quantitative and qualitative: exponential shifts in the amount of textual production—of documents, copies, records, and papers—cannot help but bring about corresponding shifts in the terms for understanding and navigating that textual production. Thus it is precisely because of this problematic that error became so central to the textual culture of the twentieth century; indeed, the rise in documents and the rise in errors are inseparable and co-constitutive. As a textual effect, error became discretely present in a new way through the human-machine negotiation of textual space introduced by the typewriter. Attending to that presence at both the microscopic and macroscopic levels sheds new light on the shape and limit of the technologically structured writing of the twentieth century. Understanding error as a central characteristic of that writing—a characteristic, moreover, that is almost always erased, overwritten, or otherwise suppressed from the published version of a text—reveals its opaquely material secret history as a record of irretrievable and indeterminate relations between multiple bodies and machines. While the typewriter declined in cultural prominence fairly rapidly following the rise of the personal computer, error complicates, disrupts, delays, and defers its trajectory toward the forgotten. Indeed, focusing on error allows us to recover what is unique and irreducible to typewriting within what is precisely most often overlooked about it. Each error on the page, each mark left unremoved, unerased, and uncorrected, opens up a media-historical detour in miniature. It offers an alternate account of the configuration of body, machine, substrate, and text that points away from both the foreclosure of Kittlerian posthumanism and the positivism and progressivism of neoliberal corporate technocracy. If we account for the persistence of error, of textual detritus and leftover, as irreducible within the textual output of the typewriter, it becomes possible to see it as a device that continually embeds its own overlooked history with each stroke. In reading that history, we have the opportunity to retain as permanent that which we often see in the postindustrial textual moment as subject to a profoundly positivist ephemerality, and as thus in need of correction, replacement, and concealment. Thus we find in the microscopic textual dissonance of typewritten error a collection of momentary marks that, in their uneasy tendency toward oblivion, stand as uncanny doppelgangers for the very technology that produces them.

In the discussion that follows, I focus on three specific domains of error within the history of the typewriter as a way of constelling such a lost history at both the micro- and macroscopic levels, tracing a poetics of inscriptive affordances and of marks on the page that are irreducibly present but almost inevitably, willfully forgotten. I begin by outlining the place of error within the specific spatial and textual circumstances introduced by typewriter technology across the twentieth century. My discussion traces the relations between error and erasure in midcentury typewriting education and then turns to office structure and labor dynamics in the post–World War II moment. I show how discussions of mailability, materiality, and pedagogy helped to frame error as a crucial factor in the historicity of typewritten text, and how the place of the typewriter within modern office space was bound up with a complex routing of information. This routing simultane-ously regimented bodies and machines and destabilized them, connecting them with one another in a flexible network of textual production that paradoxically solidified error as part of the inscription process. My second site of inquiry is Andy Warhol's 1968 novel *a*, an avant-garde text that relies on typewritten transcription to rehearse and explode the circumstances of the modern office. By placing a radical pressure on readability through the novel's constant stream of unedited, unproofread, spatially irregular transcription, Warhol interrogates the position of the typewriter in order to raise questions about the role of physical presence, contact, and accident within the multiply mediated writing of the postwar period. I conclude with a discussion of the contemporary performance group the Typing Explosion. The Typing Explosion consists of three women who work in silence as an assembly line using vintage typewriters to produce what they describe as "poetry on demand."[13] I show how the Typing Explosion offer in their work a deeply historiographic reexamination of the relations between gender, technology, and poetic expression within late capital culture in ways that establish a critical dialogue across time between the typewriter and contemporary digital writing machines. In each of these three situations of typewriting, humans and machines engage in a manner that is neither wholly collaborative nor wholly dictatorial on the part of either entity but is instead marked by the irreducible possibility of error. This mode of inscription bodies forth both the textual complexity of the typewriter's mechanized inscription protocols and the historical complexity of its place within the writing technologies of the twentieth century.

Deformations of the Page, Assemblages of the Office: A Poetics of Error and Erasure

Structured and standardized through the keyboard, the typewriter builds error into the act of writing. In contrast to the more open writing systems that precede and follow it in history, writing by typewriter is a process of largely irreversible selection from a limited set of options present within the predetermined space of the keyboard. In part because of the ways in which constraint shapes its affordances, error and accuracy have been vexed issues since the early years of the machine. The Remington upstrike machine used by Twain and other early commercial adopters stands as a paradigmatic example of these issues. As its name suggests, rather than its typebars striking downward onto paper in a manner open to the eye of the typist, the upstrike machine struck upward from below, concealing the impact of inscription from view. Gitelman notes that this technology was "a black box: work entered, product emerged. What happened in between may have seemed mysterious to some and self-evident to others, but it was not a public or a human matter, only a secretarial and technological one. The machine's upstrike design seemed to refute the possibility of error, however unrealistically, and in removing the act of inscription from the human eye seemed to underscore its character as a newly technological and automatic event."[14] As Gitelman's description suggests, the error-free pretense of these early machines was ironically inseparable from realities of design that made them all the more prone to error. Indeed, the visibility of subsequent frontstrike technology became a primary selling point as an alternative to upstrike machines "because of the nature of writing, not typing, or at least because of the nature of error, not success."[15] Thus even the more correct and visible frontstrike format was typographically successful only in the sense that it emulated writing in terms of its greater potential for accuracy, or at least changeability. The broader persistence of error, by contrast, became a governing axis in how the body and the eye related to the machine across its history.

Indeed, twentieth-century typewriting discourse imagined error as irreducible from and inherent to typewriting, a sort of necessary evil of the increasingly textual workplace. In their 1960 manual on teaching typewriting, Allien Russon and S. J. Wanous open a chapter titled "Typewriting Errors and Corrective Measures" with the claim that "[e]rrors in typewriting, like taxes, are always with us, no matter what our philosophy of education may be. . . . [T]he problem of errors creates a serious dilemna [sic], and obviously something must be done about it."[16] Within the Taylorist operations of the emergent modern office, authorities on typewriting and typewriting instruction saw error as a breakdown in the pathway between source, mind, body, machine, and paper, the result of one of "a great number of fairly complicated psychomotor adjustments" taking place incorrectly.[17] Different authors in the literature on typewriting education offer a range of different taxonomies of error. Frederick Lyman Wells's 1916 study divides errors into four orthographic categories—"omissions, substitutions, transpositions (metatheses) and additions"—thus highlighting the textual end product itself as the central site of error, while Russon and Wanous divided the results of a 1926 study of sixty thousand errors by D. D. Lessenberry into three major categories of error taking place at the juncture between fingers and keys: "(1) errors made by striking the adjacent key, (2) errors made by striking the home key [a key in the center row of the main area of the keyboard] instead of the key above or below, and (3) errors made by a general confusion in the use of vowels."[18] While both of these systems are spatially determined, their shared emphasis on the writing subject rather than the material constraints of the machine as the source of responsibility for error is worth noting. Jane Clem similarly emphasizes the typist as the source of error, grouping errors under "three general heads: errors of mind, errors of motion, and errors of machine. A small percentage of the errors made by typists are errors of machine. Typists are not machines and are, therefore, more capable of error than a typewriter."[19]

Yet if to err is (at least primarily) human, it is the distinct property of the typewriter to retain those errors. Whereas the autocorrection software of computer word processing would be quick to transpose the text "hte" or "teh" into "the," an uncorrected typewritten document retains these strange, defamiliarizing strings of characters. In doing so, it marks not only the technological limitations of the typewriter's capability for self-correction but also the specific, instantaneous confusion in the timing of the fingers that preceded and produced the error. Indeed, precisely what massive error studies such as Lessenberry's seek to capture is a kind of mechanical shadow history of the typing body, a totalizing history of all possible errant bodily movements over the space of the keyboard. While "hte" and "teh" are superficially reducible to the same semantic meaning—a mistyping of "the"—each of them nonetheless records a different series of movements in space and time. These recordings, moreover, are insistently opaque encodings, as opposed to the automatically resolved marks of word processing or the ambiguous marks produced by handwriting. They provide a trace that is palpable, but not fully comprehensible; even taken as a collection, the taxonomies above cannot account for every possible or actual error.

While most typewriting and business educators agreed that error would inevitably appear within typewritten documents, thus necessitating that typists learn how to erase and correct, the process itself of correction raised complex questions of inscription and historicity, adding a further layer of dissonance and disruption to the already unstable materiality of typewritten text. Perhaps the most primitive and immediate method of type correction is typing over an error with a string of x's and retyping the intended word so that, for example, "hte" becomes "xxx the." Yet the correction this action provides is a vexed one at best: it marks the error in a double, palimpsestic fashion, recording the process of covering the error rather than making it disappear from the page. Modern business culture considered such an effect permissible in private, "personal-use typing," where "the work is designed only for the typist's own reading," but not in documents intended for a more public circulation.[20] Given the textually conflicted history that cancellation simultaneously masked, recorded, and reproduced, wholesale erasure was often a more desired mode of correction. In the discourse of twentieth-century typewriting and typewriting education, erasing was understood not just as a technical and textual necessity but indeed as a complex skill to be mastered through practice, the subject of full chapters in many texts and much debate across the field, attesting to how complex and material a practice erasure was understood to be. In a 1969 typewriting manual, for example, Leonard J. West notes, "Ease (speed and quality) of erasing depends on at least three things that have nothing to do with stroking proficiency: quality of the paper erased on, use of the right kind of eraser for that paper [a standard disk-shaped eraser for regular use or a soft eraser for erasing on thin paper or removing the marks of an erasure], and darkness of the typewriter ribbon."[21]

Here in the banalities of mechanical affordances and workplace protocols, in the semantics of how to parse the stages of typing text, we find a multilayered inscriptive aporia. Errors were perhaps the most discontinuous and defamiliarizing elements of any typed document, yet also often the most ephemeral; conversely, erasure was intended to render both error and itself invisible, literally absent from the record, yet it nonetheless inevitably left visible traces except when performed absolutely perfectly. Given that an individual typewritten document might be discarded, rewritten, duplicated, and otherwise iterated any number of times in various ways, the complex circuit of error and erasure casts a long shadow over how such iterations might shape the totality of textual production, and what they might mean in turn for larger questions of inscription, substrate, authorship, and textuality. Indeed, the deceptively clean, error-free status of the final version of a given typewritten document constitutes a kind of epistemological deception at the level of the microscopically bibliographic. Russon and Wanous felt that "[s]tudents should know that employers are more concerned with mailable typing in offices than they are with the numbers of erasures made. In fact, if the erasures are not noticeable, they may be assumed to be nonexistent."[22] This last sentence posits an uncanny double negative: the paradox of unnoticeable, nonexistent removal stands as an unstable hinge not just of the mailability of a given document (whether it is effectively "clean" enough to circulate publicly) but indeed of its deeper materiality, its historicity, the place of the substrate in its discursive meaning, and the very nature of its layered condition as a document. If we cannot see error—or at least the evidence of its removal, its absenting from the page—that error effectively does not exist within the finished document, and for some eyes never existed to begin with. Perfectly removed from the document, it disappears from its history and memory as well. Yet so many educators writing on typewriting give so much attention and concern to erasure as to suggest that it is nearly impossible to perfect, posing an inscriptive impossibility that bends and circles back on itself: to be removed from view, errors must be erased; when erased, they disappear not only from the document but from history altogether; yet such an erasure can never fully take place.

Thus the typewritten page functions as a palimpsest not only in its visible text but also in its blank spaces, characters and whitenesses layered over each other in an invisible record of inscription. In the closing lines of the final full chapter of *Scripts, Grooves, and Writing Machines*, Gitelman argues, "The newest immediate aspect of [modern] textuality was probably the sound of blank space, as the spaces between words and lines of type had to be created, rather than simply 'left' blank as they were in the production of handwritten pages. In typewriting, space on the page was *made* as well as *used*: writing newly involved 'writing space.'"[23] Such spaces were written through error and erasure as well as through the simple movement of the carriage: viewed through the lens of error and erasure, each space on the typewritten page stands as a potentially infinite accretion of marks that no longer exist, removed from the space and time of the document.[24] Matthew Kirschenbaum describes the "peculiar nature of electronic objects" as inhering in "their remarkable staying power and their fugitive abandon."[25] In the paradoxes of typewritten error and erasure—in the ragged materialities of the page, at varying turns ink-bled, carbon-copied, crumpled, smudged, pristine—we find an analog ancestor of the peculiar textual condition Kirschenbaum sees within electronic information, an earlier instance of inscriptive affordances shaping textual production. In a manner that is precisely contradictory to its intended end, erasure persists as often as it disappears, and through this persistence, so too remain the traces of error. The moment of error, then, stands as an inscriptive crux between the typewriter's permanence and its erasability, between the uniform iterability of text printed on the fly and the irregular idiosyncrasy of each and every stroke, each and every random, mechanical character on the page.

If individual character spaces were each microscopic sites for the embedding of error within the process of typewriting, the structure of the modern office itself was the macroscopic counterpart to those spaces. Inseparably wedded to the typewriters that populated it, the office functioned as a space in which the errors produced in the act of typing could potentially be corrected, but could also be reinscribed, retained, augmented, multiplied, and circulated. Thus the mode of textual production present in the office is dramatically different from that present in the image of the Great Man author, or even in the similarly common situation of the dictating author and his (often female) amanuensis. The synthesis of standardization and instability that the typewriter concretized and made visible is perhaps the defining characteristic of the modern office.[26] Changes in the demographic makeup and the technological infrastructure of the office over the course of the second half of the twentieth century further intensified this tension within the office and the texts that it produced. Gender was a pivotal issue in the interpersonal dynamics of the modern office, and there has been increased scholarly attention in recent years to the question of women in secretarial and office positions and to the relation between women and type-writers in particular.[27] Much of this critical work has framed the emergent presence of women in the twentieth-century office in terms of control and resistance, and this conversation has provided important context for my thinking here. However, rather than pursuing these terms as such, my aim here is to build on this existing work in order to show how the configuration of typewriters and bodies in the postwar office managed information in a manner that was unstable and highly indeterminate, setting in play a constantly shifting politics of inscription. Indeed, as the structure and staffing of the postwar office population changed, the mistransmission of information became possible at every step of textual production and at every level of power.[28] The protocols of writing in the office were highly standardized: one office-management handbook from 1947, for example, dictates that paper should move through the office "entirely in a forward direction," with "no turning back or criss-crossing."[29] Yet the actual process of textual production, the configurations of typing bodies, and other office arrangements could be more complex and heterogeneous, changing sometimes hourly, as well as over longer periods of time, depending on fluctuations in staffing and workload.

The multiple technologies of transcription available in the office compounded the complexity of these interpersonal transcriptive relations.

Executives could dictate material in person to a stenographer or typist or to a dictation machine for later playback. Gitelman describes the office's distributed network of composition as one instance of "the interval between authoring and inscribing, an attention gap that could variously contain authoring agents and inscriptive means. . . . In business typing the interval between authoring and inscribing became cluttered with a variety of possible means, the stenographer, dictaphone, or tentative rough draft that joined the skill and gender of the typist, the engineering and design of the typewriter. Typing didn't create the gap, it only called new attention to it, prolonging and stylizing it in new ways, complicating intention, adapting and supplementing the logic of the hand and pen and telegraph."[30] Indeed, this clutter of machines and bodies exponentially increased the possibilities for error and mistransmission with every new sequence of transcription and every new connection in such a sequence, shaping and reshaping text through a complex constellation of gender, authorship, and technological affordance. Each time a given document was dictated, read aloud, read from shorthand notes, typed, retyped, copied, revised, corrected, or otherwise transmitted among the office's network of authoring bodies and machines posed a potential opportunity for textual deformation. This complex, nonlinear trajectory of inscription, transcription, erasure, correction, and duplication was designed to produce professional, "finished" copy but in reality could not help but generate a discontinuous collection of discards, drafts, and misstarts alongside each "finished" document.

Within such a context, error serves as the evidentiary mark of a process of textual production based not on any individual author's style or level of linguistic or technical proficiency, nor on any single moment within the course of textual production, but rather on the movement of information through multiple different physical spaces, registers of authority, power dynamics, and technological mediations, multiple spaces in the open clutter of the office's inscriptive interval. At both microscopic and macroscopic levels, the systematization of textual production that inhered in the typewriter and elsewhere in the office molded written text in ways that often refused that systematization and reversed its effects. Perhaps the greatest evidence of this destabilization is the opacity of error, the way in which a given instance of error points the way toward a document's textual history yet simultaneously refuses a clear narrative of that history. In the final typewritten iteration of any given document, it is impossible to trace the specific impact of the office's variously complementary and contravening forces or to relate them to previous or subsequent samples. Each document produced by the typewriter, each piece in the massive corpus of postwar corporate inscription, exists as the unique result and record of an individualized sequence of body-machine interfaces and technological marks. While a given document's particular errors might help to differentiate it, they can never fully clarify or contextualize it, instead offering up a history by way of a kind of textual negative, an inverse image of the final text defined by that which is simultaneously left uncorrected and left out.

From *a* to A and Back Again: The Alphabetics of Transcriptive Form

Andy Warhol's *a* revels in the aesthetics of error, the duality of the left uncorrected and the left out. Warhol's novel both rehearses and explodes the affordances of the modern office as a system for producing text. It purports to be comprised of twenty-four hours of conversations among the members of Warhol's Factory studio, taped by Warhol with a portable cassette recorder, transcribed on typewriters by four women, and published as a constant stream of unedited, unproofread text.[31] In turning to *a*, I intend to provide a diagnostic example of how literary writing might seize on the simultaneous persistence and ephemerality of typewritten error in order both to create art from the inscriptive affordances of the modern office and to deploy that art toward a broader inquiry into the materiality and historicity of the typewriter as a writing system.

The typewriter is a central (if often invisible) force within much of modern literature, a subject for some authors (T. S. Eliot's "typist home at teatime" in *The Waste Land*, for example, or Mina Harker's secretarial transcriptions in Bram Stoker's *Dracula*), a source of inspiration for others (perhaps most famously James in his later years), and undoubtedly a de facto means of production for countless others.[32] Most literary texts that engage typewriting do so at a narrative or thematic level—through attention to what, to modify Craig Dworkin's framework, might be described as the typewriter in the text. Warhol's novel, by contrast, hinges on the typewriter of the text, using the machine not only to narrate, theorize, and perform its own effects within literature but also to record the transcriptive work of the typewriter as literary material in and of itself.[33] The novel is not the product of a single authorial typewriter, but rather the product of a complex typewriting authorial network. It offers an aesthetic capture of the operations of the modern typing office, a blank polyphony that documents the bodies and machines of the office in their own dissonant idiom. At the center of this system is the ambiguity of error and the alternate textual trajectories it points toward: by retaining mistranscription, misspelling, misattribution, and numerous other forms of error in the text of a novel, Warhol makes the limits of typewritten transcription visible within the domain of the literary.

With its disjointed, syntactically difficult narrative, its thematic concern with information technology, and its profoundly technological mode of production, *a* sits at the intersection of two artistic trends of the late twentieth century, drawing on both the discursive, formal, and ontological play of high postmodernist fiction and the reproductive, found-art images of postmodern pop artists such as Roy Lichtenstein, Robert Rauschenberg, and Warhol himself. Indeed, *a* generates a number of characteristically postmodern textual effects—what Brian McHale describes in terms of "'alloverness,' a flood of stimuli all of equal importance, lacking hierarchy or syntax" and "deliberate nonfluency: the construction of sentences so awkward (to the point of ungrammaticality) that it is the sentence-structure itself that fixes the attention"—not through singular human authorship but rather through precisely the same sort of technological focus that underlies the mass production used to produce visual art in Warhol's Factory studio.[34] Additionally, *a* shares its concern with media technology not only with Warhol's visual work but also with the work of a number of formally experimental postmodern writers, including but not limited to John Barth and William S. Burroughs. In this sense, its highly mediated formal experimentation stands in almost diametrical opposition to Jack Kerouac's approach to the typewriter as a transparent conduit in the writing of *On the Road*. *a* replaces the "spontaneous bop prosody and original classic literature" of Kerouac's novel with the prerecorded "aimless conversation and waiting around" of the Factory, posing a sort of typographic bookend to "the long sixties, extending from the late fifties to the early seventies" that Marianne DeKoven sees as the timespan for the emergence of the postmodern.[35]

However, the techniques that Warhol's novel employs are subtly yet crucially different from both the literary strategies of these authors and Warhol's own visual strategies. *a*'s mode of production replaces the reproductive work of the Factory's silk-screening with the transcriptive work of an office within that Factory; these techniques involve neither the overdetermined technical constraints used by Barth nor the randomized cut-up and fold-in techniques used by Burroughs, but rather something in between and outside of both categories.[36] Indeed, Barth and Burroughs draw on a tradition of literary technique rooted in the 1960s avant-garde and the experimental inventions of high modernism. *a*, by contrast, locates aesthetic innovation and friction in the collective banalities and accidents of the typing office, producing experimentation from the preexisting circumstances of clerical labor rather than from literary conceit. Viewed along these lines, it participates within a genealogy of what Alan Liu calls "destructive creativity," in which "the office . . . becomes the target of iconoclastic art" via "a destructivity that attacks knowledge work through technologies and techniques internal to such work."[37] Although *a* avoids the directly oppositional approach Liu imagines, the dissonance it reveals within the typewriter system might nonetheless be seen as a similarly internal critique of the practices of technologized information labor, drawing connections between the working protocols of the literary and the clerical. Indeed, what is at stake in this critique is not just the politics and power dynamics of knowledge work in the modern office or the subversive poetics of the typewriter as an artistic machine but also the very notion of the transcript and the archive themselves—the local history produced by the technology, and with it the global history of the technology. By saturating one of the typewriter's most common products (the office document) with one of its most common and unique but also most commonly erased textual effects (the error) Warhol imagines both the novel and the transcript as dysfunctional textual histories, and in doing so imagines print text as a substrate for recovering and remembering forgotten textual and technological moments.

The text of the novel, originally presented with very little contextualizing information and demarcated only by breaks indicating different sides of the tapes used and irregular labelings of speakers, is a highly discontinuous document at all levels. The layout of the text shifts forms at random, words are misspelled and seem to be left out on a fairly frequent basis, punctuation is irregular, and indications of who is speaking come and go and change format without explanation. The narrative of the novel, such as it is, is equally disjointed, with a constantly changing mass of characters gossiping, listening to music, taking drugs, and traveling around New York City without any larger direction. Warhol himself, who goes by the alias of Drella in the novel, remains largely laconic and even silent for long stretches, while Ondine, the star of Warhol's 1966 film *Chelsea Girls*, dominates much of the conversation that makes up the novel's text. *a*'s narrative events often invoke the media system surrounding the text and the Factory in general. Indeed, the work of the Factory seems to be less the production of art objects (even in the Warholian sense) than the mediation of information; the novel's narrative of "aimless conversation and waiting around" is, more specifically, a narrative of waiting—often in vain—for information and media technology to arrive clearly and concretely. Many recurring plot elements, moreover, center on ways in which mediation is absent or nontransparent: Ondine and Drella miss the delivery of a video camera at the Factory; Ondine leaves a beloved record by the opera singer Maria Callas behind in his travels; and various characters misdial phone numbers or are answered with busy signals ("I just dialed the hospital again and I got information," one unattributed voice tellingly complains).[38] In foregrounding the instability of information as it moves across the networks of the Factory and of contemporary media culture more generally, these events resonate and converge with the novel's formal confusions, producing a text in which the mistransmission of information at the level of narrative is often itself mistransmitted at the level of inscription and transcription.

Given how *a* tests readerly stamina and aptitude without offering much in the way of traditional literary compensation, critical reaction to Warhol's novel at the time of its publication was for the most part predictably harsh. While some reviewers saw the novel as having merit in its implicit claims about language,[39] most dismissed it outright: a critic for the *New Yorker* called it "a totally boring jumble," and Sally Beauman's review for the *New York Times* critiqued the book's documentary project as an authorial failure to generate narrative development or even readerly interest.[40] Beauman saw *a* as Warhol's imposition on the reader to "struggle through the 451 pages of Ondine; at the end we will be left, like [Warhol], with just . . . Ondine." She objected to the novel's mediated construction as much as to its central character: "Ironically 'a' is not ultimately even realistic. Most of it—I suspect because the tapes didn't pick up connecting pieces of conversation—is incomprehensible snippets and gobbets of talk. Because Ondine's brain seems irretrievably addled with amphetamine, most of what he says takes the form of grunts, squeals, and bad puns. It's frightening to think one can be bored by this sort of willful self-destruction, but one can. On film, Warhol's people live; they evoke responses; pruned down to a transcript they lose all identity, they all sound alike, they evoke nothing, not even compassion."[41] Reactions such as these make clear the readerly expectations of comprehensibility and narrative development against which Warhol positions a.[42] In this sense, as Dworkin notes, the novel's "explanatory subtitle"—a novel—"might be understood as an attempt to establish a ground against which the project as a whole can be better understood (or against which the knowing deviations from the defining conventions of the novel can at least be registered)."[43]

As Dworkin's reading of the novel's subtitle as a deliberate announcement suggests, the unreadability that the contemporary reception charges a with is neither a shortcoming nor an indirect consequence, but rather precisely the desired effect that Warhol seeks through the novel's complex production system. This system is designed to generate a productive and provocative undecidability rather than a refusal of readability or reading altogether. The indeterminacies of mistranscription and typographical error provide a textual manifestation of the narrative misconnections, miscommunications, and missing information that define working life within the media system of the Factory. Thus the novel's readers, implicated within this system of technological undecidability, must labor under the same conditions of incomplete comprehension as its characters, treating the page as an unstable record and speculating about the bodily and mechanical trajectories that produced its disjunctive marks. In addition to signifying for this local ambiguity of the novel's narrative world, a's form also makes a broader argument about the writing technology used to produce it: in retaining and foregrounding the confusing, challenging fabric of the typists' unedited transcripts, Warhol suggests that the discrete spatial characters of the typewriter produce greater specificity than other writing systems at the level of the letter, but not necessarily greater clarity or precision at any broader level of meaning. He says of the novel, "I wanted to do a 'bad book,' just the way I'd done 'bad movies' and 'bad art,' because when you do something exactly wrong, you always turn up something."[44] Within such an understanding, the transcript's divergences from typographic, orthographic, and narrative convention are not easily dismissed evidence of incomprehensibility as such, but rather the most jarringly apparent traces of a complexly distributed writing process in action—a process, moreover, that demands to be read with an eye toward questions of affordance, inscriptive poetics, and the temporality of the media archive.

Warhol's desire to "turn up something," then, refers to two related dimensions of the novel. Firstly, the production of a "bad book" "turn[s] up something" in the sense of a claim to generic innovation and revision: by saturating *a* with the orthographic and semantic confusions that Dworkin describes as "knowing deviations" from novelistic convention, Warhol offers a model for an extreme expansion of the categories of the novel and the literary in general. Warhol's allusion to turning up also highlights the more specific, and indeed fundamentally technological, amplification that this expansion entails, increasing both the potential for and the persistence of ambiguity within the text by making mediated transcription the central operation of its production. By foregrounding ambiguity in this way, Warhol produces a series of moments within the text in which the material and physical contingencies of technological mediation come to bear on the act of writing in a manner that circumvents traditional literary aesthetics to present a mode of writing that directly records its own modes of technological inscription and mediation rather than reflecting on them thematically or discursively. In the reading that follows, I trace these moments across the various material domains of the book in order to consider how it uses typographic experimentation to excavate the poetics and historicity of typewriting itself.

Although the novel is a transcript in the sense that it contains a written record of speech and other sound on Warhol's tapes, it frequently presents this sonic information in formats that diverge from the spatial conventions of transcript formatting as visible in legal or journalistic documentation. By changing the novel's layout back and forth between such a conventional transcript format and numerous other formats that use multiple columns and shifting blank space, Warhol and his typists manipulate the architecture of the page in ways that index the complex, unstable intertwining of bodies and machines in the space of the Factory office. Lucy Mulroney describes three main typographic styles—"Style A takes the form of 'Two columns, with one-em dash hanging indention for the over-run of speeches.' Style B takes the form of 'a solid, full-measure page' with only a two-em space inserted between speakers. Style C also takes the form of a full-measure page, but with 'a new line for each speech'"—along with a "plethora of variations" that "complicates any reading of standardization" with regard to the novel's layout.[45] Distributed on the page in these different forms, the words of the novel's personae register as units of information that occupy space character by character, word by word, and line by line, form and content entangled in irregular patterns that throw the materiality of text and inscription into relief over and above the capture and documentation of sound or action.

While the most frequently occurring example of this arbitrary spatial division is (fittingly enough) Style A, which first appears on page six, the novel begins with three lines of transcribed sound (which I discuss further below), and then shifts to Style B's straight transcript, devoid of line breaks, almost as if the typists were attempting to minimize space on the page between words and character's lines.[46] The novel then abruptly shifts to Style A in the middle of page six without any meaningful reason. This format does not present two simultaneous streams of speech or the alternating speech of multiple characters, nor does it intrinsically allow the space of the page to hold any more text than a conventional transcript format (and it certainly holds considerably less per page than Style B). It instead charges the architecture of the page by dividing its surface, foregrounding the typewriter's role as a machine for rationing that space. Faced with this spatial division, the reader must effectively read the space of the page twice, skimming over each column one time. This motion forces the eye to move in a more fully mechanically regimented fashion than it would in reading a traditionally arranged novel, thus causing it to echo the predetermined movements of the typewriter carriage and the element. Mulroney notes that Arnold Leo, the Grove Press editor for *a*, "realized it might be easier for readers to follow if it were formatted other than as a full page of running text."[47] Yet the difficulties of each individual format and the discontinuities among them both dramatically contravene such a possibility, producing a text that demands material, visual, and cognitive labor to read as well as narrative and interpretive labor. In Mak's terms, then, the physical *is* the conceptual on these pages; the work of reading inheres in spatial form as content. The varied formatting of the novelistic page reveals its status as an inscriptive format of print literary textuality, imagining the novel as a kind of distorted corporate transcript of the Factory's Office.

The presence and effect of blank space in the novel's various formats is crucial to this labor dynamic. In contrast to the textual density of Styles A and B, the moments of relatively conventional transcription in Style C begin to resemble the script of a play or the text of a free-verse poem rather than that of a novel in their relative spaciousness. Yet what is at stake here is ultimately not generic distinction but rather the manner in which the typewriter can marshal the presence and absence of text on the page in ways that bear no regular commensurability with the duration of speech and sound being transcribed. Factors such as the speed of speech or of interchange within the conversation have little to no bearing on the relation between text and blank space on the page. Instead, the spaces to the right of each line of spoken conversation fluctuate in length dependent on the relation between the typewriter's production of textual space in that line and the predetermined width of the page. Thus these spaces—irregular in length but nearly all considerably sizeable—function as repositories of textual silence that bears no direct relation to sonic silence. In the context of the novel's more nontraditional layout formats, these spaces, seemingly merely the function of the convention of aligning printed text on the left-hand side of the page, become newly visible as attenuated spaces left behind by the marking mechanisms of the typewriter.

Thus while on one hand, Warhol points to the presence of flexible textual strategies within perhaps typewriting's most banal form, namely the transcription of preexisting material, on the other hand he suggests that these flexibilities (and, equally importantly, the meaning generated by them) derive from largely arbitrary affordances of the technology and the page, regulated by the preexisting spacing functions of the machine, and thus in large part quite literally out of the hands of the typist. The more conventional moments of Style C come and go fairly quickly amid the more common and more extensive sections of Styles A and B, a fact that would almost seem to suggest that they were crowded out by the greater textual density of those formats. Yet their relative rarity serves precisely the opposite function: more noticeable precisely because they are less common, these sections foreground the embedded nature of textual space and silence throughout *a*, even and especially in its less immediately apparent forms—the novel's paragraph breaks, the space between columns in its two-column sections, and indeed even around individual letters themselves. Striking, emphatic instances of the written space Gitelman saw as the first and perhaps farthest-reaching legacy of the technology, they cannot help but stand in for information from the initial sonic tapes—echo, background noise, the overlap of voices, hiss and static—that is often palpably absent from text on the page. Suspended between tape recording and typing, the architecture of *a*'s pages bodies forth a textual poetics of mediality and loss.

At a more microscopic level, the novel's distortions and disjunctures of language further raise the question of what is lost and gained through its transcriptive network of bodies and machines. The first lines of *a* exemplify this problem, articulating the limitations of technologically mediated writing in accurately reproducing the sounds it transcribes:

> *Rattle, gurgle, clink, tinkle.*
> *Click, pause, click, ring.*
> *Dial, dial.*
> ONDINE—You said (*dial*) that, that, if, if you pick, pick UP the Mayor's voice on the other end (*dial, pause, dial-dial-dial*), the Mayor's sister would know us, be ***(busy-busy-busy).***[48]

Standing at a pay phone on a New York street, Ondine swallows a handful of amphetamines and unsuccessfully attempts to call his friend Rotten Rita, who also goes by the name of the Mayor. His actions are as difficult to transcribe and to read as they are for him to carry out. How quickly do the sounds in these lines follow after one another? At what pitch are the "clink" of Ondine's pill bottle and the "ring" of the dial tone? How long does each "dial" on the rotary phone take? Lacking explicit attention to issues of frequency, timing, and simultaneity (as well as any number of others) that are central to this material on tape, the text of this typewritten transcript is markedly incomplete, incapable of reproducing even this most banal sonic information. Of course, these limitations are present in the transcription of speech as well as in how the novel represents the sound of inanimate objects. Thus while it is somewhat more comprehensible than the first three lines, the transcript of Ondine's first words is ultimately no more faithful to whatever sonic material might be on the source tapes. The text can at least partly capture the repetition present in unrehearsed conversational speech—Ondine's almost stuttering "that, that, if, if you pick, pick UP"—but it cannot transcribe the simultaneity of Ondine's speech and the sounds of his actions—"(*dial*)," "(*dial, pause, dial-dial-dial*)"—as they occur and are recorded on tape.

Thus, at its outset, Warhol's novel seems to play out what Kittler considers to be the crucial dividing question of modern media technologies. For Kittler, while the typewriter's capacity for information storage is limited to "the finite and arranged stock of its keyboard," the phonograph—a sonic precursor to Warhol's portable cassette deck—is unique in its ability to record virtually everything, "all the noise produced by the larynx prior to any semiotic order and linguistic meaning" as well as "the physiological accidents and stochastic disorder of bodies" beyond vocal expression altogether.[49] These first lines of *a* would seem to substantiate Kittler's claim: the typewriter's attempt to reckon with the problems of sound through textual manipulations such as capitalization, boldface text, italicization, and parentheses falls far short of the scope of the tape recorder, failing to convey the complexity and density of Kittler's (admittedly idealized) "noise of the real."[50]

Yet as the conversation between Ondine and Drella continues, the novel begins to register the unique internal problems of the typewriter as an inscription technology operating in conjunction with the human body. Punctuating the transcript, these irregularities refuse classification as either incidental effects of the typewriter or direct transcriptions of recorded sound. Several lines after his first attempt at a call, Ondine contemplates taking a cab across Central Park before trying to make another phone call, asking Drella, "Are there difFERent places" where they could call Drella's answering service.[51] This capitalization of the middle syllable of the word "different" presents a markedly different manipulation of text from that of the earlier capitalization of "pick UP" or Ondine's question of "If we go through, through the park, is there ANY place we can keep calling[?]."[52] It is both visually irregular, occurring in the middle of the word, and sonically irregular, as if suggesting an unusual rhythmic emphasis. Another instance of this effect several pages later makes clear what is actually at stake in these modifications. As Warhol and Ondine search for somewhere to have break-fast, Ondine remarks, "Oh there must be some restAUrant."[53] Close attention to the QWERTY layout of the typewriter keyboard reveals that while this textual irregularity could be an accurate transcription of an unusual vocal inflection or of a distortion in the recording, it could just as likely be a record of the typist's hand accidentally striking the caps lock or shift key as it struck the "a" key, and not releasing that key until after striking the "u" key. In contrast, Ondine's comment that "If there's any kind of subterfuge [he has] to use, it has to be very obvious nad very funny" fits more clearly in the category of bodily typographic error in its uncorrected confusion of the sequence of letters in the word "and."[54] Yet the novel's lack of explicit differentiation between these different kinds of modification of text makes it impossible to tell which is in play at any given time, thus producing an irreducible undecidability through its technological mode of production.

a is, in this sense, the inverse of the midcentury typing manuals I discussed in the previous section, a collection of errors without a clear taxonomy. Far from being "finite and arranged," as Kittler says of the typewriter's textual mechanics, this undecidability produces a multiplicity of potential pasts: there is no clear pathway spelled out from the transcript's text back to the sonic content of the tapes, only the suggestion of a constantly multiplying array of potential recorded histories present in the tapes, themselves laid over by the array of potential histories of transcription present within the typewritten characters of the novel. Viewed through the blank spaces and ambiguous characters of *a*, the typewriter appears as a machine of aleatory distortion, writing spaces that are layered and littered with invisible, latent inscriptive pasts.

By publishing the typescript of the novel, complete with these ambiguities, as the final version, Warhol uses the text to invoke typewriting as a profoundly bodily production of semantically opaque information, an irreversible generation of marks through a series of bodily movements and moments of contact with the machine. These errors are not only "the most important parts of the book," but indeed derive their importance from being some of its most clearly typewritten parts.[55] They trace the incomplete, random process of transcription, presenting bare, defamiliarized marks gesturing not toward any "noise of the real" present within the original event, but rather toward bodily action that can never be fully or definitively retrieved or reproduced. Thus Warhol shows that the typewriter's distinctive capability is paradigmatically not to record "the physiological accidents and stochastic disorder of bodies" in a wholesale fashion, but rather to present the end result of those accidents and that disorder at a remove, encoding them through the space of its keyboard such that they are perpetually just out of the grasp of comprehension, chance movements that can be fully reaccessed only by chance. Approaching this question of capture and chaos, Mulroney notes that the novel "navigates between, on the one hand, an interest in appearing completely unedited and, on the other hand, a simultaneous interest in ever so gently helping readers move through the narrative," and that it achieves this complex synthesis of the air of randomness and error with readability and continuity through the manner in which Warhol "thoroughly manipulated" duration and content on the page.[56] Such manipulation would seem to suggest that the novel's conceit of chance is largely a contrivance and a misrepresentation. Yet as Mulroney herself demonstrates, error and chance are still central to its effect, made possible by its multiauthorial network and thus by the "denial of authorship" that Warhol exhibited toward the novel as well as his paintings.[57] This authorial strategy locates error across two complexly commensurable approaches: the first of these is chance, namely the inconsistencies, incorrectnesses, and barriers to reading that emerge accidentally in the production of the text. The second is intentionality, namely the barriers that are introduced through deliberate intervention, whether that intervention takes the form of direct editorial manipulation or—perhaps even more importantly—of making the editorial choice to retain the effects of chance in some places but not others.

Yet the carefully managed moments of difficulty Mulroney traces through the novel's manuscript stages are largely at the level of conventional novelistic consumption—they raise questions and inconsistencies of narrative, chronology, voice, and presentation—rather than at the level of microscopic textual materiality and transcriptive work. She reads *a*'s challenging form and explicit sexual and drug-related content as means by which Warhol and Grove generated an artificial scandal around the novel's publication, and in keeping with this intent, the textual difficulties she focuses on are primarily moments of difficulty for the novel's intended readers rather than for its multiple authors. Yet it is the alphabetic form of the novel that retains and records the scene of inscription most microscopically and palpably, and thus *a*'s inconsistencies in spelling and its transpositions of letters and repetitions of words seem to be more granular and to require a more complex historicization. If these textual idiosyncrasies cannot be accounted for as the result of the genuine presence and persistence of error through the transcription process, they could only otherwise be explained as having been intentionally produced and inserted during that process, requiring a meticulous attention to detail that seems unlikely and goes undiscussed in Mulroney's account (or any other less thorough accounts of production). Thus even accounting for the manipulations and constructions she documents, it seems safe, and indeed perhaps necessary, to consider error to be irreducible from *a*'s text, as it is from the text of any document.

Over and against the histories of artificial textual dissonance Mulroney traces, these accidental errors represent moments of inscription whose histories cannot be fully retained or recuperated. These problems of writing in turn produce problems of reading, ones that put pressure on questions such as narrative and voice to broach questions of inscription, affordance, and mediality. Once present in the final printed version, these typographic confusions cannot be filtered out of the reader's sensory and aesthetic experience in the way that sonic or visual noise can be diminished in postproduction or ignored by the trained ear or eye. They must instead be encountered and assimilated by the reader (to the extent that they can be) in order for him or her to continue following the flow of the novel's text. As the reader becomes more skilled at assimilating these confusions over the course of the novel's 451 increasingly fragmentary and opaque pages, they consequently absorb less and less of the actual textual material of the novel. Cognitively eliding these confusions, skimming over the text's localized disruptions in the interest of a simpler, more general and linear understanding of "what happens" in the novel, is at once both a seemingly necessary reading strategy and an interpretive evasion that Warhol anticipates and impedes. By rendering *a* incomplete and irresolute through the retention of error, he forces the reader to oscillate between reading the novel superficially and reading it completely, character by painstaking character; each method offers its own forms of clarity and comprehension as well as its own interpretive blind spots.

"How Are We Going to Write 'Oouh'?": Error, Transcriptive Undecidability, and Warhol's Leftover Typists

Through a number of interjections by the women who typed it, *a* documents the standardization of error across the breadth of the office's typewriter system as well as within the scope of the single body-machine interface. These interjections are *a*'s clearest and most immediately readable traces of transcriptive undecidability, raising the problem of the complex and distributed task of transcription within the modern office environment that Warhol mimics by hiring the typists. The presence of the typists in the production of the novel becomes most deeply visible in the text at these moments of aporia, precisely the sorts of problems that it is traditionally the typist's job to avoid in favor of determinacy, clarity, transparency, and faithfulness to original material. These moments thus mark tension at the procedural, authorial level as well as at the textual level, with the bodies, machines, and protocols of the office ceasing to deliver their traditionally intended results. What appears within the text in the place of these results is a blunt registration of the unattainability of clear and faithful transcription. Although the typists mark problems in transcription through these interjections, and at certain points also provide glosses on those problems, they rarely rectify them or make the text transparently readable, nor do they accept responsibility for problems or assign responsibility for resolving them. Indeed, to take such redemptive and restorative actions would be wholly contrary to the stated project of the novel. In marking transcription problems in such a blank fashion, the typists' interjections offer a complex, immanent critique of the typing office's larger network of textual production, presenting the problems of transcription as inevitable and irreducible within that network. The text that results suggests that the unstable operation of transcription that the novel undertakes is a norm rather than an aberration, and that transcription itself is paradoxically neither a broken operation nor a fixable one, but rather a mode of writing that necessarily must contain disruption within and precisely because of its standardizing structures and directives. Following the lines of Warhol's critique, tracing these microscopic ruptures in the circuitry of the typing office, we might also see within those ruptures the fragmented pieces of a larger history of typewriting, a media poetics of the paradigmatic postwar writing technology written in that technology's own detritus and leftovers.

Several different forms of transcriptive instability appear over the course of the novel. Many of these are meaningful or allusive in a way that suggests a clear, deliberate intervention into the novel's aesthetics and thematics by one or more of the typists. In these moments, a typist often raises the aesthetic problem of transcription through a sort of medial pun, a slippage in meaning that self-consciously points toward the problems of moving information from tape-recorded sound to typewritten text. For example, a conversation between Ondine and the character Rink Crawl centers on the homonymy between Callas (as in the opera singer Maria) and the skin condition known as a callus:

> O— . . . Oh ooh, my callas. Oh ho.
> R—Your calls. He's worried about his callas; it can't even sing.
> O—My callas is hurting me.[58]

Dworkin writes of this exchange, "The pun that might otherwise be taken for a transcription error is corroborated by Ondine, who exclaims: 'Your calls. . . .'"[59] Yet I would suggest that the process taking place here is more complex and distributed than Dworkin's either/or dichotomy between pun and transcription, between deliberate linguistic confusion and accidental mechanical confusion, can account for. After all, the typist transcribing the scene is in on the joke as much as the two men speaking, if not more so: by transcribing (almost) all of the instances of the word in question—those that refer to the "sing[ing]" opera diva as well as those that refer to the "hurting" skin condition—as "callas" rather than "callus," she produces a transcript that is neither an accurate, transparent record of verbal punning nor an incorrect, error-ridden record of straight-faced, humor-free speech but instead locates the complexity and confusion of the joke at least partly in the act of transcription itself. To type "callus" at any point here would be to imagine the joke as transparent and easily moveable across the different media in play—and thus not as a joke at all. Instead, the typist arbitrarily compacts the two spellings into one, using the resonance between them to mark the ambiguity and limitations of transcribing this or any spoken material (a set of conditions that is extended and made more directly visible in the typing of "calls" for "callas"). Through this deliberate compaction, the transcription of the novel becomes visible as a stage in the production process in which information is at turns lost, transformed, distorted, and set into question, rather than merely transmitted.

In other moments, the novel's characters themselves articulate this difficulty more explicitly, acknowledging the position of the typists and adding further layers to the problem of transcription, as in this unattributed exchange:

> [I]f you're all woman there's no need to be a transvestite.
> Uheauh.
> How are we going to write "Oouh"?
> It's hard but we'll find a way.
> Uheauh. We have to get, there's . . . my throat.[60]

This passage imagines the act of transcription as at once broken and reconnected across two distinct temporalities of information production. In switching back and forth between "uheauh" and "oouh" in the moment of typing, the typist performs the instability of typed transcription within the structures of office. Yet this instability is of course already embedded in the taped source material by the speaking characters, who knowingly discuss the difficulties of putting such a nonverbal expression into text. As they do so, they explicitly include themselves in the writing process: the question they raise is not "How are the typists going to type 'Oouh'?" but rather "How are we going to write 'Oouh'?" This inclusion suggests a poetics of transcriptive writing that begins before playback of the tape and typing of the text, at the moment of the initial speech act itself. Such a poetics both accommodates the textual aporia visible here and elsewhere in the novel and imagines that aporia as the product of a distributed process of textual production incorporating multiple human and technological agents, a process that is always collaborative, but never complete. Indeed, the novel's moments of tension between sonic and typewritten information suggest that transcribed text—and by extension perhaps any mediated text—never sits stably within one field of information, even when it has seemingly reached its "final" site of storage. It flickers between different fields in microscopic increments, bearing the marks of the multiple conflicting and complementary agents that shape it.

The typists' most substantive interjections within the novel often appear as direct annotations, qualifications, or questions about the immediate material they are working with. In these moments, the typists break both the flow of transcribed sound and speech on the page and the flow of transcription itself. Their textual insertions register information that is wholly outside of the material of the tapes, thus making explicit the uneven, additive condition of multiagented transcription within the Factory office. Left unresolved in the final published version of the text, these interjections suggest that the fundamental problem of transcription is not one of eliminating ambiguity but rather one of addressing and contextualizing that ambiguity as irreducible; perhaps more so than anywhere else in the novel, the mailability that stands as the practical ideal of typewriting instruction gives way in these moments to a complex lack of resolution reverberating through the text's typed copy. At times the issue raised by a typist's question is one of simple sonic accuracy: "I thought you had the pill out (pillow?) She looks just like—Disconnected lines? (or Did you connect the lines?)."[61] Interspersed with Ondine's speech, the typist's questions here pose possible alternate conceptions of the sonic record at stake, material divergences that lie both within and outside the "main narrative" of the transcript. In many cases, these questions become a means of complex, explicit self-fashioning and self-reflexivity within the text, as when one of the typists annotates her own transcription of Ondine singing along with a Callas record: "[Y]'know and it's just when you get 'Throngera (*singing along in Italian—check the record or Ondine*) aschulta' where there's no pause—'familia, sculta' (*singing again*) she can't take, you can't take a rest there where there's no rest, what is she singing? Who wrote it?"[62] The typist's troubling of content and authorship through her brief note to "*check the record or Ondine*" both parallels Ondine's own far more logorrheic expression of confusion and explicitly raises the unanswerable question of the novel's larger network of production. Is the "record" the typist refers to the specific Callas LP being played or the more general recorded material of the tapes? To whom is this note addressed, and what sorts of informational relays does it invoke through that address? Is the typist writing to herself for later reference? Or is it a note from one typist to another who was supposed to review and revise the transcript but never did? Or is it a note to Warhol, or to Factory foreman Billy Name, who was responsible for marshaling the galleys through publication, or to Grove editor Arnold Leo, or perhaps even to the reader? Although the communication could have been intended for any of these recipients, the novel's deliberately uncorrected condition leaves these questions unanswered. Thus in comparison to textual errors committed solely by a typist, which inhere at the individual typographic, physical, or cognitive level, these annotative instabilities function as metaerrors of a sort, moments of textually and aesthetically productive breakdown in the office's transcription network. Rather than pointing toward a simple correction in order to achieve mailability, they leave any number of potential transcriptive relations open, each with its own dynamics of power, authorship, and technological investment.

Just as each individual interjection negates the possibility of a clear transcription or reading of the novel at the same time that it annotates and adds to it, it is equally impossible to generalize an authorial role for the typists from the novel's multiple kinds of interjections. Through these impossibilities, Warhol offers an aesthetic tracing of the distributed structures of subjectivity and authorship within the office. It would be tempting to claim either that the moments of interjection in *a* are the marks of a sort of successful authorial coup, through which the typists repeatedly announce themselves as having the most clear, stable, and autonomous voice(s) in the novel, or that they serve as rare exceptions to a pattern of the discipline and silencing of female voices in the novel's world. At various moments, each of these roles comes to the fore. However, given the dramatically dispersed authorship of the novel, neither of these perspectives can fully account for the role of the typists' voices. Reflecting on *a*'s transcription process in *The Philosophy of Andy Warhol*, Warhol expresses dissatisfaction with the skills of the typists, complaining that "some kids came by the studio and asked if they could do some work, so I asked them to transcribe and type my novel, and it took them a year and a half to type up one day! That seems incredible to me now because I know that if they'd been any good they could have finished it in a week. I would glance over at them sometimes with admiration because they had me convinced that typing was one of the slowest, most painstaking jobs in the world. Now I realize that what I had were leftover typists, but I didn't know it then. Maybe they just liked being around all the people who hung around at the studio."[63] Warhol seems to speak here as a traditional office manager, dissatisfied with the typists' work ethic and with what he sees as their phony, overwrought commitment to accuracy; his description of the typists as "leftover typists" suggests that *a*, with its constant uncorrected errors, interjections, and disruptions, can similarly never be anything more than a weak, peripheral byproduct of technocapital textual production—a leftover novel, as it were. Indeed, the fact that the typists' work is uncredited suggests that his contempt is at least partly sincere and straightforward. In this sense, his exploitation of anonymous female labor to produce the novel constitutes a literalization of his infamously vampiric manipulations of women in the Factory (his alias, Drella, after all, is a portmanteau of Dracula and Cinderella).

Yet the penchant for ephemerality, excess, and waste that runs throughout Warhol's work suggests a more complex perspective than this initial dismissal suggests. Shortly before he discusses *a* in *The Philosophy*, he explicitly champions the leftover, particularly in its embodied female form, as a crucial form of aesthetic labor within the processes of modern media production: "When I see an old Esther Williams movie and a hundred girls are jumping off their swings, I think of what the auditions must have been like and about all the takes where maybe one girl didn't have the nerve to jump when she was supposed to, and I think about her left over on the swing. So that take of the scene was a leftover on the editing-room floor—an out-take—and the girl was probably a leftover at that point—she was probably fired—so the whole scene is much funnier than the real scene where everything went right, and the girl who didn't jump is the star of the out-take."[64] The scenario Warhol imagines here seems to situate the leftover as a category roughly equivalent to trash: the proverbial celluloid left on the cutting room floor, the accidental, incidental detritus of mass media culture left to be forgotten—or, as in the case of much of his visual work, reclaimed and recontextualized. When we understand the leftover in this sense, we see Warhol and the typists working (although certainly not collaboratively) to perform a media poetics of the typewriter by retaining errors in the published text of the novel. In chapter 3, I consider celluloid cinematic materiality through Akira Mizuta Lippit's understanding of the shadow archive, an archive that preserves through forgetting and oblivion; here Warhol and the typists incorporate a shadow archive of usually forgotten marks and inscriptive movements within the pages of *a*, the raw material of a media poetics defined by dead ends and lost histories. Warhol's conception of the leftover within these marks also imagines a complexly accretive relation to temporality: the leftover text of *a* is not what is disposed of and then reclaimed, but rather what remains, the totality of textual accumulation that persists on the pages of the novel as a kind of flattened palimpsest, recalibrating moments of error toward a complex alternate history of textual labor that circulates through the novel.

The typists' moments of entry into the novel foreground a mode of subjectivity and intentionality that shapes the text in crucial ways without being teleological or exegetical with regard to its content or authorship. Warhol's retention of the typographic problems produced by these four leftover workers emphatically shapes the aesthetics of the novel in their image, as a massively leftover novel written at the disjunctures among the multiple human and technological subjects involved in its production. By presenting four female typists as such crucial elements in *a*'s production network, Warhol sets in motion a limit-performance of the mechanics of the typing pool, a collection of anonymous women assigned to transcribe a massive omnibus text. Thus as a female group, the typists serve not only as transcribing agents in the production of the final text but also as signifying agents within a performative critique of the dynamics of gender and technological capital.[65] Their bodies are loosely and flexibly connected to one another, to the devices around them, and to the body of Warhol himself as the ostensible author of *a*; they are the unstable crux of Warhol's engagement with the bodily and authorial problems of transcription and textual labor in the second half of the twentieth century. How, then, does the novel, produced in such large part by the unseen and uncredited labor of these female bodies, imagine the bodily dynamics of the work of transcriptive textual production? How does Warhol seek to imagine and transform the body within the space of the typing pool? What macroscopic technological histories do these bodies gesture toward in the microscopic textual histories in which they participate?

The marks made by the typewriter in *a* encode a history of bodily movement and (re)configuration that can never be fully retrieved. The individual characters produced by these machines serve as points of condensation and compaction for that history, coding the bodies that produce the novel as indeterminate and aleatory precisely because of their involvement in this textual production. In order to offer a fuller picture of the technological history traced by this compaction, I want to return briefly to one of the exchanges from the novel that I quoted earlier:

> [I]f you're all woman there's no need to be a transvestite.
> Uheauh.
> How are we going to write "Oouh"?
> It's hard but we'll find a way.
> Uheauh. We have to get, there's . . . my throat.[66]

By switching back and forth between "oouh" and "uheauh" spellings, the typists not only perform the impossibility of complete transcription, as I suggested earlier, but also provide a textual parallel to the condition of a man being "all woman." The association of "all woman" with these nonverbal communications identifies it as inexpressible through "normal" verbal speech and constantly in flux; in the context of the Factory's queer culture, it imagines a sort of gender play at the extreme, a level of performative refashioning so deep that it vastly outstrips the performative refashioning the novel's characters attribute to transvestitism. The concept of being "all woman" appears frequently in the conversations of the novel's male characters, most often in an abbreviated form as "A. W.": one character is described as "dEFinitely A. W.," while another is "A. W., not asexual."[67] Through its purely alphabetic nature, A. W. represents the fluid sexualities and bodies of the novel's characters and producers constituted in the form of typewritten text. It invokes women, men (who within this schema are always also women), and last but not least the particular and particularly ambiguous body that circulates through the text largely in silence: A. W., of course, stands for Andy Warhol.

If we take A. W. at its face value as a typographic mark made for the body as well as by the body, it becomes effectively impossible to know with any clarity or stability exactly which embodied characters or kinds of characters these typewritten characters stand for in any one given instance. A. W. is a textual means of foregrounding, transforming, and intermingling the bodies within and around the text—characters and authors, typists and typewriters, men and women, straight and queer—but also a means of concealing them. It is at once all, some, and none of these bodies. Scattered throughout the novel, this multilayered authorial signature invokes the all-woman group that types the words of the novel and the "all-woman" group that speaks those words. Each group uses the technologies at its disposal to make marks that both hide and reveal the other group, with A. W.—both the authorial mark itself and the ostensible author himself—as perhaps the most complex and compacted textual secretion of all. Yet as with any and all of the novel's marks and bodies, A. W. and Andy Warhol offer only the microscopic endpoint of a massive history of bodies, machines, and information circulating through space, interpenetrating and recombining with one another in combinations that cannot be extracted from the mere characters on the page. Like the text of the novel as a whole, A. W. occupies space but refuses any singular location: we can never know how each mark traveled through the Factory's transcription network, which hands produced each mark, which bodies each mark set in motion, or which bodies each mark brought into contact with one another.

To understand *a* as a deliberate leftover—as the encyclopedic, overwhelming typewritten surplus of a "finished" novel that itself does not and cannot ever exist as finished—is to propose that the bodily, procedural, and textual affordances of the typewriter have the potential to bring about a writing system with a set of conditions different from either the illusory polish and inspiration of the literary genius or the alleged mechanized circumscription of the secretarial technician. The content of *a* is simultaneously initial, transitional, final, and residual. Its systemic textual confusions present a vision of the transcriptive writing of postwar technoculture as a mass of potential and actual leftovers, moments of varying degrees of imperfection and imprecision that resist elimination from the act of typing. The potentiality for error that Warhol's novel exploits exists within all typewriting, even and especially if it is often eradicated in editorial correction and revision. Indeed, attending to the microscopic material specificities of the typewriter reminds us of the ways in which modern technological writing is often a highly embodied and multiauthorial practice even in the initial stages of production, regardless of the detached, polished façade of any seemingly finished product.

In attending to the relation between standardization and error as the central characteristic of typewriting's materiality in this chapter, I have attempted to offer a theory of this embodied, multiauthorial condition as capable of existing across, and thus of complicating, simple boundaries between collaboration and contestation, intentionality and contingency, the biological and the technological, the literary and the corporate, and, perhaps most importantly, between writing as a material product and as an immanent process. Of course, few texts traverse all of these lines in the way that *a* does, while many purport to transcend them in their seemingly finished states. Indeed, just such a transcendence is one of the central objectives of both the mainstream publishing industry and the corporate textual protocols that *a* renders so carefully and carelessly in pastiche. Yet the typewriter sits at the oblique intersection of all of these lines, a modern technology with the capacity to shape the aesthetic, subjective, and material dimensions of writing without necessarily imposing a fixed teleology on them. Within the complex writing system of the typewriter, the materiality of text manifests itself in the overwhelming probability of localized, idiosyncratic disruptions rather than in any larger predetermined horizon of aesthetic, subjective, or political possibility; error is both potentially irreducible and potentially invisible, marking textual and technological history through both its presence and its absence.

The complex synthesis of permanence and ephemerality that characterizes error as a crux point of typewritten text is also characteristic of the typewriter itself. Although it seems unlikely that Warhol intended it as an augury of things to come, *a* appeared close to the beginning of the end for the typewriter as a writing machine. The IBM Selectric first appeared in 1961, revolutionizing typing by replacing individual frontstrike type hammers with its golf ball–style "element." It quickly came to dominate the market, accounting for approximately 75 percent of all electric typewriter sales in the United States by 1975—one might even imagine the typists in Warhol's factory using this ubiquitous, iconic midcentury machine to transcribe the tapes of *a*. Yet as much as the Selectric revolutionized typing, it was also the "last typewriter" in many ways, as its sales began to drop as quickly as they had risen as part of a general decline in typewriter sales in the late 1970s as word processors and desktop computers became increasingly popular.[68] Understood through the lens of this abrupt turn toward obsolescence, caught at every level in tension with its own assimilation into the invisible, the typewriter sits in a contingent, conflicted place within the history of postwar writing machines, and as such it also makes visible the contingency of that larger history. In making possible microscopic errors within mechanical writing, it makes visible the macroscopic instabilities and nonlinearities of media history—the profoundly invisible ways in which our understanding of the history of modern writing is perpetually subject to disjuncture, repetition, transposition, and discontinuity across text and time.

Coda: Exquisite Bodies, or, How to Compute without Computers

Each of the first three chapters of *Archival Fictions* explores how a work of contemporary print literature engages the materiality of analog media, demonstrating how print authors write new narratives of media history through formal figures of error, erasure, disappearance, distortion, anachronism, decay, and combustion. While these works and my analyses of them operate within a framework of pastness and obsolescence (albeit often in order to complicate and counter those concepts), the codas that close each chapter transpose the concerns of the literary work in play to a more recent historical moment in order to consider how the materiality and historicity of these analog forms of inscription circulate within contemporary digital culture. Thus as a way of closing chapter 1, I want to turn to the contemporary performance group the Typing Explosion Union Local 898 as the exemplar of a complexly historiographic approach to the poetics of midcentury typewriting.[69]

If typewritten text offers us a back-door entryway into the textual production of the postwar period through error, what might it mean to produce such text in the contemporary moment? Like many analog media formats—perhaps most visibly and notably vinyl records—typewriting has had a retro renaissance in the early twenty-first century, appearing as a nostalgic fetish object everywhere from the much-touted modernist *mise-en-scène* of the television series *Mad Men* to the hipster culture of urban locales from Portland to Brooklyn. Darren Wershler-Henry, writing in 2005, notes twenty-five pages of typewriter-related items on eBay, much of which is advertised as vintage in a manner that plays on consumers' equations of history and class prestige: "Through the magical application of one adjective, apparently anything can be equated to a fine wine, and therefore rendered worthy of the attention of a connoisseur . . . or, conversely, anyone interested in such 'vintage' objects must necessarily *be* a connoisseur, even if the adjective has become nearly meaningless."[70] A search for "vintage typewriter" in 2021 on Etsy, an ecommerce site smaller than eBay but more specifically geared to vintage goods, yields nearly six thousand items on 124 pages. Much of the typewriter's nostalgic appeal, like that of any old media format, derives from its air of authenticity and tangibility. Jessica Bruder of the *New York Times* notes, "In more than a dozen interviews, young typewriter aficionados raised a common theme. Though they grew up on computers, they enjoy prying at the seams of digital culture. Like urban beekeepers, hip knitters and other icons of the D.I.Y. renaissance, they appreciate tangibility, the object-ness of things."[71] Of course, this "object-ness" draws its appeal in large part from its detachment from the actual materialities of working conditions at the moment of the typewriter's prominence; like all nostalgic purchases, buying a typewriter in the twenty-first century allows access to an image of history from a distance, without requiring entry into the dynamics of power, gender, and labor that characterized the twentieth-century office.

The Typing Explosion, in contrast, revisits the materiality of typewritten labor not as ornament or nostalgia but as the foundation of a deeply historically engaged aesthetic practice. Active from 1998 to 2004 (with a brief reunion in 2006), the group consisted of three women then in their late twenties and early thirties, performing both in established performance and theatrical venues and in what they describe as "guerilla poetry construction on the sidewalk or in an office."[72] In their performances, the three women enter the performance space dressed in vintage 1960s secretarial clothing and take their seats at a long table behind three manual typewriters. Audience members approach the table and have the chance either to select poem titles on index cards stored in a card catalog or to write titles of their own choosing on a blank card. The first typist in line then takes the card and begins typing a poem for that title. The three typists then work collectively on the poem, passing it back and forth and communicating with one another through a secret code of bells, horns, and whistles. They work on up to three poems at any one time, circulating them back and forth, before handing completed, certified copies to the audience members who originally submitted them, for the price of one dollar.

This performative restaging of the postwar typing pool relies on a highly complex and overdetermined relationship to cultural and technological history. With their deadpan retro aesthetic and their collective, deliberate anonymity—they operate under the shared alter ego of "Diane," as if taking on a single hypergeneric persona of the postwar working woman[73]—these three performers look at first glance almost like the noncharacters of Cindy Sherman's *Untitled Film Stills* come to life, unlocatable types adrift in the pastiche of postmodern culture. Yet what is most strikingly relevant about this aesthetic is not its detached referencing of the past. Indeed, this aesthetic critically marks a constant cultural cycle of idealized technological memory, in which the nostalgia that Kittler expresses for handwriting gives way to subsequent nostalgia for the typewriter. The group's appearance also registers the extent to which the secretarial aesthetic is newly (re)current on a wide scale, as these three artists resemble hipster working women in any major American cultural center as much as they resemble the lost archetypes of 1950s working femininity, if not paradoxically more so. In being about nostalgia, their work is about the present. As much as they perform the aesthetic of the corporate past—indeed, precisely because they perform this aesthetic alongside so many other similar young women— they register as textual and cultural laborers within the technology and aesthetics of the current moment. Beyond their underlying recreation of the past, their work constitutes an intervention into the dynamics of the retro rather than a deployment of those dynamics as such. Exposing and exploiting the undead state of the typewriter, the Typing Explosion lays its operations against the operations of contemporary digital culture, and in doing so they offer a performative rewriting of media history through the typewriter and its textual output.

While the group's intent is precisely not to reify the typewriter as it is traditionally understood, their project of thinking across different moments in media history nonetheless entails a certain amount of political and historical negotiation and recalibration: they announce their practice as a departure from what might be understood, from one ideological stance, as the alienation of the subject produced by late capital's dispersion of the body through the computer. As one member puts it in a documentary on the group, the audience is "face to face with us and with the creation of art and I think that that's something that isn't the same as if we were typing on computers and it was coming up in other people's cubicles across the city. So what makes the Typing Explosion engaging . . . is that we're face to face with people."[74] Yet their performance subverts the professed and presumed transparency and immediacy of this predigital communication space in a number of ways. While the performers and the audience are indeed "face to face," they interact without speech or verbal expression other than the words they produce on the page. Moreover, the typists' "secret language" of "bells, horns, and whistles" seems intended as much to confuse and constrain the audience as to provide the artists with a means of internal communication, if not more so.[75] This system makes a dramatic claim on the gendered embodiment of typewriting: although the female body is linked to the machine here, the silence and anonymity of the typing pool under this connection is a force of aesthetic collectivity rather than of workplace subordination or subjective foreclosure as Kittler sees it, a revision that relocates communication and aesthetic production from one-on-one spoken conversation to the circulating itinerary of the typewriting body and the typewritten page.

Thus the work of the Typing Explosion finds its aesthetic center in the bodily production and circulation of texts and documents, in the immanent act of typing rather than in the content of any given typed document as such. The members of the group describe their work in mechanical terms, as "preparing a document for the person that was in attendance," and they note the importance of excluding the words "poetry" or "poem" from the title of the group, to say nothing of the choice of "typing," with its technological implications, over the more generalized term "writing," or even "typewriting."[76] The artists sit in a line and describe their work as "poetry on demand" as if part of an assembly line, and their work echoes the surrealist poetry-passing game known as "exquisite corpse." Yet their work differs crucially from both of these modernist models in that the poems of the Typing Explosion move nonlinearly, randomly, and recursively, circulating repeatedly through the hands and machines of the three performers without any predetermined path. Such a process is neither a rebellion against Fordist technological labor practices nor an attempt at random poetic collaboration as such, but rather both a subversion of the aesthetics and labor protocols of technologically determined, office-based writing and a natural extension of them. In this sense, the Typing Explosion harnesses "the chaos of the writing pool" of postwar corporate culture in a manner that pushes that chaos to its logical extreme.[77] This gesture is similar to Warhol's work in *a*, yet while Warhol positioned transcription as a limit form of writing, foregrounding the opacity and error that inevitably emerge as information moves through different bodies and different media, the Typing Explosion works in the opposite direction, pushing writing to the verge of transcription. One member of the group describes their performances as a "bold representation of [their] true sel[ves]," but also notes that they do not have "time to really read what the other person has written, but as you're threading it into your machine your eyes will just sort of gaze as you go down the page, so you'll sort of pick up these buzzwords, or you'll glance at the title and you'll get a general feel about the poem."[78] Taken together, these contrasting descriptions understand the artists' bodily and even mental contact with the textual material at hand as at once both deeply invested with affect and also ephemeral and tangential, as the byproduct of routing information rather than as a context for direct "writerly" attention in any conventional sense.

Moreover, the group's practice performatively pushes through the structure of the typing pool to model an approach to textuality and information that resonates with the distributed, multiauthorial connective systems of digital culture. Within both paradigms, information is a source of identification and attachment as well as a quantity that is easily moveable, revisable, and exchangeable, shaped and constituted by its circulation through a network comprised of multiple different spaces, machines, writers, and readers. As one of the members says of the group's writing, information constituted in this way conveys an "urgent human voice" rather than "an individual voice."[79] This comparison implies a writing practice that is more urgent and more human precisely because it is not individuated in the manner of the traditional isolated literary author at the typewriter. Indeed, the use of the term "voice" here seems almost inaccurate, given that expression here emerges as much from performative procedure as from any expressive poetics on the page, if not considerably more so. In performing this conception of technological writing, the Typing Explosion dismantles the nostalgic oversimplification of the typewriter as a machine that produces clinical, stable writing from a monadic position. They offer instead a vision of the typewriter within contemporary culture as a supplement and a predecessor to the computer, a kind of genealogical ancestor not just to its form factor as an object but also to its circulatory mechanics and protocols. Indeed, while the physical resemblances between the two devices are evident enough—their similar shape and size, their keyboard placement and layout, the location of paper and screen as the respective locations for typed text—the typewriter seems paradigmatically different from the computer precisely in its mythos of isolated, individual authorial work. The Typing Explosion works to undo this mythos through their emphasis on interconnection as both a means and end to their work. Their visible passing back and forth of poems echoes the operations of both the typing pool and the computer network in that it draws attention to the often-invisible flow of information through technological infrastructures past and present, throwing into relief how both machines in question rearrange the micro- and macroscopic spaces around their production of text. The image of three textually connected typewriters takes on the appearance of a prototypical computer network, while the deliberate secrecy and inscrutability of the group's system of bells, whistles, and passes both recuperates the unpredictable yet easily ignored textual mechanics of the typing pool within the present moment and also reveals that mechanics as the technological ghost underlying the seeming exactitude and seamlessness of every digital transmission.

Indeed, this rearrangement of space attains its greatest dispersion in the group's distribution of their work to the audience. The group's poetic material begins in the form of titles chosen from the group's card catalog, moves from the audience member's hand to one performer's hand, becomes a poem through its circulation through the hands and machines of the all of the performers, and finally returns to the hands of the audience member, who may share it with others in the audience, take it home, discard it, or otherwise store or disseminate it as they see fit. Taken as an ongoing practice over many performances, this distribution amounts to the mediation of material from one consolidated, highly structured space of storage to a randomly shaped, radically distributed network. The group also retains a carbon copy of each poem it produces, a collection that constitutes a third, hidden space for their work, shadowing and doubling its public circulation from within private storage. Thus in their typing hands, media poetics takes shape as the composition and circulation of documents, but also as what Current describes in midcentury office culture as "[t]he ready multiplication of documents," a practice that both saves and wastes time and labor.[80] Such a practice invokes both the masses of paper produced within twentieth-century corporate culture and the seemingly weightless backups and copies of contemporary cloud-based digital storage, tracing a history of modern data storage in which dispersion and consolidation, public and private, and paper and digital continually mirror and recall one another. Which is more stable—the typed poem or the carbon copy? The closed card catalog or the scattered publication? The monolithic collection or the single sheet? The hard-drive file that can be seemingly seen and touched on one's personal computer or the distant copy deep in a nondescript server farm? Each format, each object has its permanences and its vulnerabilities, its malleabilities and its discontinuities.

The differences between typewritten and computerized communication are of course myriad and present at every level, as common as the similarities I have traced through the work of the Typing Explosion. Yet the connective dialogue that they stage across media history, laying the typewriter alongside the computer, with the typing body as the means of connection across time, suggests that the typewriter's ghosts of technological instability are never fully banished. They locate the typewriter and the typing pool as present and current within the moment of the computer, subject to an uncanny, untimely return. This archaeological work reveals not just the complex, chaotic prehistory of the computer, nor just the chaos of the computer's own inscriptive and circulatory operations (a question I consider more fully in chapter 4), but rather, far more importantly, the return of the typewriter itself as a historical trajectory that is simultaneously permanent, ephemeral, and discontinuous. Striking keys and passing papers, the group writes a history for the machine in the shape of the very marks it inscribes on paper. Their performances imagine a dead technology as momentarily, contingently, repeatedly alive. In doing so, they imagine the media history of the twentieth century not as an inexorable historical march from one system to the next, but rather as a field constantly overlapping itself, characterized by recursion, residues, error, and the disjunctive, unpredictable reappearance of writing bodies and machines across time.

CHAPTER TWO
Unheard Frequencies

Kevin Young's *To Repel Ghosts* and the Analog
Aesthetics of the Turntable

Only when gramophonic reproduction breaks down are its objects transformed.
Or else one removes the records and lets the spring run out in the dark.
—Theodor Adorno, "The Curves of the Needle"

Of Tinfoil and Type: Sound after Inscription

Inscription is the shadow history of the phonograph. The record player, the technology perhaps best known as the first mass-produced means of one-way public listening—the ancestor of playback technologies from the cassette and the compact disc to the MP3 and the audio stream—was initially designed as a two-way technology, a machine for writing sonic vibrations as well as reading them. Thomas Edison's first phonograph, which he presented to the offices of *Scientific American* in 1877, worked in a manner that bore an uncanny resemblance to conventional stylographic writing. The device captured sound through a mouthpiece and diaphragm, passing these vibrations on to a needle that would emboss them on tinfoil wrapped around a metal cylinder that could be turned by a hand crank in order to inscribe sound over time. A second pairing of needle and diaphragm could then be used to read the indentations on the foil in order to play back the recorded material at a later date—sound mediated back and forth through the pen, as it were.

The technical parameters of the phonograph's scene of inscription—the sharp implement carving marks on a thin surface in an up-and-down, hill-and-dale pattern—dovetailed with the print-centric media culture of the late nineteenth century to ensure that this new technology took shape in relation to the old technology of writing, each one shaping and shaped by the other. As Lisa Gitelman notes, "[T]he fugitive sounds captured by the phonograph meant what they did because of the ways they might resemble and—particularly—because of the ways they had to be distinguished from the only other snare available: inscriptions made on paper."[1] Douglas Kahn similarly sees early phonography not just as a singular technological process but also as a larger "dramatic shift . . . in ideas regarding sound, aurality, and reality," a shift that moreover "linked textuality and literacy with sound through inscriptive practices."[2] This linkage, Kahn suggests, was part of a larger "intensification of inscription" in the late nineteenth century, by which phonography set in motion a rethinking of what it meant to write, not just in terms of the greater capacity for informational complexity and density provided by sound recording but also at the level of substrate and inscriptive materiality. This rethinking turned on a shift from alphabetics to material forms: from "the accumulation of simple lines arrayed in an alphabetic system that could be grouped, read, and written" to a more expansive conception, held at turns by both modernist artists and inventors alike, of "the single line of inscription [as invested] with unlimited signs of life."[3] Such a line could be found at any number of turn-of-the-century technological sites, from sound recording to the proliferation of new mechanized writing and drawing devices to the wider applications of "the graphic method of representing automatically recorded curves" across scientific disciplines.[4]

In the context of such an intensification, the graphic dimensions of Edison's first talking machine, "potent with read/write functions," might be seen as simultaneously a function of technological possibilities and affordances, an example of the formative impact of print culture on the device, and a mediatic engagement with and refiguration of that impact.[5] After all, the very word "phonograph"—Edison's brand name for the device, and a term that would become one among several (gramophone, Graphophone, and paleophone, to name a few) in subsequent years—derives from the Greek *phoné* and *graph*, meaning sound or voice and writing, respectively. While the turntable, the most prominent twentieth-century descendent of the phonograph, is best known as a means for consuming prerecorded music, Edison originally designed the phonograph to record telephone messages for office use, in order to provide a more exact and efficient substitute for written and transcribed communication. In an 1878 list of potential uses for his invention (often enumerated in histories of sound technology), Edison notes "the reproduction of music" as only one of ten possibilities, among letter writing, audio books, "the teaching of elocution," the "family record," "music-boxes and toys," speaking clocks, "the preservation of languages," note taking for educational purposes, and the recording of telephonic communication.[6] Historians often remark on the diversity of possible applications included in Edison's list, as well as the fact that music, ultimately the primary application by a wide margin, is only one of ten. More notable, however, is how many possibilities focus on recording by everyday users as well as or in addition to playback. Such a predominance underscores how deeply Edison conceived of the phonograph as a writing machine, a device for the production of records (broadly understood) rather than their consumption.

Tinfoil recording was initially economically successful, but over time the demand for recorded sound came increasingly from the mass entertainment audience rather than from the corporate sphere, a market shift that brought with it technological and material shifts. The conditions of consumption in the mass market were more receptive to the wax-disc-based gramophone introduced by Emile Berliner in 1887 than to Edison's tinfoil phonograph: while discs were read-only, they were cheaper and easier to mass-produce. Capacity was also an issue. Tinfoil could hold approximately two minutes of recorded sound, a timespan suitable for short communications, while discs could hold closer to four minutes, lending themselves more fully to popular songs and other prerecorded content. In addition, as Alexander Weheliye notes, the fragility of tinfoil as a medium proved problematic: "The tin foil on which sonic information was by then being imprinted could only sound out what it had recorded twice or thrice at a maximum, and the hand crank to power the phonograph was so delicate that slight shifts in speed altered and/or distorted the content completely."[7] Thus the paper-like qualities of the phonograph—the material affordances that made it at least potentially and initially viable as a two-way technology of recording and reproduction—were the undoing of that very same two-way capacity.[8]

Thus, as with the technology of the typewriter in chapter 1, we find in the technology of the phonograph another slant history of paper writing in the dead media of the twentieth century, another skew trajectory that begins in innovative explosion and ends in obsolescence and (in this case, at least) nonfunction, leaving print textuality nonetheless dramatically transformed in its wake. For Friedrich Kittler, the phonograph looms as a foundational object in the history of modern inscription: "[A]ll concepts of trace," he claims, "up to and including Derrida's grammatological *ur*-writing, are based on Edison's simple idea. The trace preceding all writing, the trace of pure difference still open between reading and writing, is simply a gramophone needle."[9] Robert M. Brain traces a different lineage for this relation by way of physiologist and protocinematic inventor Étienne-Jules Marey's collaboration on the graphic method of representation with linguists Michel Bréal and Charles Rosapelly. As Brain notes, the work of Marey, Bréal, and Rosapelly was contemporaneous with Edison's, but with "scientific rather than commercial aims, specifically to give new laboratory foundations to the science of linguistics," most notably in relation to the foundational linguist Ferdinand de Saussure, who was Bréal's protégé.[10] Brain's connection of the graphic method of the mechanical line to the larger history of signification, particularly Saussure's concept of the signifier as an acoustic image, offers a compelling intellectual lineage for these ideas, while Kittler's reading of Edison offers a material one. And while Kittler's lineage is undeniably a deeply romantic and mysticized one, collapsing the history of modern inscription into the slender space of the phonographic needle, the same might be said of the treatment of the line as a totalizing mark within the history of the graphic method that Brain traces.

Indeed, both narratives—each with its own limitations and extremities—inform how we might understand the history of phonographic inscription. Yet in light of two related distinctions between these narratives, my thinking below draws most directly on the Edisonian. Firstly, while both Edison's and Marey's systems allow for the inscription of sonic information, Edison's allows for playback as well; as the 1877 *Scientific American* recounting his demonstration puts it, a "complete phonograph or sound writer" makes it possible to "translate the remarks made" as well as to make them in the first place. Secondly, while Marey's system was broadly applicable across scientific domains, Edison's was understood as decidedly bookish from the outset, precisely because of its playback function: *Scientific American* describes this write-read function as being "as if, instead of perusing a book ourselves, we drop it into a machine, set the latter in motion, and behold! the voice of the author is heard repeating his own composition."[11] My discussion below builds on this bookish capacity for two-way exchange—and on the related questions of inscription and substrate, and of distortion and inexactitude, that emerge from it—using those questions to trace a media poetics at the intersection of phonography and print writing.

Chapter 1 of *Archival Fictions* suggested that attending to the obsolete technology of the typewriter provided critical insight into media history and its relation to print literary production. I showed how the radical formalism of Warhol's *a* surfaces both the centrality of error to typewritten text and the typewriter's uncanny, liminal place in media history. The turntable and the vinyl record occupy a similar historical position. Just as the typewriter has been superseded by the digital technology of the computer, so has the turntable by the compact disc, the MP3, and the audio stream (as well as by a number of other technologies—8-track tape, cassette tape, digital audio tape—that are themselves now also superseded). Like the typewriter, the turntable circulates somewhere between the dustbin of history and the rarefied sphere of the retro—the preference that vinyl enthusiasts show for the professed authenticity and warmth of the LP bespeaks the same nostalgic impulses on which the Typing Explosion's pastiche of postwar office culture plays. Thinking the media poetics of the phonograph through the literary, then—retaining their shared inscriptive capacity as a kind of shadow history connecting the two—consequently opens up cultural, discursive, and material dimensions of the device that were lost to recording technology overall until much later in technological history, drawing into relief a complex, discontinuous trajectory marked by fits and starts, presences and absences. Indeed, reading the literary codex and the sonic disc as formats alongside one another—and moreover tracing how one format reads and writes the other—sheds light on central theoretical issues of media poetics such as inscription, memory, and materiality: the ways in which sound relates to writing not just as sense but as storage. What characterizes the mediality of paper in dialogue with vinyl, and how, following Craig Dworkin, might we view these substrates as formal devices and sites for the enactment of media poetics? How do the architectures of the page and the book represent and respond to the affordances of sound technology? How might we read the history of the phonograph and its descendants—the turntable and the LP record—alongside the history of the print codex book? How, moreover, might the book itself write this history?

In order to pursue these questions, I turn in this chapter to Kevin Young's *To Repel Ghosts: Five Sides in B Minor* (2001), a print text structured as a collection of records and focused in part around the life and work of the contemporary African American painter Jean-Michel Basquiat. Basquiat's work approaches the culture and history of the African diaspora through a catalogic aesthetics, building dense, often palimpsestic surfaces that combine expressionistic figuration and allusive text to render a complex, nonlinear history of modern Blackness. In using Basquiat's life and work as an avenue to consider the triangulated intersections among the book, the vinyl LP, and the painted canvas as surfaces for recording, storing, and circulating history—African American history in particular—Young develops in *To Repel Ghosts* a formal-material media poetics and politics of the poem: in terms of both content and form, the book thinks through both the politics of race in America and the ways in which those politics are entwined with different technologies and substrates.

Young describes *To Repel Ghosts* as an "extended riff" on Basquiat rather than a straightforward biography, with the artist and his work serving as "a bass line, a rhythm section, a melody from which the poems improvise."[12] *To Repel Ghosts* resembles any other conventional print codex as a physical object; it is not, in Pressman's sense, materially bookish. Yet Young divides its pages through an elaborate conceit of its being a collection of vinyl sides. Rather than apportioning it into sections, subsections, and poems, he structures it as two discs, titled "Zydeco" and "Mojo," each one divided into several sides, each side containing various numbers of tracks: "Zydeco" includes the sides "Bootlegs," "Hits," and "Takes," and "Mojo" includes "B-Sides" and "Solos." This organizational strategy resonates both in spite of and because of the book's conventional materiality. After all, its pages and sections can never actually be vinyl discs or grooves—nor could even the most radical codex experimentation—and as historically and materially close as the inscriptive processes of tinfoil and paper are, they are also fundamentally different. The phonograph emerged from a cultural environment dominated and determined by print writing, and its tinfoil indentations bore "structural as well as functional comparisons" to print inscription.[13] Yet both these early recordings and those that later followed on wax constituted divergences in the history of inscription as much as continuations. As Gitelman notes, phonographic inscription introduced into public culture a strange new paradox of records that were illegible to human eyes: "No person could read recordings the way a person reads handwritten scrawls, printed pages, or musical notes, or even the way a person examines a photograph or drawing to glean its meaning. Only machines could 'read' (that is, 'play') those delicately incised grooves."[14] However, in another layer of paradox, these "talismans of print culture" say something precisely in saying nothing: "illegible and yet somehow textual, public, and inscribed," they silently point back to print culture, yet in their illegibility and their nonalphabetic nature, they reflect that print culture as a culture of objects as well as a culture of language and text.[15] Illegibility and opacity, then, are key to the dissonant convergence between phonography and alphabetic textuality. *To Repel Ghosts* is most urgently about sound technology precisely in the fact that, like any and all books, it can never be sound technology; this paradoxical incompatibility becomes the foundation for a speculative mediatic poetics, in which Young applies pressure to the formal affordances of the poetic codex in ways that shed light on the affordances of a sonic format that the format of the codex can glimpse, limn, and echo but never reproduce.

This speculative poetics bears on the historicity of contemporary media culture as well. Like the members of the Typing Explosion in their invocation of the midcentury secretarial pool, Young turns to the phonograph in *To Repel Ghosts* not out of nostalgia, but rather in order to draw a complex history of technology, tracing resonances and tensions between contemporary digital formats and earlier analog media. In focusing on the record as an inscriptive object, Young remains historically faithful to the media technology of Basquiat's time, yet he also makes a larger claim about the stakes of mediation and media history, one that hinges on the inexactitude of the analog as a crucial aesthetic, theoretical, historical, and material lever. The analog appears across *To Repel Ghosts* at the levels of poetic device (the lyrical figure of the analogy itself), structuring conceit (the inexact, analogic relation between the LP disc and the print codex as storage media), and mode of inscription under consideration (analog sonic signals in contrast to digital ones). Explicitly thematizing and drawing connections between these different resonances of the concept, Young uses the poetics of *To Repel Ghosts* to argue for a conception of technological materiality and media history that is itself analog. Such a conception of inscription and storage over time not only includes and at times privileges individual analog technologies in particular but is itself indeed defined by the imprecision, inexactitude, and indirect approximation that define analog media. A phonographic and alphabetic history of Basquiat and the African American cultural genealogy that informs his work, *To Repel Ghosts* functions as the paper descendant of Edison's tinfoil sheets, a collection of etched, scratched surfaces that are more readable to the eye than those early recordings, but also store similar textual, material, and historical complexities of their own, tracing the contours of sonic technology through print textuality.

Book and Record, Archive and Absence

In a number of the structural and formal specificities of *To Repel Ghosts* (which I trace below), Young appropriates the generic procedures and structures of other media while simultaneously distorting and overturning them. Precisely in modeling his text in the image of a series of records and a series of Basquiat's paintings, Young explicitly claims the impossibility of completing such a gesture faithfully. The paradoxical nature of this formal claim on mediality answers the aesthetic call Weheliye makes in *Phonographies*. Writing in opposition to Derridean thinking regarding representation and repetition, Weheliye argues on behalf of "not repetition with a difference so much as the repetition *of* difference[.] . . . This repetition of difference does not ask how 'the copy' departs from 'the source' but assumes that difference will, indeed, be different in each of its incarnations. . . . As a consequence, records, CDs, cassette tapes, or mp3 files should not be thought as attempting to replicate a lost immaculate source/original but as events in their own right."[16] Anticipating Sterne's format theory, Weheliye advances a schema here that differs both from Derridean grammatology and from several key prevailing critical theories of reproduction. The storage formats in the media landscape he sketches are not copies that shatter the cult value of the original in the Benjaminian sense, nor are they exactly copies without an original in the Baudrillardian sense. They are all copies (if only in the sense of existing in multiplicity) that are themselves originals: distinct and disconnected from one another in their material and technological parameters, but paradoxically also resonant (in all senses of the word) with one another precisely in their differences. Viewed from this perspective, "the original/copy distinction vanishes and only the singular and sui generis becomings of the source remain in the clearing": the format through which information is stored matters precisely because of the complex and contradictory similitudes and differences across multiple formats.[17] Each object of storage, as Weheliye suggests, is itself an event, not only a marker or record of time but also an entity that occupies time itself in its specific objecthood. Taken together, these objects accrete to a larger trajectory of media history that is resolutely discontinuous, uneven, and analog, even and especially if some of the objects in question are themselves digital, as in the case of his catalog.

Thus before I turn in earnest to the poetic "tracks" that make up the bulk of *To Repel Ghosts*'s pages, I spend considerable time and space on a number of elements in its paratextual apparatus as a way of outlining how the book itself functions as an object engaged in media-historical inquiry attentive to questions of mediality, race, and the analog broadly understood. As its subtitle—*Five Sides in B Minor*—suggests, this apparatus collectively makes the speculative mediatic claim that *To Repel Ghosts* is not a series of poems at all, but rather a collection of "sides," groupings of recorded sonic tracks on vinyl discs. Both in spite of and because of its impossibility, this conceit of the print text as a sonic artifact pervades its apparatus. In addition to its prefatory poem, its visual frontispiece, and the visual pages that demarcate its various recorded "sides" through images of the surface of a record (all of which I discuss in greater depth below), *To Repel Ghosts* includes a set of "liner notes" as well as an acknowledgments page that details the text's production and publication history in sonic terms, describing it as an "album" and an "LP," noting where it was "[r]ecorded" and "[r]e-mixed," and prefacing lists of previous publications of various tracks with descriptions such as "[s]ingles from this album first aired on the following stations" and "[o]ther cuts have since appeared on compilations including."[18] For Young, invoking the vinyl record as a model through these gestures is not an authorizing or authenticating strategy but rather one that both allows and forces the codex of *To Repel Ghosts* to engage in a range of dissonant, uneven recognitions with other media technologies. All of this apparatus exemplifies Gérard Genette's conception of the paratext. As understood by Genette, paratexts are the elements of a book that frame the author's main text, encompassing everything from the materiality of the cover to elements such as section headings and running titles that constitute the architecture of the page.[19]

Paratexts constitute "a zone not only of transition but also of *transaction*," a textual space that "enables a text to become a book."[20] In the case of *To Repel Ghosts*, the question of paratextuality is also a question of mediality, of how the spatial, textual, and material affordances of the literary codex refer to the affordances of the vinyl record. To modify Genette's definition, this book's paratexts enable its text to become a record—or at least to purport to do so on the surface when it never truly can.

This question of paratextuality and mediality is also a question of race, history, and power. In producing a book that explicitly presents itself as something other than a book and, more specifically and more importantly, as an artifact of sonic technology, Young stakes out a critical project at the intersection of modern media history and African American literary history.[21] The formal-material conceit of the book's apparatus and organization as a collection of five vinyl sides invokes two crucial antecedents for engaging this intersection. Firstly, the book's titular five sides suggest a potentiality to deliver on the technophilic wish of the protagonist of Ellison's *Invisible Man* as he hides underground in the novel's preface: "Now I have one radio-phonograph; I plan to have five. . . . I'd like to hear five recordings of Louis Armstrong playing and singing 'What Did I Do to Be So Black and Blue'—all at the same time."[22] Young's work offers a formal enactment of Ellison's foundational narrative scene, exemplifying Weheliye's claim that "a subject of sonic Afro-modernity, while breaking with purely visual and linguistic paradigms of subjectivity, comes into being in the crevice made by the audiovisual disjunction engendered by the phonograph."[23]

Indeed, *To Repel Ghosts* imagines in its paratextual conceit an Afro-modern subjectivity that is palpably, explicitly phonographic and audiovisual, as I suggest below. Yet the sides of Young's book also reach back to an earlier source text of sonic Afro-modernity, providing a particularly, deliberately mediated instance of the "Talking Book" that Henry Louis Gates, Jr., cites as a founding object in the African American literary canon.[24] Anticipating by more than a century the fantasies of Edison's audience at *Scientific American* for a technology that allows the book to "read itself," the talking book first appears in African American literary history in the narrative of the enslavement of James Albert Ukawsaw Gronniosaw, first published in 1770.[25] In a moment of thwarted literacy within Gronniosaw's narrative, the book in question, a Bible, "speaks" to Gronniosaw's Dutch enslaver, but "ha[s] no voice" for him, only a "rather deafening silence." "For Gronniosaw," Gates writes, "the book—or, perhaps I should say, the very concept of 'book'—constitute[s] a silent primary text, a text, however, in which the black man f[inds] no echo of his own voice."[26] The talking book, for Gates, is the "ur-trope of the Anglo-African tradition," the object in which the "curious tension between the black vernacular and the literate white text, between the spoken and the written word, between the oral and the printed forms of literary discourse, has been represented and thematized in black letters at least since slaves and ex-slaves met the challenge of the Enlightenment to their humanity by literally writing themselves into being through carefully crafted representations in language of the black self."[27] For Maurice Wallace, the talking book "also stand[s] in for the fantasy of writing, generally, to posit, as Freud claimed, 'the voice of the absent.'"[28] Wallace's description makes visible how the talking book is, in addition to being a cultural trope for signification, an imaginary media technology—a narratively represented textual object in which questions of oral and inscriptive meaning and memory swirl together and intertwine. Weheliye understands the Gatesian "speakerly texts" of the African American tradition that follow from the foundational scene of the talking book—work by authors such as Pauline Hopkins, W. E. B. Du Bois, Zora Neale Hurston, Ralph Ellison, James Baldwin, Nathaniel Mackey, and Toni Morrison—as "sound recordings . . . writings [that] suggest a different way of merging the *phoné* and *graph* than the technology of the phonograph, underscoring how sound and writing meet and inform each other in the annals of twentieth-century African American literature."[29] Couched and layered in paratexts, Young's text short-circuits the *phoné/graph* merger, imagining a literalization of the talking book, a codex that itself imaginatively stores sound through writing.

At the same time, however, it also redoubles and reworks the terms of this merger. *To Repel Ghosts* is a "speakerly text" that shares the same concerns with the intersection and interdependence of sound and writing as the abstractly sonic recordings produced by the authors Weheliye lists. Yet it does so not only as speakerly or as a text but also as a material storage object that reflects on the stuff of both domains, situating itself at the intersection of alphabetic and sonic inscription. In this sense, the text constitutes a detour in the sonic history of African American literature from the metaphorically phonographic to the literally (if speculatively) phonographic. Young merges *phonè* and *graph* because of the technology of the phonograph rather than in spite of it, imagining a playerly text, composed of records on paper that demand to be confronted through their material trappings rather than naturalized and domesticated as conventional print text.

What does it mean more specifically, then, to structure a printed text in the form of a set of records? One way to understand such a gesture is as a particularly complexly mediated instance of what Joseph Conte describes as the "procedural form" of postmodern poetics, which "consists of prede-termined and arbitrary constraints that are relied upon to generate the context and direction of the poem during composition."[30] What happens, though, at the convergence of form and affordance, when the constraints for a print text derive not from alphabetics, language, or print itself but rather from another media technology altogether? For Young, it is precisely the constraint of the fantastical, unplayed, and unplayable quality of the "records" comprising *To Repel Ghosts* that makes them viable objects for writing, a materially imaginative constitution of the talking book. Indeed, like the book in Gronniosaw's narrative, Young's paper records are deafeningly silent as well, storage media that exists to be played back but cannot be. Their silence broaches the question not of the power dynamics of individual literacy or communal social agency, but rather of how reading, writing, inscription, storage, and playback shape and situate media objects and their histories, and how those objects themselves represent history (both their own and that of the larger culture in which they circulate). In order to trace the shadow history of phonographic inscription, recuperating material that is unread and unplayed, Young positions the codex as a storage format for that which cannot be read. Through this conceit of the book as playerly record, he troubles the question of readability in order to invoke a larger history of sound technology that is shadowed by and shot through with the fraught questions of reading and writing themselves.

Just as Young uses the affordances of the record to throw alphabetic reading into relief and into question, the form of the book conversely puts pressure on the affordances of the record as a media format. The material content of each side in the text refuses clear correlation with the material dimensions of an actual phonographic side: the number of tracks varies from seventeen on the shortest side to thirty on the longest, and the page count varies from fifty-five to almost eighty. Young's organization raises a number of questions as to how written text might analogize the generic procedures and material dimensions of the record—how much time does the "playback" of a page take? How (if at all) do variables such as line length affect that time? How many poetic tracks could the physical space and information capacity of a phonographic side hold? Moreover, beyond the generalized questions of how a printed book might procedurally appropriate the constraints of a record, the particular sequence of sides Young constructs contains disparities in dimension and scope (the differences in side length, for example) that would be effectively impossible to attain in the pressing of an actual analog record. Indeed, as emphatically as *To Repel Ghosts* announces the record form as its procedural conceit, there seems to be virtually nothing of the record about it other than the highly contingent concept itself: what appears to be a complexly evolved procedural form is ultimately the disjunctive effect of addressing another medium at a close material level. By imposing the affordances of the vinyl record onto the structure of *To Repel Ghosts* only to simultaneously transgress them, Young tests the analogic limits of written text and the codex format, unfolding the ways in which the affordances of a record (its duration, segmentation, and bandwidth, among others) can be imaginatively broken, broken down, reconstituted, and otherwise transformed through outside interpretation from another media form. Thus just as Young structurally transforms and radicalizes his literary work through sonic, technological "constraints . . . formulated without literary precedent," producing a textual aesthetics that is "obviously made, deliberately assembled" in the image of the record, he conversely interrogates the material structure of the record as a medium for storing information through textual representation.[31]

These contradictory commensurabilities between the book and the disc as storage media—the analogic relation between these two analog media, to frame the relation more pointedly—find their first expression in *To Repel Ghosts* in the short prefatory poem that begins the book. This untitled poem is the book's first paratextual element and indeed the first piece of information inside the book, appearing before both its frontispiece and the page listing Young's other publications. It appears entirely in italic, lowercase characters, centered on the page:

> *distortions clicks & pops*
> *from analog equipment*
> *are part of the fabric*
> *& only contribute*
> *to the garment's uniqueness*
> *& sound quality* [32]

These six lines weave together multiple strands of closely related plays on words: "sound" registers both in its sonic sense and as a marker of the stable, reliable "quality" of the "garment" in question, while "analog" connotes both a specific format for sonic technology and a larger mode of semantic, aesthetic, and informational relation. Similarly, Young's use of fabric and a garment as key images in such a prefatory piece draws an implicit resonance between text and textile, underscoring the material nature of the work to come. Indeed, the multiple resonances of many single words in the prefatory poem provide points of connection among different fields of meaning—the technological, the textile, the textual—that are all conceptually and verbally interrelated, but are never completely interchangeable. As the self-reflexive place of "analog" as a central term within these relations suggests, these domains are themselves analogues, entities that are comparable and share a conceptual overlap without being wholly reconcilable. Through the centrality of this term and concept to the poem, Young provides a version in miniature of the text's argument as a whole, advancing a media poetics and a vision of history (both of Basquiat himself and of the sonic technology around him) that together adopt the analog signal as both content and form.

Thus through these inexact comparisons, the poem encapsulates both the paradoxes of the phonograph as an inscriptive machine that I raised above and the paradoxes of writing across media that Young throws into relief in adopting the phonograph as a model for print authorship. The accuracy and "distortion" that the poem articulates and performs become visible as co-constitutive properties of the phonograph and book as "analog equipment," each one dialectically requiring, opposing, and producing the other. Similarly, the sonic authenticity that the poem promises on behalf of the text as a whole is an explicitly and deliberately distorted authenticity, transformed and transmuted by external forces such as time, sonic limitations, and material decay, but also by the way in which Young manipulates the book's discontinuous, nonnarrative text as a seemingly faithful record of Basquiat's life, work, and times. There is no explicit mention of a record as an object within this poem perhaps because there is no credible record in the sense of an unimpeachable fidelity, only a series of analog variations. This prefatory poem, then, crystallizes *To Repel Ghosts*'s paradoxical media-historical claim: the book is a collection of discs as specific objects, but to call it a record in the broader sense of the term would be precisely to ignore the analogic instabilities that define those discs for Young. Conversely, rather than standing as a deviation from some sort of one-to-one replication of another media form, Young's simultaneous embrace and circumvention of the procedural conceits of the record form is a necessary, explicit claiming of the unachievability of precisely what the text purports to be: to use Weheliye's terms, it promises a record and delivers an event. These gestures suggest that in order to write in the shape of records, it is necessary to do so in categorical difference from the record, not as an indirect consequence of untranslatability between the two forms but rather as a productive means of accessing the aesthetic energy produced through such a dissonance. The distortion that emerges as a governing principle through this approach is not a necessary evil to be minimized, as in the eyes of technocratic positivism, but nor is it a wholly resistant gesture that undoes the controlling cultural work of that positivism. Rather, as this prefatory poem itself argues, it is literally and figuratively part of the fabric of intermedia relations, an irremovable result of working across different systems of inscription and storage, translating and circulating informational material across time.

Analog and Apparatus, or, *Ceci n'est pas une disque*: Generic Experimentation as Media Theory

A number of visual paratextual features within *To Repel Ghosts* extend this analogic approach to intermedia relations and media history. The first of these to appear within the text is a reproduction of Basquiat's *Now's the Time* (1985), a plywood disc nearly eight feet in diameter painted to resemble the Charlie Parker record of the same name.[33] The surface of Basquiat's wooden "record" is starkly minimal, its blackness interrupted only by two white rings to demarcate the outside of its label and its spindle hole, and by text denoting the title and artist, "PRKR" in Basquiat's orthographically compressed, small-cap writing. His turn to the sculptural in this piece (a relatively rare instance in his work overall) accentuates the materiality of the record it represents, exaggeratedly expanding its physical dimensions while reducing its semantic dimensions, replacing the record's regular, concentric phonographic groove with the organic irregularities of wood grain and compacting the explanatory text of its label. Like a low-fi version of one of Claes Oldenburg's oversized sculptures of everyday consumer objects, Basquiat's profoundly unplayable disc transforms the Parker record into a monument to the opacity and distortion that information gathers

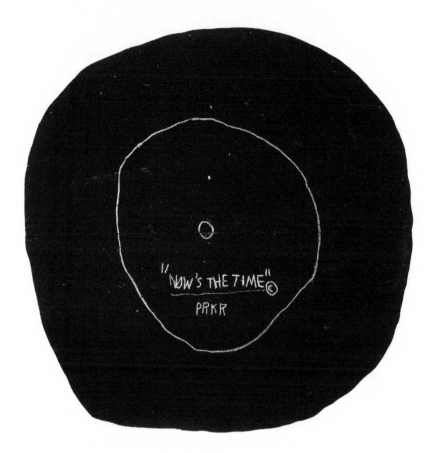

Figure 1. Jean-Michel Basquiat, *Now's the Time*, 1985. Acrylic and oil stick on plywood. © Estate of Jean-Michel Basquiat. Licensed by Artestar, New York.

as it moves across different media. Young's inclusion of this image on the frontispiece further extends Basquiat's transpositional visual play: the oversized, textured, three-dimensional artwork becomes a flat, textureless image smaller than a human hand, and indeed smaller than any actual record. The full impact of this transformative frontispiece depends on a reader's prior knowledge of the original Basquiat work (as well as perhaps of the original Parker record). Yet the image as it is within the text, directly across from the text's title, subtitle, and attribution—these sides are "sung by the author"—nonetheless conveys the virtual impossibility of putting work in other media transparently into or onto the printed page precisely by announcing Young's attempt to engage in just such a project.[34]

Young's choice of this particular Basquiat piece at the opening of the book—rather than, say, a more commonly representative painting from his oeuvre—also invokes an array of multiple histories and temporalities discontinuously overlapping across the book and the multiple media it represents. To take the painting's title and inscription at face value as a kind of annunciation, *when* exactly is the "now" in question? At what time, and how can we as readers know and situate ourselves in relation to it? What documents or records, what systems of inscription and memory, exist alongside this reticent, minimalist surface in order to help us locate, retain, and replay this now? If we acknowledge, following Weheliye, that every object of storage is itself an event, we also have to acknowledge that this event occurs and recurs across multiple temporalities and multiple media—repetition of and as difference. Are we in the now of Young's twenty-first-century paper authorship? Of Basquiat's 1980s work with paint, canvas, and (at least in this case) wood? Of Parker's 1945 recording of the composition to tape for release on vinyl as part of the now-legendary Savoy Sessions?[35] Of Edison's talking machine announcing the moment of its own emergence as a "celebrated author-orator" in the late 1870s?[36] All of these technologies and temporalities are in play and in contact with one another here, their simultaneity layered and laminated within the opaque surface of Basquiat's recontextualized object, a kind of media-historical palimpsest that gains further depth from the phonograph's status as the first technology able to, in Edison's words, "store & reproduce automatically at any future time the human voice perfectly."[37] Any time this record plays, it seems, whether on vinyl, wood, or paper, it is always all of these nows.

The pages that mark off and introduce the text's different sides through-out the book display a sequence of even more minimalist "records." Each of these pages consists of a black circle with a small white circle at its center and white and gray text across it, enumerating the names and numbers of the disc, the side, and the various tracks included within it—for example, disc one is titled "Zydeco," and side one of disc one is titled "Bootlegs" and comprises twenty-seven tracks, all listed on the image at the beginning of the side. These meta-Magrittean pages extend the work of the frontispiece more fully into the domain of the literary as a format; even more so than that introductory image, they are and are not records, registering as blank, flat surfaces on paper, etched with textual, alphabetic information. They function as minimalist icons, at once both reproducing and distorting their imaginary counterparts in the real world of the vinyl LP, and also as visual analogues of the Basquiat painting on the frontispiece. Much as Young's incorporation of "Now's the Time" distorts Basquiat's distortion of the original Parker record by transposing it into the domain of print textual-ity, these pages work toward a similar mediatic point from the opposite direction, distorting the conventional table of contents into the form of a disc. The stark contrast of black and white space on these pages stages a complex play on scale and synecdoche. While the image seems at first to represent the black center label of a LP with a white spindle hole in its center, it also demands to be read at a wider spatial scale, in which the black space represents the entirety of the disc and the white space represents the central label on that disc.

This second reading of the disc image inverts the proportions and visual polarities of the first reading, a vertiginous optical gesture that announces the text's form and content as constantly in flux. Text, image, and object reverberate against one another on these pages to produce a highly mediated and materially engaged instance of the worlds embedded within worlds that Brian McHale cites as a central trope of postmodernist fiction, a sort of *disque en abyme*, so to speak.[38] Of course, a crucial difference persists between Young's structural conceit and the majority of the worlds within worlds of postmodernist fiction described by McHale. Whereas the structures dis-cussed by McHale take place at the narrative level, within the ontological worlds of the novel, Young's records exist outside of the narrative, diegetic world of the text's content or "plot," to the extent that there even is one—this is the mediatic worlding of the poem rather than in it, to adapt Dworkin's terms. Indeed, in the absence of a unifying narrative for the poems collected in *To Repel Ghosts*, these discs register not as metanarrative devices but as metaobjects. They are imaginary media artifacts rather than penetrations from a narrative world, produced by Young in relation and response to Basquiat as a cultural practitioner yet bearing no narrative or historical connection to him as a historical figure or character in the text. The sides that make up *To Repel Ghosts* are the text in material terms, yet somehow they are not of the text in discursive terms.[39] This tension finds its extreme in the ontological and technological problem embedded in the fact that the book is divided into "five sides," as alluded to in its subtitle. This description makes perfect sense in the context of the language of jazz culture, connoting a collection of five recordings. Yet when read more literally it takes on a paradoxical impossibility. How can a collection of two-sided vinyl records ever have five sides? How can disc one—or any disc, for that matter—have three sides? If we take into account another detail from the deep history of phonography—namely that disc recordings were one-sided until the early twentieth century—Young's uneven division becomes somewhat clearer, yet not necessarily more stable.

Indeed, Young's speculative recasting of writing through the thick materiality of the phonograph gives it the surface trappings of that medium, yet the complexities of *To Repel Ghosts*'s paratextual apparatus serve as a reminder that the material affordance storage capabilities of the phonograph are neither as stable nor as clear as they might seem. This setting of two technologies of inscription and storage against one another through visual form serves as a self-conscious reflection on the histories those technologies serve to record as always already subject to distortion and disruption, precisely because of their status as recorded. The book's paratextual apparatus imagines those histories—of Basquiat, of African American culture, of the phonograph, the disc, and the page themselves—as complexly analogic both individually and collectively, swirling back and forth in space and time, blurring and hissing into one another because of the technologies in which they are embedded, at turns distorted, secreted, and uncovered through the protocols of inscription and storage that the text claims on behalf of print writing. In the sections that follow, I turn to the poetic text of *To Repel Ghosts* itself in order to consider how Young uses literary form to trace these protocols.

Tracing Distortion: Analogues and Catalogs, Indexicality and Inexactitude

In the same way that *To Repel Ghosts*'s paratextual elements accumulate and circulate around its so-called main text without articulating any clear narrative cohesion, the book's poetic tracks themselves similarly accumulate in a way that forestalls a linear historical trajectory. Their subjects include events from Basquiat's life and representations of his paintings, but also thematic and historical material that resists cohesion in being only indirectly related to him. These "non-Basquiat tracks," so to speak, frustrate the narrative coherence that the text's ostensible biographical focus seems to promise: tracks such as "Jack Johnson," a twenty-two-page, multisection monologue in the voice of the titular African American boxer, for example, or "Oleo," a compressed portrait of the performer Bert Williams, represent material wholly outside of Basquiat's life itself and only indirectly related to his artistic work. The track "Monarchs" exemplifies this overall antinarrativity on a microscopic level. As the section I quote below illustrates, "Monarchs" consists entirely of excerpts from the lineups of the Kansas City Monarchs, "*Kansas City's Own / World Colored Champions*" of baseball, as the track's subtitle notes, from various years ranging from 1920 to 1945:

1920

Arumi	rf, 2b	
Blukoi, Frank	2b	Philippines
Carr, George ("Tank")	1b, rf	California[40]

Although these tracks exist together in the same book with one another and with the tracks that focus directly on Basquiat, and often share common concerns, they are emphatically not detours, digressions, or deviations from a singular central or main path of the Basquiat life narrative. Indeed, while many of the figures addressed in these tracks—Johnson, Williams, and the Monarchs, among others in the text—are the subjects of Basquiat paintings (although not necessarily the paintings rendered in *To Repel Ghosts*), the lines of filiation between these multiple spheres are never spelled out or even directly articulated.

On the contrary, they relate paratactically, through a complex analogical commensurability rather than through direct, one-to-one connection or continuity. Thus the book fits the criteria Brent Hayes Edwards advances for a serial poem: "[A] book-length work composed of discrete individual poems, clearly interrelated but not assembled into a suite or sequence with a discernible narrative arc, epic ambition, or programmatic frame. Without the well-wrought urn of the single lyric poem, so familiar in English-language volumes of poetry as to be taken for granted, the reader is challenged to find new ways to navigate the book as a unit. . . . Serial form is paratactic rather than hypotactic, heterogeneous rather than systematic."[41] Following from my discussion of *To Repel Ghosts*'s structure and paratextual apparatus thus far, I will show in this section how the book's serial poetics serves explicitly and directly as a media poetics, a means for representing and interrogating the phonograph as a storage medium alongside the codex. Indeed, the navigational challenges of this text are in particular challenges that invoke and intertwine the history and materiality of these two media.

In this sense, the book's poetic seriality serves alongside its paratexts as another means by which the conventions of the record and the print codex trouble and reconsider one another, opening onto a larger interrogation of how these media might store history. Both media can be consumed linearly, but they do not necessarily need to be. Although a record's tracks exist in a sequence, that sequence need not bear or impose any intrinsic meaning; the forward motion of the needle through the single ongoing groove of a record tantalizingly suggests a narrative coherence and temporal continuity that can easily be undone through the selection of a single track from the predetermined sequence. While this potentiality is present within the print book, dominant practices of literary reading since the emergence of print have often suppressed such discontinuous reading. Peter Stallybrass argues, "One cannot move easily back and forth between distant points on a scroll. But it is precisely such movement back and forth that the book permits. It not only allows for discontinuous reading; it encourages it." Yet, as Stallybrass notes, much of conventional narrative literature from modernity onward has treated the codex as a scroll: "The novel," for example, is "a brilliantly perverse interlude in the long history of discontinuous reading."[42] *To Repel Ghosts* foregrounds the book object's openness to discontinuity. On the one hand, it contains too much material outside of its chronologically progressive narrative of Basquiat's life, work, and death to merit consideration as a novel in verse: its text juxtaposes moments that exist within a biographical trajectory against isolated, one-time historical events and documents without explanation or connection, and in large part seemingly without any larger integrating rationale. Yet that very trajectory provides too much of a continuity and occupies too much of the book to make it a collection; indeed, precisely through the prominence of the Basquiat narrative within the book's mass of information and history, Young invokes the narrative coherence of the novel and the conventional codex precisely in order to leverage against it. He promises the continuity Stallybrass attributes to the scroll and the novel and then deviates from that continuity, not merely encouraging but indeed forcing discontinuous reading in ways that resonate with the material affordances of both the print codex and the phonographic disc. Faced with the book's mass of text, the reader must choose (although in reality they can ultimately only vacillate) between attempting to read linearly, in the front-to-back, beginning-to-end manner of the scroll or the novel, "where the teleological drive from page to page mitigates against dipping about or turning back," and attempting to read discontinuously and isotropically, in a manner that approaches the book as a loose manifestation of the archive, a material collection of textual information without any larger organizing principle.[43]

Within this archival mass, associations and references cluster, interweave, and overlap in Young's language. Indeed, the same convergences that *To Repel Ghosts* models at the level of paratext and technological form also take place at the level of the word. The first track of disc one, side one, "Campbell's Black Bean Soup," embodies this approach. As its title suggests, the track documents a first meeting between Warhol, famous for painting Campbell's soup cans, and Basquiat—the titular "black bean/being"—at the latter artist's studio. The track's language extends the referential network set in place by its title: "Basquiat stripped / labels," Young writes, "opened & ate / alphabets."[44] These three lines layer a complex network of allusions and double meanings—a self-conscious poetic fabric, to use the language of the prefatory poem. Basquiat's "stripp[ing] labels" points both to his specific deconstructive dismantling of Warhol's imagery in several collaborative paintings later in their careers—his neoexpressionistic approach materially disrupting Warhol's characteristic brand-logo silkscreens—and to his role as an artist who broke racial boundaries, with his widespread popularity within the predominantly white art world of the 1980s dismantling cultural determinations that had previously limited the prestige and visibility an African American artist could attain. Likewise, Young's claim that Basquiat "opened & ate alphabets" refers again to Warhol's iconic soup cans (specified as "chicken // & noodle" in the next lines of the track), but also to the dense textuality of his canvases.[45] The deliberate polysemic overload of lines such as these serves to accumulate overlapping, uneven meanings within individual words in a manner that points toward analogously overlapping and uneven relations between media technologies; Young's style exaggerates poetic technique in order to position it as an analogue for mediation itself, a means of triangulating between print writing, painting, and phonography.

While this poetic strategy has specific implications for the phonographic record as an object in particular, it also speaks to Young's concern with analogy and the analogic more broadly. The short track "Pork," which I quote in its entirety below, exemplifies this practice:

> Ham, Sons of
> Ham hock
> Ham i.e. showoff[46]

"Pork" is the shortest track in *To Repel Ghosts*, yet precisely because of this it is the most telling and concentrated enactment of Young's poetic principles in the book. The track is literally and figuratively indexical, a condensed catalog of unarticulated resonances and contiguous meanings related to the titular term. Its terse language and discontinuous form suggest that there are complex, overlapping relations between the terms in play, but never make explicit what those relations are. Moreover, those unnamed relations are themselves always close but never synonymous, a tension raised in the way the indexical form of the track situates them: these multiple uses of "ham" are not semantically interchangeable, nor are "pork" and "ham," nor even are "ham" and "showoff," in spite of and because of their being linked by an equating "i.e." Indeed, Young's grouping of these uses under a single title serves to underscore differences and discontinuities in linguistic and cultural valence as much as similarities.

Young's use of indexicality and inexactitude as a poetic device fittingly reaches its apex in *To Repel Ghosts*'s index, a paratextual piece that comes virtually at the end of the book, after all of the discs, the liner notes, and the acknowledgments. The index consists of a single page of cultural referents seemingly appropriated from Basquiat's paintings and rendered in small caps to indicate their status as direct quotations, arranged in alphabetical order by last name (where applicable) and ranging from "SYKES, ROOSEVELT" to "VIRGINIA MINSTRELS," as if the page were an arbitrary excerpt torn from a larger index of some sort.[47] It seems to promise the reader a means for accessing Young's text nonlinearly and discontinuously yet deliberately, seeking out references within the text to these particular figures and institutions. Yet this access is ultimately a dead end, at least at the level of surface practicality: the index is wholly without page numbers, and virtually none of the items in it appears within the poetic tracks of *To Repel Ghosts*, with the notable exceptions of "TWAIN, MARK," which appears several times in the track "Undiscovered Genius of the Mississippi Delta," and "VICTOR RECORDS," the record company referenced in the title of "Victor 25448 {1987}," a track that takes its name from the Basquiat painting of the same name, which in turn refers to the Victor catalog number for the 1936 recording "Little Old Lady."[48] Yet it is precisely in its lack of direct, clear referentiality and navigability, in the opaque, inexact histories it encodes, that the book's index most closely echoes Basquiat's work. Indeed, with its short, catalogic lines, its form on the page echoes the form of Young's poetic tracks proper, as well as the dense textuality of many of Basquiat's own paintings.

The artist, too, employs text on the canvas in a manner that is both literally and figuratively indexical. In a 1983 interview, curator Henry Geldzahler suggests to Basquiat that his inclination toward copying and listing words in his paintings produces "indexes to encyclopedias that don't exist," a Borgesian claim to which Basquiat responds obliquely, "I just like the names"; when Geldzahler patronizingly characterizes Basquiat's cultural syncretism as reflecting "an interest in all kinds of intellectual areas that go beyond the streets, and it's the combination of the two," Basquiat replies, "[I]t's more of a name-dropping thing."[49] Basquiat's response here resonates both idiomatically and physically: his works engage in a practice of cultural and historical reference—"name-dropping"—by literally dropping names and other words into space, allowing them to hang paratactically around one another on the canvas, producing an indexical effect without invoking the clear referents (real or imaginary) implicit in the encyclopedias Geldzahler imagines. Jeffrey Hoffeld suggests that this practice of inscription is at least partly shaped by Basquiat's intensive study of a monograph by Leonardo da Vinci. Hoffeld claims that Basquiat appropriated not only the specific contents of the book but also several crucial elements of its aesthetics, both the "astonishing mix and range of subjects" juxtaposed on the page in its voluminous index and the "overallness of treatment" through which da Vinci produced pages "undifferentiated, spatially or otherwise, by their specific content."[50] Regardless of the extent to which da Vinci in particular influenced Basquiat, the parallels Hoffeld draws between the two underscore the ways in which Basquiat's practices treat indexicality as a specialized kind of inscription, one that Young claims as an intermedia poetic strategy and an approach to the architecture of the page—his appropriation of Basquiat's text is also, more deeply, an appropriation of his working practices with text.

I consider how Young applies this methodological appropriation to a history of phonographic inscription in my discussion of his "Discography" poems in the section below. First, however, in preparation for that discussion, I want to situate more fully Young's use of the index and indexicality as analogic devices in relation to the larger history of the book. The index is a paratextual device that is unique to print culture and the print codex. Within the constrained continuity of the scroll, which precludes nonlinear textual navigation, the index is unnecessary and irrelevant, and within the irregularities and idiosyncracies of manuscript books, it is inaccurate—only with the segmentation and standardization of print does the index become a valuable tool, allowing the nonlinear, discontinuous navigation that Stallybrass notes. In the case of longer texts, the role of the index became progressively more crucial: Janine Barchas, writing of Samuel Richardson's *The History of Sir Charles Grandison* (1753), describes this role as forcing "physical oscillation between narrative and paratext . . . [t]he novel's extensive index, by demanding a non-linear approach, exerts an even greater hold over [] reading and interpretation."[51] Young's use of indexicality claims this hold, but to no direct or discrete end. Discontinuous, nonlinear reading leads in this case not to greater precision or specificity but rather only to a more deeply discontinuous and nonlinear history traversing the codex.

Thus we find in Young's poetics a particularly complex and idiosyncratic formulation of the relation between the two structuring principles I have traced thus far, analogy and indexicality. To the extent that these concepts can be traced or charted across different paper media, common sense might suggest the following connections: the continuity of the scroll, with its inexact locations of particular passages and its smooth, indivisible spaces and movements between those locations, would seem to resemble and perhaps anticipate the protocols of analog media such as the phonograph, while the precise, discontinuous, and indexable locations of the codex would seem in their nonlinear configuration to more closely point toward digital media forms.[52] Yet *To Repel Ghosts* disrupts these historical parallels. The items in its index—as well as so much of the poetic language in so many of the book's tracks—point not to clear destinations within the text, Basquiat's paintings, his biography, or the histories of contemporary art and African American culture that he draws on and exists within, but rather elsewhere. They invoke phantom texts and objects, entities that hover outside of the strict domain of the text like the "encyclopedias that don't exist" Geldzahler imagines orbiting Basquiat's textual work. Discontinuity in this instance points not toward instantaneous, discrete leaps between locations in language, text, and time, but rather toward the gaps between those locations, spaces that cannot be mapped precisely but register only through distortion, static, and inexactitude. The deliberate afunctionality of Young's index, its refusal to direct the reader to a clear, existent textual location, claims the codex as a format on behalf of a history of analog media and the analog production and storage of information. Taken as a whole, then, *To Repel Ghosts* collects the material of an analog history around and through Basquiat, but refuses to codify or order it at the level of language. Yet what might initially seem like a conventionally poststructural serial poetics based on the endless slippage and regress of signification ultimately reveals itself when viewed alongside the book's paratextual apparatus to be a materially embedded media poetics of the analog, a textual, linguistic structure through which Young traces a complex and internally contradictory model of the storage capacities of modern media.

Fittingly, given *To Repel Ghosts*'s attention to Basquiat and his work, these analog relations appear perhaps most dramatically in relation to the artist's paintings themselves. For example, just as the blankly stated indexical

Figure 2. Jean-Michel Basquiat, *Pork*, 1981. Acrylic, oil, and oilstick on glass and wood with fabric and metal attachments. © Estate of Jean-Michel Basquiat. Licensed by Artestar, New York.

meanings enumerated in "Pork" relate to one another through the complexly dissonant convergence that characterizes the analog for Young, so too does the track overall relate to Basquiat's painting *Pork* (1981).[53] Basquiat's *Pork* is painted on a door: the main panel of the painting, occupying the lower two-thirds, is dominated by a black-skinned, red-eyed head topped with a bristling, undulating halo, a sort of dark, distorted angel. A variety of other marks circulate around this head, including the word "pork" itself, a painting of a cardboard box marked with the words "top" and "*peso neto*" (Spanish for "net weight," a frequently appearing phrase in Basquiat's work), a series of repeated block capital h's—HHHH—and several patterns of curlicues and arrows that resemble fences. Above this main panel, the six panes in the original structure of the door contain multiple other marks: a pie shape with one slice missing; a smiling, almost cartoonish African American head with a flattop haircut; repetitions of the letter R and of the word "TAR" (another common word in Basquiat's work). Other than including the word, this painting is not "about" pork in any larger thematic or representational sense; it bears an opaque relation to its title that is characteristic of Basquiat's approach to textuality and source material in general, an approach that Young's track and his analogic poetics overall in turn appropriate and extend.

In fact, the track "Pork" is not about the painting *Pork* at all: whereas many of Young's tracks named after Basquiat paintings also list the year of the painting in question in their titles—for example, "Hollywood Africans {1983}" or "Fois Gras {1984}"—"Pork" has no such annotation.[54] Nor does the track employ small caps to mark its text as a direct quotation of writing in Basquiat's painting—if, of course, the text in the track were even in the painting to begin with (to my knowledge and in the scope of my research, the text in the track "Pork" does not appear in any of Basquiat's paintings). Young's constellation of words, references, and meanings in "Pork" is his own, a gesture in the manner of Basquiat, analogous to his indexical textual work, but not, so to speak, in the direct image of the painting. This emphasis on the analog at all levels consequently points toward a revision of ekphrasis, the poetic genre often understood, following James Heffernan's definition, as "the verbal representation of visual representation."[55] Through Young's self-conscious, explicit, and multilayered attention to multiple media and the comparative relations between them, the central question of ekphrasis becomes one of storage rather than content, of the format that form allows—the question not only of what each medium might store but also how it might do so. Yet when considered against Basquiat's approach, this shift in focus seems to bend back on itself: after all, what other kind of ekphrasis can there be in relation to a painting that is almost entirely textual to begin with? How might poetic, analogic thinking across media forms serve to rethink the history of those forms? In the section that follows, I turn to two tracks where Young explicitly raises the question of ekphrasis, textuality, and phonography as grounds for thinking about print writing as a storage mechanism for analog cultural and media history.

Warped Grooves, or, "Thriving on a Riff, aka Anthropology": Discography without Discs

Having traced a general outline of Young's use of indexicality and analogic mediation in the section above, I now turn to the question of the phonographic in particular as a mode of media poetics in *To Repel Ghosts*. What does it mean to write not only a given record's sonic content but also the process of phonographic recording and playback and the object of the record itself—to produce an inscriptive event that records the event of inscription in another medium? How does the poetics of analogic overload that Young establishes as a working process in alphabetic writing approach the question of the analog itself as enacted and embedded in the material dimensions of another storage medium? Young's writing about records in *To Repel Ghosts* is nearly always already a multiply mediated process, as he stages it largely through Basquiat's paintings. Thus his textual representations of records are not simply tracks about records but rather tracks about paintings about records—paintings that are, as I discuss below, themselves often predominantly and at times even entirely textual. Dworkin's concept of the substrate as a formal device is again crucial here, revealing how the relations among the different inscriptive surfaces at play—the disc, the canvas, and the page—point to the need for a more complex conception of ekphrasis, one that takes account of the mediatic landscape of the modern and contemporary periods.

In a critique of much of ekphrastic literature and of interart and intermedia theory in general, Willard Spiegelman argues that the critical consensus through which "ekphrasis is generally taken as a 'verbal representation of visual representation' needs some modification when one contemplates . . . at a double remove."[56] Stitching an analog fabric among different media through this "double remove," Young uses the materiality of the phonographic disc and of Basquiat's painterly use of text to rethink the materiality of codex-based print text as well. His use of form in representing phonography self-reflexively situates the architecture of the print page within a history of phonographic storage, in the process reconfiguring that history through the architecture of the page. To consider how Young theorizes a media poetics of phonography through literary form, I focus in this section on the two tracks titled "Discography," for two related, if perhaps also contradictory, reasons. Firstly, as suggested by their title, these tracks engage explicitly with the phonographic disc as an object and with its circulation through and constitution of Black culture and history. Yet conversely, by taking up phonography by way of the visual and textual registers present in Basquiat's *Discography* paintings, these tracks also explicitly represent the Black history and poetics of phonography as multiply mediated, shaped by the constraints of the medium and also of the other media that store this history.

Within the context of the multiple intertwined modes of inscription that inform these tracks, the term "discography" merits particular consideration for the multiple meanings that resonate within it. Just as "phonography" literally derives from the Greek for "sound" and "writing," "discography" connotes discs and writing. Yet as the very presence of the disc as an a priori in this situation, both materially and etymologically, suggests, the relation between these components is complex and multidirectional. "Discography" connotes writing onto discs, the inscriptive production of unreadable records that emerged in early phonographic culture. It also connotes writing about discs in the catalogic, archival sense, referring to "a catalogue raisonné of gramophone records" or to "the study of recordings."[57] Yet neither of these meanings sits well with the inscriptive surface of the print page. As Gitelman suggests, the grooves of the phonographic disc cannot be read via alphabetic print text, and as the dead-end catalogs of *To Repel Ghosts* show, the print codex cannot map the full scope of a discographic history. Thus the discographies that Basquiat and Young produce are mediated metadocumentations of records as storage media rather than in terms of the sound they store. Over and above presenting discography as content—poems or paintings about discs or music, for example—they seek to do discography through visual and alphabetic form, tracing how different media store one another, and in many instances how they fail to do so faithfully or comprehensively. As a practice, discography yokes together these storage systems while at the same time keeping them perpetually paratactically distinct, as analogic modes of inscription reverberating across multiple surfaces. In the black holes and collapsed parallels of intermedia ekphrasis, both Basquiat and Young represent media objects by pushing against their limitations as storage objects, tracing a history defined by dissonance, disjuncture, and inexactitude.

Basquiat's paintings *Discography (One)* and *Discography (Two)*, both from 1983, provide one point of entry into this complex system of representation and inscription.[58] Both paintings consist of white block-letter inscriptions on black backgrounds, detailing the personnel and a partial track listing for Charlie Parker's famous Savoy Sessions of November 26, 1945, and August 14, 1947, respectively. Commonly considered one of the most important recordings in modern jazz, the Savoy Sessions also featured Miles Davis, Dizzy Gillespie, and Max Roach, and produced crucial takes of canonical bebop compositions such as "Koko," "Now's the Time," and "Billie's Bounce." In each painting, Basquiat lists the name of the group that played the tracks listed (Charlie Parker's Reebopers [sic] and the Miles Davis All-Stars for compositions *One* and *Two*, respectively) and the pertinent players and their instruments, and lists a number of tracks recorded by that group, including numerous instances of multiple takes of the same composition—five separate iterations of "Billie's Bounce," for example, or four of "Nows the Time" [sic], or two of "Koko." Each painting also has several unique elements as well: *One* lists the location and date of its session and includes a square enclosing a listing of the record sides in questions (sides A–D), while *Two* includes crossed-out credits for Teddy Reig as producer and Harry Smith as engineer, as well as the Savoy catalog number and side and track placement for most of the takes listed (the first take of "Milestones," for example, is recording number 3440–1, and is on side F, track 1).

These paintings embody what W. J. T. Mitchell calls "ekphrastic fear": "the moment of resistance or counterdesire that occurs when we sense that the difference between the verbal and the visual representation might collapse and the figurative, imaginary desire of ekphrasis might be realized literally and actually."[59] Mitchell's concept predominantly pertains to visual images as conventionally understood—as paradigmatically nonverbal and nonalphabetic, or at least not solely verbal or alphabetic. In these cases, ekphrastic fear comes from the possibility that the verbal might accomplish the impossible task of representing the visual with perfect totality and accuracy. In the case of the *Discography* paintings, Basquiat exploits this fear to an almost uncanny effect, collapsing the chasm between verbal

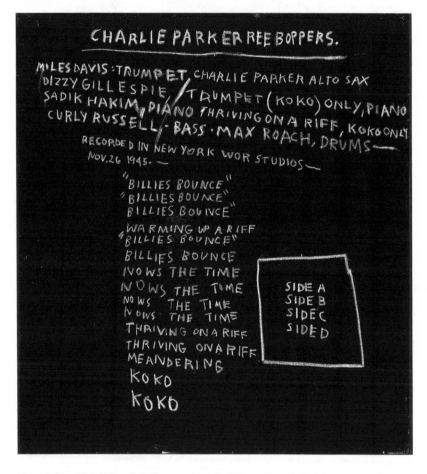

Figure 3. Jean-Michel Basquiat, *Discography One*, 1983. Acrylic and oilstick on canvas. © Estate of Jean-Michel Basquiat. Licensed by Artestar, New York.

and visual from a direction opposite what Mitchell describes by producing paintings that verge on being ekphrases of themselves. Thus any ekphrastic fear in this case stems not from the representation of the object as a visual artifact but from the virtual eclipse of the object as a material artifact by the operations of transcription. The visual that is usually so distant and different from the verbal is rendered here as effectively nothing but the verbal; the medium of phonographic storage is the only message of the medium of these minimalist canvases.

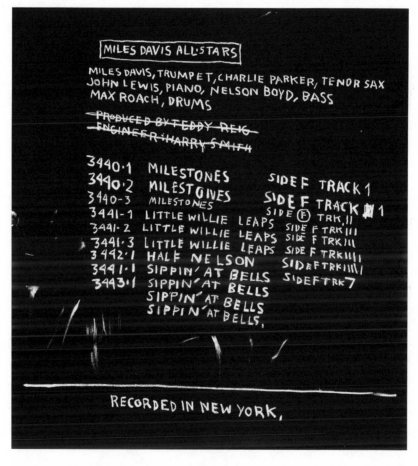

Figure 4. Jean-Michel Basquiat, *Discography Two*, 1983. Acrylic and oilstick on canvas. © Estate of Jean-Michel Basquiat. Licensed by Artestar, New York.

As canvas renderings of the album copy for these recordings, these paintings are the visual representation of a particular kind of verbal representation—not the poet approximating the work of the artist but the artist approximating the work of the archivist, recording and organizing the metadata of the albums' sonic data, and achieving an uneasy kind of visual poetry in the process. As in the case of the indexical qualities of Young's poetry and many of Basquiat's paintings, part of this uneasiness derives from the formal qualities of these works, each track title resembling a poetic line, building toward an archival found poetics. Yet just as much uneasiness conversely comes from the archival discontinuities and inexactitudes that these lines serve to register. These paintings are effectively back covers of Parker albums without the albums themselves: paratexts without texts, metadata without data. Precisely in their attention to the discrete individuality of each take that they list, they explicitly acknowledge their inexact relation to the actual recordings in question. The process of enumerating personnel, track listings, and other information simultaneously marks the sounds on record and makes clear the inability of text to transpose them: however sonically different four consecutive takes of "Now's the Time" may be, listing each of them without further description or qualification self-reflexively underscores the impossibility of a transparent rendition or representation of sonic material within the textual-visual realm of Basquiat's paintings. Undifferentiated by any description, these track titles become iterative and indexical, mute marks of storage that write particular moments of sonic history but cannot recuperate the content of those moments. Thus Basquiat's paintings imagine discography as an inevitably incomplete process of transcription, a mode of writing media history that does nothing more (but also nothing less) than register its own inexact compatibility with the recorded sound it purports to transfer and store within another medium.

Young's tracks "Discography One" and "Discography Two" take these paintings as their highly inexact points of origin. Young separates these tracks from direct connection to the *Discography* paintings in a number of ways: firstly, their titles differ in punctuation, lacking parentheses, and, as in the case of "Pork," they have no datings to link them to the specific paintings in question. Moreover, these tracks do not transcribe the text of the *Discography* paintings in any substantive or sustained fashion. Thus the aesthetics of the analog are once again in play in these tracks, as Young riffs on Basquiat's methodology in order to imagine a materially informed practice of alphabetic discography within the format of the print literary codex rather than directly describing the *Discography* paintings themselves as objects. Indeed, if these tracks are direct discographies of anything, it is not the Savoy discs that serve as the basis for Basquiat's paintings but rather the phantom discs of the book's own five sides. Catalogues raisonnés of discs that cannot be touched or held, these tracks attest to a media history of recorded sound that can never directly reproduce the inscriptive capacities of the phonograph, instead only etching the outlines of its materiality on the page.

"Discography One" consists of individually titled subsections focused on a series of famous figures in the history of jazz: Louis Armstrong, Parker, Billie Holiday, Lester Young, and Max Roach. All of these artists figure in Basquiat's work, but virtually none of the sections of the track (with the notable exception of "Now's the Time," which I discuss below) pertains to actual paintings. Instead, they function as generalized aggregate portraits of the musicians themselves, staged through Young's characteristic polysemic puns and allusions, often invoking the phonographic in uneven, indirect ways. "Stardust," for example, traces Holiday through "Billie's Bounce," the bebop standard named for her and referenced numerous times in Basquiat's *Discography* paintings, implicitly making Basquiat's own discographic strategies part of the portrait:

"BILLIES BOUNCE"

"BILLIES BOUNCE"
Miss Holiday's up
on four counts

of possession[60]

"Satchmo" imagines Armstrong's complexly dual racial and cultural image as a minstrel figure and an innovative artist as constituting the two sides of an imaginary record. "SIDE A" of this record consists of black

wax grooves
going round
in an endless

endless grin

clearly derived from minstrel iconography. "SIDE B" offers a diametrically opposed vision of Armstrong as a complex sonic producer capable of "out-play[ing] / Beezlebub on a good // day," his record's "labels spun // too fast / to read."[61] Here the phonographic trumps the alphabetic, with the material operations of the turntable rendering the textual illegible.

"Now's the Time" extends this approach in its attention to the Basquiat painting of the same title that serves as the frontispiece for *To Repel Ghosts*, both describing the piece as "blacked wood / warped" and appropriating its text:

"NOW'S THE TIME"
underline
PRKR[62]

In the same way that the pages introducing each side of *To Repel Ghosts* distort its frontispiece (which, as I have suggested, itself distorts Basquiat's sculptural painting, which in turn distorts the Parker record), this poem foregrounds tension and dissonance across formats by forcing the manually created visual material of the painting of "Now's the Time" into printed alphabetic text: "underline" stands in for the actual line of the painted label in a manner that reproduces it while simultaneously highlighting the inexactitude of that reproduction. This inexactitude reverberates back down through the layered accretion of analog mediations that precedes the poem, from the frontispiece to the painting to the actual record and finally to the Parker performance itself captured on that record. Each of these artifacts exists as the product of an inexact, interdependent dialogue across different forms of storage that are themselves defined and connected by their incompatibilities.

Young asserts in the track's epigraph that it is "*made from original/ masters*," a claim that seems to connote both the artistic mastery of the musicians represented and the concept of master recordings that often precede mass phonographic pressings—a concept that suggests the capture and storage of some essential distillation of the artists that the track subsequently derives from.[63] Yet the idea of an original master in such a context seems out of place on several counts. Firstly, technological history is largely indeterminate and inconclusive in this area. The earliest master recordings were pressed directly onto phonographic discs before being duplicated, while the use of magnetic tape mastering in place of phonographic mastering first appeared in the 1940s. All of the artists Young describes in this track recorded across this timespan, making it difficult to theorize the technological relation between mastering and the phonograph in this context in a fixed, singular way. More broadly, there is no systematic, singular sequence of relations that can be traced among the media objects and artists invoked by "Discography One," precisely because there is no one single master original object. Even in the case of Young's "Now's the Time," which draws directly and explicitly on Basquiat's painting, the multiplicity of takes on that composition as enumerated in Basquiat's *Discography (One)* makes it impossible to imagine a singular referent. Thus the "original masters" of this track manifest as yet another deliberately inexact incarnation of *To Repel Ghosts*'s phonographic history piling up over multiple temporalities, multiple analogic "nows" across multiple media. As Weheliye suggests, each media object here is an event in its own right, paratactically reverberating against those before and after it but irreducibly different from them in terms of its format's textual and material affordances. Each object is an original because it is a copy, bearing within itself the static-drenched, distorted images and sounds of the past; analog history inheres across these artifacts in the perpetual newness of inexact reproduction.

Young extends this methodology in "Discography Two" by directly appropriating the discontinuous and often disorienting text of Basquiat's paintings to constitute the entirety of the track's text. If "Discography One" foregrounded a Black phonographic politics in the poem, focusing on the cultural legacy of a series of crucial jazz artists, "Discography Two" engages Basquiat's work in order to imagine a corresponding politics of the poem, deploying a form and process shaped by questions of the archive in order to imagine Black subjectivity in "the audiovisual disjunction engendered by the phonograph." Thus this track's divergence from the *Discography* paintings is even sharper than that of "Discography One": its text comes not just from sources other than those particular paintings but also from a collection of paintings that address jazz and phonography in dramatically uneven ways, constituting a discography virtually devoid of actual discs and even of music altogether. For example, the section "Jazz 1986" contains the text "CHARLIE PARKER REEBOPPERS" and titles of several Parker compositions ("MARMADUKE" and "STEEPLECHASE"), but the lines that follow these references seem to resist any context for or connection to this discographic information, and indeed the section as a whole seems largely arbitrary in its choice of text:

> MARMADUKE
>
> MAMADU
>
> STEEPLECHASE—
>
> CHARLIE PARKER REEBOPPERS
>
> GUANO
>
> FUEGO
>
> "A IMAGE OF VICE"[64]

Yet while such a poetics is radically discontinuous and nonnarrative in its arbitrariness—seemingly the logical extreme of Young's paratactic, indexical form—it is paradoxically also exact in that arbitrariness. Through this approach, Young reproduces Basquiat's catalogic effect without reproducing his canvases themselves altogether, approaching "the poem as a material object" in order to theorize through it a cultural politics of form.[65]

The section titled "Quality," for example, is based on Basquiat's 1983 work *Untitled (Quality)*, and consists of key words from the center swath of that almost entirely textual painting, centered on the page to echo the visual form of the painting:

> POSTOAKOES
>
> REST IN PEACE WHO TRUST?
>
> WARM AIR FRONT

MASS SLUMS

CUTTHROATS

DUST BOWL[66]

While these units of text, the first lines of the section, are undoubtedly front and center at the top of Basquiat's painting, they are not the only lines in that area of the painting, and although some nearby lines in the painting appear later in the poem, many do not appear at all, while others appear only partially or outside of any sequence in relation to the layout of the painting. Moreover, the wholly textual form of Young's track smooths over the painting's lines, arrows, cross-outs, and other marks that sit somewhere between the alphabetic and the imagistic. The entirety of "Discography Two" consists of poetic lines such as these, which reproduce Basquiat's words exactly at the level of language yet can never exactly reproduce his canvas at the material level of orthography and inscription. This technique surfaces a productive paradox in the friction of intermedia transcription, suggesting that repetition is the logical conclusion for approaching Basquiat's textual work on the printed page, but also acknowledging that exact repetition is ultimately an impossibility, capable only of producing a continuing series of media objects, each in its own format, each with its own independent and interrelated affordances.

In transcribing Basquiat's text inexactly, much as in the case of the "underline" in "Now's the Time" of "Discography One," Young makes clear which kinds of inscription print writing cannot capture or copy. As the gap between Basquiat's so-called painted original and his so-called printed copy widens, Young's aesthetics of inexactitude reaches further beyond the bounds of the page as a formal device to invoke other modes of inscription and storage; the marks and textual dimensions of Basquiat's paintings that alphabetic print cannot store become the material of an elusive history of the paintings that in turn stands in within Young's book for an elusive history of phonography itself, a discography that could never be accomplished in alphabetic writing, only gestured at through the mediatic work of form. Thus Young engages in what Kittler describes as the writer's celebration of "the very opposite of his own medium—the white noise no writing can store."[67] He records not the unrecordable, but rather the state of unrecordability itself—the stuttering, rippling proliferation of the media event across multiple surfaces and multiple temporalities. The text of the paper poet verges asymptotically on that of the canvas painter, the difference between the two visible only in the minute—yet ultimately uncloseable—gap of meaning between a given unit of text on the canvas and that same unit of text on the page. In remastering Basquiat throughout *To Repel Ghosts*, then, Young both standardizes the artist's inscriptions and at the same time renders them more deeply analogic, setting them adrift across a distorted history of writing, marks and media that can be collected, but never securely fixed in time.

The closing track of *To Repel Ghosts*, "Retrospective," finds Young and Basquiat deep within analog media history, albeit immersed in the materiality of the television rather than that of the phonograph. In its final lines, Young addresses Basquiat within the context of an imagined late-night televisual signoff:

> If only
> you'd said so
> long like a television
> station, signed off
> the air—Star
>
> Spangled Banner
> blowing before bars—
> red, yellow,
>
> more—color—
> before brief
> black—the static—[68]

Imagining both the discrete isolation of colors in the "bars" of a test pattern as well as their reconsolidation in "static," these lines eulogize Basquiat as an analog media practitioner. While Young addresses him directly here, he also makes oblique reference to the short-lived rock band known as Gray, and before that as Test Pattern, in which Basquiat played a central role.[69] In this context, such a reference becomes not only a biographical anchor but also a self-referential emblem for the technological and aesthetic practices that underlie both Basquiat's and Young's work. Young sees the dissonance of mediation as a constitutive element of the production, transmission, and storage of information, one that shapes the meaning-making capacities of analog technologies such as the codex, the phonograph, the canvas, and the television, but perhaps also the capacities of digital technologies such as the hard drive, the MP3, and—again, also—the codex. In this sense, then, it is not only the individual media that are treated as analog in Young's work but the larger history itself of those media. To write such an analog history of media entails not only writing about analog technologies as subjects— media history in the poem, to modify Dworkin's terms—but also writing in the modes of those technologies at the level of textual form—the media history of the poem. But it also means allowing the uneven indexicality of the analog to inform the codex at all levels: language, architecture, paratext, affordance, objecthood. Through a media poetics rooted in the inexactitude of the analog, Young imagines a modern media history that emerges from the dissonant reverberations between phonographic and alphabetic inscription.

Coda: Playing Paper

Records were once—briefly, vulnerably, permanently—paper too. In the early years of recorded sound, it was not uncommon to produce paper prints of sonic content that had first been captured and stored by means of other media. For example, the 1877 *Scientific American* article recounting Edison's first demonstration of the phonograph also includes a strange paper form of the recording he played back, an extended sequence of dots and lines that the editors of the magazine described as "of course absolute facsimile, excepting that they are level instead of being raised above or sunk beneath the surface."[70] This transcriptive imprint of Edison's early tinfoil recording is a strangely liminal intermedia text—neither set type nor phonographic groove, an inscription that cannot be read by the eye or the needle. Yet the paper prints of Emile Berliner's gramophone discs are perhaps even more uncanny. Circular in form, with their etched grooves captured as fluctuations in lines on the page, they look to the twentieth-century eye strikingly like LP records made out of paper, eerily prefiguring the faux-objecthood of Young's section frontispieces and bending that print representation back on itself across time.

Several of these paper discs have been found, dating from the late 1880s and early 1890s.[71] Patrick Feaster, media preservation librarian at Indiana University Bloomington, has converted these prints from paper inscription to digital sound as follows:

> First, I take a high-resolution scan of the print and convert it from
> a spiral into a set of parallel lines through a polar-to-rectangular-
> coordinates transform. Next, I "cut" the individual lines and "paste"
> them end-to-end to create several long, narrow strips. After repairing
> any breaks in the line, I use a "paintbucket" tool to create two separate
> bands of varying width—one with the area below the line filled in
> white, the other with the area above the line filled in white. Next, I run
> these images through ImageToSound, a program that converts them
> into WAV files as though they were variable-area optical film sound
> tracks. Finally, I combine the paired WAV into stereo files, stitch the
> successive pieces together, sum to mono, and voilà—we have sound![72]

A storage medium initially produced without a playback technology, these
paper records were, for all practical purposes, obsolete at the moment of
their creation, serving only as a kind of indexical marker of the innovation
of sonic recording and inscription, a repetition event that pointed toward
a silent dead end. They encode information in a dramatically different way
from actual phonographic recordings, and cannot be sonically played back
using the technology of their day, yet they signify for sound in multiple
ways at once, intertwining the inscriptive approach of Edison and the
graphic method of Marey and his colleagues in a single mark. The use of
digital scanning and conversion that Feaster describes makes it possible to
convert these paper objects to sound without damaging them or sacrificing
accuracy in a way that seems unique in technological history, so much so
that they almost seem to anticipate their potential digitization some 120
years after their production.

Yet setting aside the possibility of such a prolepsis, these gramophonic
prints also offer us a glimpse of an interstitial moment in which paper and
print inscription play a striking role within the history of a modern media
technology (the protocinematic paper prints developed by Edison's studio
that I discuss in chapter 5 are another such moment). Berliner's invention
of disc-based recording provided a crucial shift in the affordability, reproducibility, and durability of recorded sound. Gramophonic prints such as
those discussed by Feaster suggest that both in spite and because of this shift
toward the wax and subsequently vinyl disc, paper and its cousin material,
tinfoil, persist as storage forms at the margins of sonic inscription—the

material fragility of the surface, it seems, is paradoxically precisely what undergirds that persistence. Indeed, these paper documents, interstitial with regard to both time and medium, illustrate how the moment in which the recorded disc rose to prominence as a format was also the moment in which it briefly took form within a mode of storage that defied playback by means of the technology of the time. They also anticipate the self-contradictory, overdetermined ways in which Young's book straddles different regimes of inscription and different moments in media history, imaginatively indexing the materiality of analog audio media through the speculative materiality of its paper paratexts. Indeed, just as the paper prints of Berliner's recordings seem to look ahead in time, anticipating a digital future with the means to read them and play them back, Young's paratextual images rely on the digital workflows of contemporary publishing to look in the opposite direction, back toward the analog past of vinyl and paper.

Playing any of the paper records incorporated within *To Repel Ghosts* in the conventional, literally gramophonic sense—putting the relevant page of the book on the turntable under the needle—would of course be instantly destructive. Paper would snag, bunch, crumple, and tear, the needle would capture and play the sounds of its own damaging effects, and sonic history would be lost, destroyed by the machine invented specifically in order to reproduce it forever. Yet perhaps this is precisely the point, or at least the greatest historiographic lesson to be learned from these vestigial documents—indeed, while the symbolic realms of paper and print can only ever encode sound rarely and obliquely at best, they nonetheless have a great deal to tell us about sound precisely through that limitation, as the unique instance of the paper print record suggests. The digital scanning and conversion that Feaster explains alleviates the physical threat of destruction: separated from the original document by a glass flatbed, the scanner's contact image sensor slides along that document in a process that bears more resemblance to photography or to optical reading than to the physical contact of touch or phonographic playback. The absence of any physical threat from this digital reading makes visible by omission the physical vulnerability that is otherwise so consistently present in other forms of reading and writing, inscription and playback, whether they be sonic or alphabetic. We might consider the highly contingent, unsound "*sound quality*" of Young's five sides as a paradigmatic example of this vulnerability.

Yet attending to such vulnerabilities across different moments in time, from the nineteenth-century paper print to the twenty-first-century poetic codex, also points us more broadly to the profoundly, productively distorting ways in which media history itself is distorted by the very media in question—by the ways in which those media construct themselves and each other. Analog transcriptions that point toward digital playback, digital images of analog recordings stored in code, vinyl discs rendered on paper, paper dreaming of vinyl dischood: each medium, each format seems to store the other just out of reach, anachronistic inscriptions and impressions secreted back and forth across time.

CHAPTER THREE
Archive, Film, Novel

Mediated Writing and Media History in Don DeLillo's *Running Dog*

Between literature and film another emulsion forms.
—Akira Mizuta Lippit, *Atomic Light (Shadow Optics)*

Discarded pages mark the physical dimensions of a writer's labor—you know,
how many shots it took to get a certain paragraph right.
Or the awesome accumulation,
the gross tonnage of first draft pages.
—Don DeLillo, "Don DeLillo: The Art of Fiction CXXXV"

[Y]ou open a file, that's cinema.
And then you weigh it. . . . It's like a novel,
because the pages are consecutive.
But because it's visual,
there's the weight of a page and the weight of the next page.
—Jean-Luc Godard, "Godard Makes (Hi)Stories"

Electronic Futures, Combustible Pasts: Missing Films and Media History in the 1970s

Chapters 1 and 2 used the obsolete technologies of the typewriter and the phonograph as sounding boards for rethinking the relations between the literary poetics of inscriptive media and media history. As I suggested, these technologies occupy strange crux positions within modern media history. Each was at one historical moment perhaps the most widely used technology of its sort—the typewriter as a writing technology, the phonograph as a format of sound media—and yet at the same time also the most imminently vulnerable to obsolescence. The authors I discuss in these chapters foreground particular elements of media poetics—the persistence of error for Warhol, and the prevalence of the analog for Young—in order to gesture in turn at the nonlinear rhythms of technological change. However, not every technocultural change is universally pervasive or wholesale; after all, even the typewriter and the phonograph persist in various contexts and contingencies, as suggested by precisely the nonlinear dynamics I have traced in the preceding chapters. Indeed, tracing such uneven trajectories of media history requires attending to residues and remainders, seeing discontinuity, absence, recursion, and rupture as central forces in technological change. Media-historical moments that reveal these instabilities open up in turn a range of problems and possibilities for literary experimentation: how might print literature represent and respond via radical formalism to the operations of a media technology caught in uneven flux between dominance and residuality? How might the architecture of the page serve to mark not only a given format of audiovisual media but also the rupture and erasure of audiovisual objects altogether? What kinds of media poetics might emerge from such an engagement with the materiality and mediality of a given technology, and how might the literary claim that poetics toward a larger project of historicizing media technology?

In this chapter, I take the literary response to the transition from film to video in the American culture of the 1970s as a testing ground for these questions. I focus on the 1970s because of the technological and cultural changes that transpired within moving-image media over the decade. Film's cultural primacy within this period served as a frequent subject for American literary novelists, particularly those who saw the medium's transformation of space and time through montage and its photorealistic representation of a world beyond the mirror of the screen as an inspiration and opportunity for innovation within prose narrative. While the visual language of film has been a shaping influence on literary form virtually since its emergence around the turn of the twentieth century, a number of ambitious novelists in the 1970s also approached film with regard to its material objecthood as well.[1] By focusing on the presence and absence of one or more films as physical artifacts within the narrative worlds of their novels, these authors underscore the materiality and historicity of film, as well as of the novel in dialogue with film. This mediatic attention to materiality deploys literary form to investigate what Gitelman describes as the "transitional states[] and identity crises of different media," moments that "stand[] to tell us much, both about the course of media history and about the broad conditions by which media and communication are and have been shaped."[2]

Perhaps the most extensive and best-known treatment of film within the American literature of the 1970s takes place in Thomas Pynchon's *Gravity's Rainbow* (1973). Pynchon's encyclopedic novel engages cinema as a technological and aesthetic mode of representation, a body of referential and cultural material, and a channel for the distribution of national mythology and propaganda. Indeed, film is arguably the novel's primary aesthetic influence: its surreal, discontinuous narrative world is simultaneously structured by the logic of cinematic montage, saturated with allusions to cinematic history (German expressionism in particular), and strewn with the apparatus of cinematic production and reproduction. John Johnston notes the "reciprocal relay effect" between the technologies of the cinema and the V-2 rocket that serves as the novel's focal structuring object, and suggests that the rocket is "connected both internally and externally to the cinema as an automatic writing machine or inscription device."[3] At the heart of this connection is Gerhardt von Göll, the director of a number of films that circulate through the world of the novel. Repeatedly disappearing and reappearing across the terrain of the novel, von Göll's films are cinematic objects that exist in perpetual deferral. For example, his pseudodocumentary about the German Schwarzkommando troop, three minutes and twenty-five seconds in running time, is artificially "antiqued, given a bit of fingus and ferrotyping, and transported to Holland, to become part of the 'remains' of a counterfeit rocket-firing site[.] . . . [A]mong ashes, charred clothing, blackened and slightly melted gin bottles, will be found fragments of carefully forged Schwarzkommando documents, and of a reel of film, only three minutes and 25 seconds of which will be viewable."[4]

The fact that this discovery is an elaborate propagandic simulation (a conceit closely connected to the status of the Schwarzkommando troop as itself a simulation) is hardly unique within the novel, as its opening lines suggest: "The Evacuation still proceeds, but it's all theater."[5] Rather, the importance of the Schwarzkommando film within the novel's media landscape lies in this simulation's predication on a specific, presumably singular object's flickering between presence and absence, and on the imagined gaps within its material history of migrations and transformations—how it might have traveled, disappeared, reappeared, and been subject to damage and deletion in order to become the cinematic object that is ultimately "discovered" at the counterfeit rocket site in Holland. Pynchon characterizes Von Göll's film *New Dope* with a similar material instability, describing it as perpetually running "under the rug. On the floor, 24 hours a day . . . a project which will never be completed. Springer [von Göll's alias] just plans to keep it going indefinitely there, under the rug" and forever inaccessible.[6] Film saturates Pynchon's novel, but in a manner that is perpetually fugitive, constantly slipping in and out of the shadows.

The novel's ultimate cinematic object, however, manifests at the level of concept on its final page, as the long-missing V-2 Rocket 00000, launched in postwar Germany, finally bears down on a movie theater in the Los Angeles of the 1970s, where "[t]he screen is a dim page spread before us, white and silent. The film has broken, or a projector bulb has burned out."[7] As Johnston suggests, "[W]e are urged to think of *Gravity's Rainbow* itself as an unfilmable movie" through this final conceit of cinematic and print materiality, as the multiple "connections (and slippages) between [cine-matic] representations internal to the novel and the novel itself" converge at a moment of apocalyptic destruction.[8] The status and significance of the novel's all-encompassing film are revealed to the reader—"us, old fans who've always been at the movies (haven't we?)"—through its detonation and eradication in this scene.[9] Given Pynchon's thick tracing of film history throughout the novel, the question of cinematic materiality and historicity matters deeply here: what might otherwise be explained as a well-worn trick of postmodern narrative, in which all that has come before is revealed to be "only" a movie, an empty, false, simulation, instead serves to close a strange loop of narrative and formal engagement between print and celluloid media objects. If the novel is indeed an unfilmable movie, it is unfilmable precisely because it seeks, however impossibly, to be that film—to collapse the architectures of the page and the screen into one.

In this chapter, I focus on how Don DeLillo engages questions of cinematic materiality and film history through textual form in his 1978 novel *Running Dog*. DeLillo has long acknowledged Pynchon as a formative influence and as the central writer of their shared generation, and DeLillo's novel shares a number of crucial traits with *Gravity's Rainbow*: both are entries in the paranoid subgenre of postmodern fiction, tracing complex conspiracies that encompass governmental, military, and paramilitary bodies, and both pair this concern with narrative attention to missing cinematic material. Yet *Running Dog* differs from Pynchon's novel in several crucial ways. Whereas *Gravity's Rainbow* is a sprawling, encyclopedic epic, *Running Dog* is more compact and constrained, and does not impose the pressures of reference or endurance on the reader that *Gravity's Rainbow* does. Published in 1978 and set seemingly in the same historical moment, it depicts an American culture more deeply and immediately enmeshed in military operations in Southeast Asia and more fully saturated by television and video. Most importantly, *Running Dog*'s formal engagement with the materiality of film takes place by way of a mode centered on transcription rather than on narrative representation, as in the case of *Gravity's Rainbow*. By anchoring the novel's formal experimentation in practices of mediatic transcription, self-consciously testing how visual information moves from one medium to another, DeLillo approaches film as a storage medium over and above a representational form. In doing so, he treats print literary writing as a means of interrogating media history through close attention to the material affordances of filmic media.

Before I focus on the media-historical work that DeLillo performs in *Running Dog*, it is important to unpack more fully the larger trope of the missing film and the conceptual leverage it provides for authors writing in the media ecology of the 1970s. The missing film provides a kind of extreme test case for the objecthood and reproductive materiality of visual media, allowing authors to map the media landscape more granularly at a moment of technological instability. In his foundational 1936 essay "The Work of Art in the Age of Mechanical Reproduction," Walter Benjamin argued that the ease with which film was reproduced and circulated was central to its political efficacy, making possible a "tremendous shattering of tradition" that could point toward new social and political modes of action.[10] By the 1970s, the material and cultural status that Benjamin claimed for film were under considerable pressure from multiple historical directions, facing threats from both the past and the future. On one hand, the electronic video images emergent as "the most likely candidate for cultural hegemony" in the 1970s offered the possibility of a world in which the complex apparatus necessary for recording and playing back images on celluloid film became obsolete and vestigial.[11] Video promised to replace this apparatus with a mobile, incidental practice of moving images made possible by new technology that quickly claimed a position as "the art form par excellence of late capitalism."[12] While the emergence of video engendered a cultural break that was partial and gradual in scope, it nonetheless shaped the media landscape in substantive ways that were simultaneously technological, aesthetic, and epistemological. Fredric Jameson claims of this impact that "one would want to defend the proposition that the deepest 'subject' of all video art, and even of all postmodernism, is very precisely reproductive technology itself. . . . If all videotexts simply designate the process of production/reproduction, then presumably they all turn out to be 'the same' in a peculiarly unhelpful way."[13] Jameson seems to reach in this formulation for a critical aporia that hinges on the materiality of media: at the same time that the process of reproduction is everywhere within video at the level of content and subject, with all videotexts delivering the same same, it is seemingly nowhere at the level of apparatus, with the mechanics of celluloid seemingly dissolving into the ether of the electronic image's instant relay. It follows, then, that video art is so insistently "about" reproduction and reproductive technology according to Jameson precisely because that technology is itself so evanescent, so invisible to the naked eye.

Such an aporia is, perhaps, an oversimplification that elides the materiality of video itself, equal in complexity to that of film (if less directly visible) but as yet largely untheorized in the early years of the technology's emergence. Yet if video's materiality still effectively remained to be seen in the 1970s, the materiality of film was conversely literally disappearing before the eyes of spectators and historians. In addition to the challenges posed by the rise of video, film also faced an increasingly severe internal threat in the 1970s as a result of its own material composition. From 1899 to 1949, nitrocellulose film, more commonly known as nitrate film, served as the primary format for recording moving images. Nitrate film is commonly thought to provide the highest-quality image of any kind of stock, and was more durable and less expensive than any other format available during the early twentieth century. However, nitrate also decomposes over extended periods, and, moreover, is highly combustible, releasing a hazardous gas when it burns.[14] This dual condition posed a dual threat in relation to the archive of early twentieth-century cinema, rendering it both highly vulnerable in and of itself and highly dangerous to anyone who handled or stored it. Although these dangers catalyzed (pun fully intended) the film community around the task of preservation from the 1960s onward, common belief within this community holds that "75 percent of all American silent films are gone and 50 percent of all films made prior to 1950 are lost" as a result of nitrate's vulnerability, while numerous fires at film archives both caused damage to the films themselves and posed danger to those who worked with them.[15] The dangers inherent in nitrate film stock not only posed a material threat to the cinematic archive but also threw into relief the urgently material status of cinema as a medium; in revealing the extreme endpoint of cinema's materiality, nitrate made visible what André Habib describes as "the central ambiguity of cinema's temporality: since its origins, it has combined the mythic time of eternal preservation with the ephemeral time of industrialized production."[16]

While this material ephemerality certainly threatens individual films as cinematic objects, it also points to a more complex historiographic paradox in terms of the medium as a whole. Nitrate's deterioration and combustion constitute the necessary condition of possibility for any critical approach to cinema whatsoever: as Paolo Cherchi Usai notes, "It is the destruction of moving images that makes film history possible[.] . . . If all moving images were available, the massive fact of their presence would impede any effort to establish criteria of relevance."[17] This paradox sets in play a kind of double bind in which, according to Cherchi Usai, "[t]he ultimate goal of film history is an account of its own disappearance."[18] To novelists in the 1970s, then, the figure of the missing film offered a way of mobilizing film's historical and material transition across the media landscape of the moment in multiple directions at once, of tracing the interpenetrations between visual media's proliferation and disappearance in different forms and formats—between its preservation and its destruction, and between its capacities as a storage medium and its own susceptibility to disappearance and deterioration.

For Akira Mizuta Lippit, this double bind of documentary persistence and material ephemerality is not unique to celluloid film as a format, but rather constitutive of the parameters and constraints that define the poetics of the archive more broadly construed. Lippit writes, "An archive is always there, just there, beyond this point, in flames. As all archives are destined to do, this archive burns, is constituted as archive by burning, by leaving the traces, or cinders, or remnants by which each archive is, in the end, constituted. This and all archives are realized in destruction, preserved by the traces of destruction."[19] More than simply pointing out the material threat of incineration to which all archives are subject, Lippit suggests that it is in the very nature of the archive to burn. The archive thus exists at once both to leverage against the loss of history and to tend inexorably toward that loss; its condition as hypomnesiac, a space of forgetting rather than of memory, is thus a profoundly material one, perpetually and inescapably subject to the heat of what Derrida famously describes as archive fever. In contraposition to the archive, which must always burn, Lippit poses the concept of the shadow archive or the "anarchive," that which archives "*otherwise*. . . . The open archive *exposes*, it reveals outward. . . . The other archive, the shadow or anarchive . . . is an archive that, in the very archival task of preserving, seeks to repress, efface, and destine its own interiority into oblivion."[20] The shadow archive, then, preserves through oblivion and erasure rather than in spite of or against it; it preserves the very absences that are the condition of preservation itself.

In *Running Dog*, DeLillo develops a media poetics of the shadow archive within and against the archive that constitutes film history. Charting the technological and historiographic tensions between the archive and the shadow archive—between perpetuity and ephemerality, memory and oblivion—he uses formal experimentation to sketch a version of film history by way of the medium's unstable materiality, defined by interwoven trajectories of storage, deletion, loss, and retrieval. Situated as it is within the context of the emergence of video culture and the disintegration of the cinematic archive, his imagination of such a shadow archive might easily be seen as a critique of postmodern mediation, a label often assigned not only to *Running Dog* but also to DeLillo's work in general. Yet to position DeLillo as a simple antagonist or critic of electronic media, or an apologist or elegist for earlier media forms, is to reduce and simplify *Running Dog*'s complex speculative reflection on the history of moving image technology. Beyond ideological implication of the reader in the generalized problem of media culture, the shadow archive that *Running Dog* traces serves as a way of delineating how the materiality of media information shapes the writing of media history and how the format of the print novel might sketch its own media history through radical formalism at the microscopic material level of specific images, texts, and objects. DeLillo imagines cinematic materiality and mediation through form within the pages of the novel, performing a series of textual gestures and operations informed by his own engagement with the cinematic archive in his research for and drafting of the novel. In the most formally divergent and inventive moments of the novel, he uses it as a format by which to appropriate the camera's operations, transcribing, refashioning, and storing cinematic material on the architecture of the printed page. Drawing on the poetics of the moving-image archive at a moment of media-historical instability, applying pressure to the affordances of the novel in a manner that is in dialogue with film but paradigmatically not in the form of film, he writes an alternate trajectory of film history through literary form.

Novelist as Archivist: Mediagraphic Metafiction and the Afterlife of Cinema

Running Dog begins and ends with a film to end all films. The novel centers on the search for the camera original of a film shot in the Berlin bunker of Adolf Hitler's Reich Chancellery just before the fall of the Nazi party in 1945. DeLillo's narrative begins with the cryptic intimation that "[a] film exists," in the words of Lightborne, a dealer and collector of erotic art.[21] From this starting point, DeLillo proceeds to spin out a number of narrative strands and conspiracies circulating around this mythical aesthetic object, detailing the efforts of various corporate, governmental, and paramilitary interests to locate, acquire, and distribute it, and ultimately revealing the film to be something entirely other than what it was initially rumored to be. At the outset of the novel, rumor has it that the bunker film is the sole record of an orgy that took place among the occupants of the bunker in the last days of the Reich, a moving image that would be "[t]he century's ultimate piece of decadence."[22] Yet at the end of the novel, DeLillo plays back within the text a film that is effectively the negative image of what has been promised to the novel's characters and readers, a disturbing and disappointing comedic inversion of its deadly serious pornography: the film turns out to be a home movie shot by Eva Braun in which Hitler performs an impersonation of Charlie Chaplin for the amusement of the elite of the Third Reich assembled in the bunker.

DeLillo situates this film, defined as it is by its seemingly extreme content, as an object of extreme singularity within the late twentieth century's culture of reproduction and simulation, variously describing it as the "[o]ne copy. The camera original" and "the master."[23] With this singularity at the forefront of the novel's concerns, the material condition of the bunker film becomes a crucial question. On finally acquiring the film late in the novel, Lightborne comments, "I have the movie [but] I haven't even opened the can. . . . I'm waiting for technical help. . . . I'm afraid the whole thing will crumble if I open the can the wrong way. It's been in there over thirty years. There's probably a right way and a wrong way to open film cans when the film's been in there so long. There might be a preferred humidity. Safeguards. Recommended procedures."[24] The issues of material fragility and contingency that Lightborne gives voice to in this passage serve as a narrative catalyst for the novel, intensifying the stakes of the search for this media object. Yet DeLillo also uses this conceit to address the materiality of celluloid film more broadly, directly situating the novel within the concerns about medium specificity and material vulnerability that characterized the technological landscape of the 1970s. In keeping with Lippit's framework, the nitrate archive DeLillo draws inspiration from for *Running Dog* tended precipitously toward incineration in the 1970s, posing a future defined by the destruction of the past.

Indeed, DeLillo's preparatory materials for the novel show a preoccupation with the stakes of cinematic preservation and deterioration to be central to *Running Dog* from the outset of the writing process. For example, his research clippings for the novel include, amid several articles on Hitler and Chaplin (both individually and as a connected pair), a 1977 *New York Times* article by Grace Lichtenstein recounting Fox Movietone News's attempts to preserve its deteriorating collection of unique World War II newsreels.[25] This grouping of research materials suggests that the material of film itself is as much of a driving force for the novel as either of the historical icons it engages. Lichtenstein's article describes a process of preservation that entails copying newsreels from the inexpensive, "highly perishable nitrate film" used during wartime onto "modern, long-lasting acetate."[26] She begins with a mock-newsreel announcement of the article's concerns that might serve as a capsule summary of the novel that it helps to spawn: "A race against time! Secret vaults and dogs with a nose for news! History crumbles before your eyes!"[27] At the same time that this archive is in danger of being erased from history, it is also potentially destructive and dangerous in its own right: according to Don Silz, an archivist and researcher quoted in the article, as deteriorating film becomes poisonous and flammable, it expands out of its container "like a cancer" and in effect thus reproduces itself even as it holds the potential to consume itself.[28] Given this conflicted material status of nitrate film as both endangered and dangerous, Fox Movietone News's transposition of cinematic material from one format to another—assuming control of its metastasizing expansion by putting it through a process of transferential reproduction—is a similarly conflicted gesture. This gesture is designed both to preserve film and to contain it; it is an intervention on behalf of film as a reproducible archival medium as well as in defense against the extreme stakes of that reproducibility and archivability.

DeLillo's attention to the problems and possibilities that emerge within such a specifically historically grounded situation of cinematic materiality and reproducibility is central to the way in which he imagines novelistic form in *Running Dog* as an intervention within media poetics and media history. Viewed within the historical and literary context of America in the late 1970s, DeLillo's focus on cinematic form and technology also extends the parameters of historiographic metafiction, a central device of the post-modern and contemporary novel.[29] By mobilizing historical and fictional media objects in the same way that novels of historiographic metafiction mobilize historical and fictional characters and events, *Running Dog* operates as a novel of mediagraphic metafiction. In the sections that follow, I show how DeLillo imagines a technological pastiche within language on the surface of the page, tracing how he stages the mediality, textuality, and materiality of the bunker film through form across a number of moments in the novel. He uses the novel's text as a means for dissecting and recombining different units of mediated information in order to examine how media technologies capture, store, and disseminate information, as well as how and where the novel might engage with those processes. Excavating, preserving, transferring, and mixing media information thus become decisive narrative operations, the novelist's means of both critically engaging the structures of media technology and, more importantly, appropriating those structures for their own purposes. Thus through the novel's formal engagements with cinematic material and technique, DeLillo situates the literary novel as a format capable of intervention within the poetics of the archive. Setting the material of the archive—what Foucault famously described as "the law of what can be said"—into play for imaginative refiguration through form, he underscores how the "system of [the event's] enunciability" that determines media history is circularly bound up in the contingent, vulnerable materiality of the very objects that that history purports to narrate and memorialize.[30]

Before I turn to *Running Dog*'s more explicit moments of mediagraphic formal experimentation, I want to demonstrate briefly how the bunker film as an artifact shapes the media poetics of the novel. Through this central object, DeLillo imagines a limit case of cinema as both a representational form and a medium in order to engage the operations of cinema at the most radical level. The bunker film promises to be the ultimate document ("unedited footage. One copy. The camera original") of the ultimate spectacular persona of the twentieth century (Adolf Hitler) engaged in the production of the ultimate moving-image genre (seemingly unmediated, orgiastic pornography).[31] For the characters in the novel, this film is both literally and figuratively unspeakable. In response to the journalist Moll Robbins's initial questions regarding the film, Lightborne can claim that it exists, but with regard to who or what appears in the film, it seems possible only to say that "[t]hings get vague here. But apparently it's a sex thing. It's the filmed record of an orgy, I gather, that took place somewhere in that series of underground compartments. . . . I don't believe it myself." According to Lightborne, his business contact has described the film as "[a] performance . . . that would surely take its place among the strangest and most haunting ever given. He also said I wouldn't be disappointed in the identities of those taking part. All this and yet he wouldn't give a straight answer when I asked if he'd seen the footage himself or were we dealing in hearsay."[32] Whether or not Lightborne's contact has indeed seen the film, this provocatively opaque hearsay is certainly the currency in usage for all interested parties, a mode of discourse that continues to dominate references to the film over the course of the novel. In a later conversation, government operative Glen Selvy, who is also attempting to acquire the film, notes vaguely that with "[a]ll those people [in the bunker], things could happen," and Lightborne later acknowledges that while there is "some basis" for believing that the film includes Hitler, "[t]he rumors have never specified the old boy."[33] As this euphemistic reference to Hitler suggests, his name is rarely if ever directly linked to the imagined content of the film.

This absence within language epitomizes the way in which the film becomes monolithic in its invisibility as a media object circulating within the world of the novel. Indeed, no direct description of the pornographic film the characters are imagining and seeking ever emerges in the novel, only language that hedges around its alleged content, seeming to say everything precisely by saying nothing—allegation and speculation, in fact, are the only forces that produce this film at all. Yet at the same time that these recurring euphemisms underscore the material and aesthetic inaccessibility of the bunker film, the actual content of "the item in question" is never less than fully clear to the novel's characters.[34] The image at the heart of DeLillo's conceit—Hitler in flagrante delicto, as it were—seems to need no description because it already exists in the collective cultural imaginary. At the heart of the novel's shadow archive of World War II, it is known precisely because it remains unseen and unaccessed, "an archive of that which has not been."[35] In fact, whether the acts imagined on film actually transpired and were recorded as imagined is far less important to the novel's characters than the contingent, yet profoundly seductive, possibility that they might have.

In this sense, the rumors of the film cater to the constellation of impulses that Susan Sontag explores in her 1975 essay "Fascinating Fascism." Like Lightborne—whose flat statement "If it's Nazis, it's automatically erotic" almost seems a parodic reduction of her argument—Sontag suggests a "natural link" between fascism and sadomasochism based on a shared quality of spectacle and theatricality: "Today it may be the Nazi past that people invoke, in the theatricalization of sexuality, because it is those images (rather than memories) from which they hope a reserve of sexual energy can be tapped."[36] For Sontag, the foundational site of this theatricalization is *Triumph of the Will*, Leni Riefenstahl's propaganda film of the 1934 National Socialist Party convention, a text of pornographic "ecstasy" in which "the leader makes the crowd come."[37] The bunker film, with its amateur mode of production and its promised images of Hitler's own ecstasy at the very end of his rule, serves as a sort of imagined negative image to *Triumph*, an aesthetic counterpoint to its epic scope and a chronological bookend to Hitler's cinematic oeuvre. Discussing the novel in relation to Sontag's essay, Mark Osteen argues that "just as fascism produces a pornography of power, so pornography, in *Running Dog*, is a form of fascist representation."[38] Yet rather than completing the equation that these arguments pose, the novel's specter of a pornographic film starring Adolf Hitler redoubles and overloads it entirely, posing a touchpoint in an alternate film history at the margins and overlaps of genre. If fascism is always already pornographic, and pornography always already fascistic, DeLillo asks, what is the status of fascist pornography? What if an example—perhaps the only imaginable example—of such an unimaginable genre existed but had never been seen? DeLillo's use of the bunker film as a cinematic limit case emerges out of this convergence of generic, ideological, and material extremities.

By posing this search for a missing film to end all films as the structuring conceit of *Running Dog*, DeLillo also anticipates "the life or the afterlife of cinema" as theorized by Gilles Deleuze in the conclusion of *Cinema 2: The Time-Image*, originally published in 1985.[39] In the closing pages of this study of post–World War II cinema, Deleuze turns to the question of the aesthetic and political potential for cinema in the face of digital technology and the then-emergent electronic image. He interweaves his consideration of this transition with a discussion of another trajectory of media change, namely Hitler's rise to power in political and cinematic terms. For Deleuze, the most compelling artistic response to Hitler's dual seizure of political and audiovisual power is the work of German filmmaker Hans-Jürgen Syberberg, particularly Syberberg's encyclopedic work *Hitler: A Film from Germany* (1978). *Hitler* consists of a massive, seven-hour stream of staged monologues and narratives delivered by a mixture of actors and marionettes representing everything and everyone from Hitler and the members of his inner circle to Thomas Edison to figures from German mythology. This overwhelming informational excess seeks to body forth in cinematic terms the devastation laid upon history by Hitler, staging a "trial" put on "by cinema . . . inside cinema."[40] If *Triumph* and the bunker film are points in one trajectory of film history, the sprawling cinematic archive of *Hitler* offers another counterpoint to both films, triangulating to form a complex constellation shaped by a range of material and discursive factors such as objecthood, scope, mode of production, genre, and the body, among others. Deleuze describes the film in language that evokes an archival poetics, as "a vast space of information, like a complex, heterogeneous, anarchic space where the trivial and the cultural, the public and the private, the historic and the anecdotal, and the imaginary and the real are brought close together . . . all of equal importance and forming a network, in kinds of relationship which are never those of causality."[41]

For Deleuze, this approach to *Hitler*'s cinematic form by way of the poetics of the archive sets in play a larger problem of history and power that hinges on similar questions of archival poetics and informational overload during and after the war: "Syberberg's powerful idea is that *no information, whatever it might be, is sufficient to defeat Hitler.* All the documents could be shown, all the testimonies could be heard, but in vain: what makes information all-powerful (the newspapers, and then the radio, and then the television), is its very nullity, its radical ineffectiveness. Information plays on its ineffectiveness in order to establish its power, its very power is to be ineffective, and thereby all the more dangerous. This is why it is necessary to go beyond information in order to defeat Hitler or turn the image over."[42] Thus just as "the camera's everywhere," in Moll's words, so are Hitler and the "pieces of information which constitute his image in ourselves" similarly ubiquitous, all-consuming, and irreducible in Deleuze's eyes.[43] The archival project of the Third Reich—the meticulous tabulation and documentation of prisoners in the camps, the constitution of human lives as nothing more and nothing less than data to be processed—is both a historical action and a historiographic one, an attempt to reshape the very production of history around its archival construction. For Deleuze, this constant archival excess that comes to define the culture of the electronic image—a paradoxical excess of nullity, no less—is thus itself a fascist condition, extending far beyond any single representation or reproduction of Hitler.[44]

Deleuze offers a response to this threat to the archive that itself hinges on cinema as a technology of the archive. For Deleuze, the central distinguishing characteristic of cinema is its self-reflexive attention to its own technological condition. Drawing on Benjamin's work on mechanical reproduction, he argues that "there is something specific to cinema which has nothing to do with theater. If cinema is automatism become spiritual art . . . it confronts automata, not accidentally, but fundamentally. . . . The man-machine assemblage varies from case to case, but always with the intention of posing the question of the future."[45] Deleuze sees this "question of the future" as dramatically fraught within the context of postwar cinema. Numerous times over the course of *Cinema 2*, he returns to the Shakespearean assertion that "time is out of joint"; in the preface to the English edition of the text, he couples it with the explanation that "Hamlet's words signify that time is no longer subordinated to movement, but rather movement to time."[46] Elsewhere in *Cinema 2*, he uses similar glosses on this line to contextualize the central characteristics of post–World War II cinema: "It took the modern cinema to re-read the whole of cinema as already made up of aberrant movements and false continuity shots. The direct time-image is the phantom which has always haunted the cinema, but it took modern cinema to give a body to this phantom."[47] The idea of cinema as haunted here is certainly nothing new, and indeed might even be traced past the origins of the moving image to the late nineteenth-century phenomenon of spirit photography, which articulated cultural anxieties regarding the uncanny, unnatural nature of time-based media technologies. Yet as much as Deleuze's vision of cinema's being haunted is formal, technological, psychic, spiritual, and cultural, it is also profoundly historiographic, a haunting of cinema by its own representation of time. This haunting self-reflexively reveals not merely the body of the past in general, but rather the particular body of cinema's own past—indeed its past as an embodied, material technology of the archive.

The afterlife of cinema Deleuze imagines, then, is not a life after death but a redoubled return of the past, of buried objects of storage and memory wrenched out of one temporality and into another. Thus in calling for artists to "turn the image over," he begins to ask how cinema might bear forth its own buried images as a way of tracing its own historicity. By attending to the material of cinematic history through form, such a practice responds to "the question of the future" not through concession or reaction, but rather through a formal practice that "confronts [its] automata" by turning inward and backward. Through the immanent critique made possible by this media poetics, cinema unearths its practices and its materials, excavating its past as a way of problematizing both the specific present moment and the temporality of media history altogether. Indeed, Deleuze argues that this moment of media-historical inquiry becomes possible precisely because of the cultural and material instability of film rather than in spite of it: "Redemption arrives too late[.] . . . [I]t appears when information has already gained control of speech-acts, and when Hitler has already captured the German myth or irrational. But the too-late is not only negative; it is the sign of the time-image in the place where time makes visible the stratigraphy of space and audible the story-telling of the speech-act."[48] *Running Dog* takes place within this time-space of the too-late, a moment of densely layered simultaneity between temporalities. The aesthetic and political potentials of cinema seem superseded within this moment by the colonizing forces of the electronic image, and just as the novel's characters themselves bear the mark of Hitler's cinematic fascism, speaking and acting through the readymade material of mass visual media, the only cinematic work that holds any significance to any of them is a document of fascist pornography. Yet at the same time, DeLillo extracts an immanent critique from the technological conditions of the too-late: against the backdrop of the emergence of the electronic, he envisions the spatial and temporal dimensions of celluloid film as newly subject to imaginative reconfiguration and recomposition, answering Deleuze's calls to "go beyond information" toward a politics and poetics of cinematic materiality by way of textual form.

DeLillo's transcriptive strategies in *Running Dog* frame the political stakes of the time-image as a project bound up with the poetics of the archive, within which cinema's "trace of historical time rendered *visible* . . . can become even more *visible* if gaps and accidents fragment and stain the film."[49] If cinema's material composition (and decomposition) render it paradoxically both more vulnerable and more visible, DeLillo extends and transposes that paradox, using transcriptive writing to imagine how the codex and the page as formats might frame the restoration of cinematic material. Richard Dienst, writing of Jean-Luc Godard's *Histoire(s) du cinéma*, claims that "the history of cinema can be told, it seems, everywhere but in cinema. Yet . . . the history of cinema is the only history that needs to be told, because only cinema has been capable of telling the story of its time. But it failed, and that is the real story."[50] DeLillo's cinematic project, then, constitutes an attempt to render this story, or at the very least to glimpse an instant within it, by intervening at the historical and technological crux of the bunker film, the layered space and time of the too-late waiting to be redirected from within it. Treating the literary as a format for mediated reproduction—producing mediagraphic metafiction by replaying key cinematic moments for the novel on the pages of the novel—DeLillo compiles a shadow archive of film through failure and absence, drawing into relief the material "gaps and accidents" that simultaneously fragment and define the history of cinema and its apparatus.

Notes Toward a Film: Materiality, Transcription, and the Alternate History of *The Great Dictator*

John Johnston claims that the characters of *Running Dog* are "hardly characters at all, inasmuch as they lack a significant mental life and seldom reveal signs of a complex psychological interiority," and that rather than having these attributes, they function merely as "sites where a particular configuration of forces and social pressures in the culture medium crystallize or precipitate out as patterned sets of recognizable interests and responses."[51] Johnston's formulation is insightful precisely in its grasp of how DeLillo's structuring of character and subjectivity in *Running Dog* echoes his structuring of the bunker film as a kind of simulation ad extremum. Indeed, Johnston's claim implies that the "characters" of *Running Dog* are not so much characters as themselves collections of images similar to the films that populate the novel alongside them. This flatness of character is a common constant within postmodern fiction, yet within the moment of technological change DeLillo focuses on in the novel, it takes on a particularly charged urgency. In this section and the following one, I read the mediagraphic moments within the published version of *Running Dog* alongside earlier versions of these passages available in the DeLillo Papers at the Harry Ransom Center. In doing so, I want both to extend the reach of Johnston's reading and reverse its emphasis. If *Running Dog*'s characters are shaped in the image of its films, as images in and of themselves, and if it is the actions and relations of the novel's characters that provide a catalyst for those films rather than the other way around, then it is those films that warrant the closest, most sustained analysis and attention. Johnston's reading marks a point beyond which consideration of character in the novel must give way to consideration of its cinematic material: if the writing of a novel around film makes the claims that he notes regarding character under the regime of the moving image, what claims does it reflexively make about writing itself—about the novel as a format, and about that format's investment in and ability to intervene within the processes of media reproduction it addresses?

The relationship between Moll and Selvy exemplifies the ways in which DeLillo mixes character dynamics and media dynamics. As Moll begins to investigate Selvy for a "series of [magazine] articles on sex as big business," she becomes sexually involved with him herself in an almost arbitrary fashion.[52] As often happens to characters in DeLillo's novels (perhaps most notably in the early sections of his first novel, *Americana*), media images permeate Moll's thoughts at key moments in their relationship. After their first sexual encounter, her mind flashes on Michelangelo Antonioni's 1970 film *Zabriskie Point*, and in "a run-on series of images" that she "half dream[s]" after a subsequent time in bed with Selvy, she imagines him "in a military setting . . . a dog tag around his neck. Maybe she was mixing Monty Clift into it, in *From Here to Eternity*."[53] In their third encounter, cinema makes a much more extensive and pivotal appearance. It colonizes traditional subjective character in a way that begins to figure a different mode of writing, one that hinges not on cultural or personal memory but rather on the material poetics of the cinematic archive as seen in the phenomenon of the cinematic revival. Heading home from a meeting with her editor, Moll randomly runs into the image of Charlie Chaplin and the body of Selvy in rapid succession: "It was late afternoon when Moll hailed a cab that took her past the Little Carnegie, where a special Chaplin program was playing. She found Selvy waiting in her apartment and decided not to ask how he'd gained entry. Bad taste, such questions. An insult to the ambivalence of their relations."[54] The two quickly fall into bed together, and after sex Chaplin's image reassumes control of Moll's thoughts: "I just remembered something. . . . We're going to the movies. I just realized. There's a Chaplin program at the Little Carnegie and we've got four and a half minutes to get down there."[55] This abrupt shift of focus on Moll's part is followed by a dramatic shift in the novel's tonality and its approach to inscriptive form and the architecture of the page: DeLillo abruptly cuts to a page-long encapsulation of Chaplin's *The Great Dictator*, the parody of Hitler that Hitler in turn parodies in the bunker film at the end of *Running Dog*.

Chaplin's film, originally released in 1940, capitalizes on the physical resemblances between himself and Hitler in order to tell a story of mistaken identity between Adenoid Hynkel, a Hitler-like dictator of the fictional nation of Tomainia, and an unnamed Jewish barber, with both roles played by Chaplin.[56] The two characters exist in parallel plots until late in the movie, when Hynkel disappears in a hunting accident. The barber is mistaken for the dictator and brought to speak at a rally, where instead of inspiring the crowd toward fascism, he abdicates his misplaced position as dictator, calling for peace, humanity, and kindness. By the moment of *Running Dog*'s publication in the mid-1970s, such a political vision was of course a profoundly obsolete dead end on multiple levels, most dramatically in its idealistic view of a liberal humanist counterforce against the rise of the Nazi party. Chaplin himself recants the naïveté of the film's parodic comedy in his 1964 autobiography, writing, "Had I known of the actual horrors of the German concentration camps, I could not have made *The Great Dictator*; I could not have made fun of the homicidal insanity of the Nazis."[57] Just as the film is politically belated, it is also technologically belated, as Chaplin's first feature-length sound film, a genre that had been popular and widespread since the release of *The Jazz Singer* in 1927. DeLillo's transcription seizes on this dual belatedness as a means of leverage for developing the novel's media poetics in terms of both form and politics. Through this poetics, he imagines an archival "rescue operation"—not of the film itself or of its obsolete politics, but rather of the historical breaks and openings it creates through this belatedness, its location within the Deleuzian too-late.[58] Indeed, this belatedness is a historiographic point of entry: both in spite of and because of it, he asks the reader to see this film as a newly open hinge point for rethinking and reconfiguring cinematic history within a moment of technological crisis, excavating and dissecting the material and temporal affordances of celluloid technology through the affordances of the printed page.

The passage in *Running Dog* that encapsulates *The Great Dictator* appears entirely in italics; spatially separated from the text around it and without any clear introduction or transition from the scene that precedes it, it visually charges the architecture of the page in a manner that signals a break—almost like a cinematic cut—from a focus on narrative form to a focus on media format. DeLillo's development of this scene from his initial notes to the final version published in the novel illustrates his engagement in a novelistic media poetics of preservation through transference that echoes the archival process theorized by Habib and described in DeLillo's own research materials for the novel. Yet this is not preservation in an idealized sense, the teleological care of the image for an imagined future. On the contrary, DeLillo's transcriptive approach underscores the necessarily transformative impact of any preservation across media formats—the complex way in which a transposed media artifact (an image transferred from photosensitive film to the code of a .jpg file, a film transferred from 35 mm to .mov, a sound from vinyl to .mp3, a text document from paper to .pdf) both is and is not the original that it serves to preserve. As Derrida suggests, such artifacts constellate "an archiving process with different states, but never one established archive."[59] The more dramatic intermedia transference staged in the novel—from light marking the substrate of celluloid to text marking the substrate of paper—only serves to underscore this irreducible complexity. After all, a paper-bound print text cannot literally preserve or store moving images, at least not with the material specificity of actual individual celluloid frames; the dissonance between these two media in terms of substrate and affordance means that every textual transcription, every adaptation, will necessarily be inexact, incomplete, unable to capture the full materiality of another medium. Yet precisely because the novel cannot materially be or contain the film, it draws our attention more closely to the archival poetics at stake within its own medium and its own moment, as well as across media history more broadly.

The earliest version of this passage appears in handwritten form in a pocket-sized notebook used by DeLillo.[60] The language in this document is highly condensed, almost as if DeLillo were actually taking notes on a screening of the film, with each phrase or fragment standing in for a scene or sequence of images. Yet precisely because of this condensed quality, this preliminary draft is notable in its striking resemblance to the final published version, both in terms of the scenes, images, and effects from the film that appear within it and, perhaps more significantly, in terms of the language used to render them. In this resemblance, the notebook text is not so much a set of notes in preparation for the imaginative act of writing the passage—raw material for authorly inspiration, as it were—as it is an initial stage of the process of mediatic preservation that ends in the published version, a first iteration of authorial transcription and manipulation of the information of the film. DeLillo's condensed minimalism within the passage frames it as a sequence of images that provide perhaps the least information necessary to retain the narrative trajectory of *The Great Dictator*. A number of the units of text that appear in the notebook reappear in the published novel with little or no change. For example, the images "infant ~~pees~~ wets on his hand" (with "his" referring to Hynkel) and "stormtroopers ~~painting~~ march and sing" appear in the published novel in sequence as in the notebook, and virtually verbatim, as "[a]n *infant wets on the dictator's hand. Storm troopers march and sing.*"[61] A scene involving the meeting of Hynkel and Benzino Napaloni (Hynkel's rival dictator and a stand-in for Benito Mussolini) undergoes similarly minor changes in phrasing and sequencing:

> There is a military display and a ball in the palace.
> ~~The dictator~~
> Invasion plans are made.
> Dictators eat limburger + strawberries.
> ~~Treaty~~.

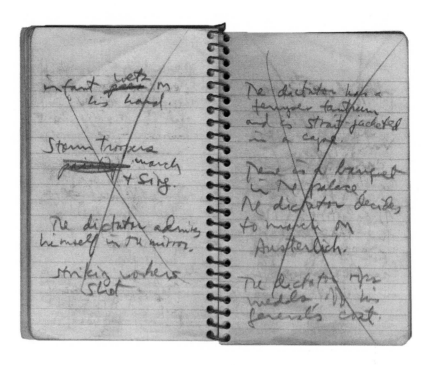

Figure 5. Don DeLillo, *Running Dog* Notebook. Reprinted from the *Running Dog* Notebook by permission of Don DeLillo and the Harry Ransom Center. All rights reserved to Don DeLillo for his own use and disposition.

becomes "*There is a ball in the palace. The dictator and his rival eat strawberries and mustard. A treaty is signed. The two men team up.*"[62] This minimal gap between versions of the passage that appear as transcriptive note taking and as final authorial writing, respectively, poses an argument of its own: it suggests that the final product is not only immediately descended from the notes in terms of content, but indeed modeled on their practice. Thus transcription and transference function as the central mode of writing here rather than as a preparatory precursor to that writing, a shift in focus and intent that conceptualizes the novel as a tool for archival poetics.

DeLillo extends this conceptualization through his material treatment of the architecture of the notebook page as a unit of storage, independent from and outside of language or text as such. In addition to individual words and phrases being crossed out in the internal process of writing and

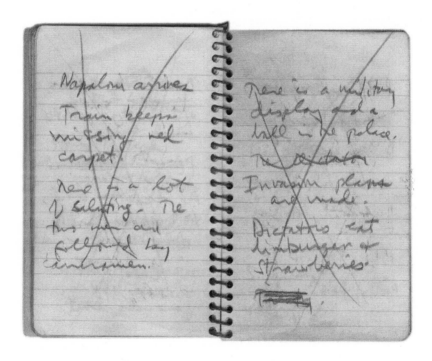

Figure 6. Don DeLillo, *Running Dog* Notebook. Reprinted from the *Running Dog* Notebook by permission of Don DeLillo and the Harry Ransom Center. All rights reserved to Don DeLillo for his own use and disposition.

revision (as visible above), each page of text-images is also crossed out as a whole with a large X, as visible in figures 5 and 6. The notebook gives no indication as to when these marks were made in the writing process or why they were made. Through this use of wholesale, large-scale Xs in addition to (and at times instead of) singular, one-by-one cancellations, DeLillo marks the pages themselves as much as what is written on each of them, if not more so. This practice claims the surface space of a given page as an operative unit of inscription and storage over and above whatever text might arbitrarily fit within its confines and whatever portion of the film that text might cover.

Within this architecture, DeLillo's Xs have the effect of a complexly contradictory system of material textual marking, registering and confirming his notes and the cinematic material those notes record precisely by cancelling them. This contradictory gesture resonates with Lippit's thinking about the archival implications of the X as "[a] writing that erases, that produces antigraphic marks. Xs. The transparent being is only there, in the fullness of its invisibility, when it can perform its own effacement. In the idiom of writing, the rhetoric of such invisibility suggests an antiwriting or erasure. . . . The destruction of graphicality must also be understood as a form of preservation: it prevents, or postpones indefinitely, the eruption of a catastrophe."[63] Cancellation preserves—it defers the material pressures of catastrophe—but only by engaging in a kind of destruction itself; the archive persists, but not without bearing and bodying forth the mark of the anarchive. Concretizing the archival tensions Lippit attributes to the antigraphic X, the Xs in DeLillo's notebook throw the film into a liminal space between oblivion and memory, erasure and writing, cancellation and preservation. In political and historical terms, the textual mark of the X here can never postpone or cancel catastrophe—it is already too late—but rather only imagine the speculative resurrection of an alternate image, an alternate history, an unseen and untouched filmic object at the margins of the shadow archive of the twentieth century. Defined by graphic cancellation of textual documentation of cinematic projection, then, the notebook itself consequently resonates as an index of the complex material and aesthetic commensurabilities between the substrates of film and paper. Pages and frames each have their own different affordances, yet both are subject to cancellation, disappearance, disintegration. In Habib's language, DeLillo's

Xs "fragment and stain" the cinematic images of *The Great Dictator* in order to preserve and transfer them, making clear that the distinctions between what is lost and what is retained, what is preserved and what is discarded, are perpetually in motion and under pressure.

The setting of the *Great Dictator* passage in italics, which does not occur until the final draft of *Running Dog*, transposes these tensions to the published version of the novel.[64] Its alteration of type stands in for the effect of graphic marking achieved by the notebook's Xs, explicitly resituating the passage as its own entity within the architecture of the page—a series of images transcribed as text, within the space of the novel but not of it. Form, formatting, medium, and materiality are closely intertwined in this gesture: using this visual device to set off and highlight a passage largely composed of deliberately flat writing, DeLillo renders the text of the passage newly visible *as* text. Palpably and materially inscribed on the page, the passage takes on an orthographic physicality intended to be seen as much as to be read. By italicizing the text of this passage in reference both to the images of Chaplin's film and to the visual effects of his own draft materials, DeLillo gives it a location of its own within the constellation of media forms and objects shaping the scene and the novel as a whole across historical time. Rather than suggesting an impossible transference of the film onto the page, the italicized status of this text lends it an almost palimpsestic effect, with the words of the passage shifted in the space of the page as if by the pressure of the sedimentation of media material under them—Hitler's massive archival project of images and information, Chaplin's cinematic response, and DeLillo's own transcriptive documentation. Deleuze claims that within post–World War II visual culture, "[t]he visual image becomes *archaeological, stratigraphic, tectonic*. Not that we are taken back to prehistory (there is an archaeology of the present), but to the deserted layers of our time which bury our own phantoms; to the lacunary layers which we juxtaposed according to variable orientations and connections."[65] Reshuffling and reorienting those layers, continually oscillating between the anarchival absence and emptiness of past time on one hand and the seeming permanence of the archive on the other, DeLillo's transcription of *The Great Dictator* traces the contours of a media object in order to reorient it as undead and unstable within media history. By transcribing and rewriting this film within the novel, setting into play and into motion the formal, ideological, and material components of its history,

DeLillo makes clear the complexly layered ways in which the larger sweep of film history is also equally subject to reorientation, oblivion, and recollection, equally dependent on the unstable, fugitive materiality of the shadow archive.

Textual Démontage, Textual Emulsion, and the Afterlife of the Novel

DeLillo uses the bunker film of Hitler that Lightborne acquires and screens at the end of the novel to exploit this fugitive materiality as a means of refiguring the media poetics of print writing. In this section of the novel, he employs the transcriptive aesthetics developed in the *Great Dictator* passage discussed above in order to sketch the "archaeology of the present" that Deleuze describes around this charged cinematic object: sifting and arranging temporal layers within the imagined frames of the film's materiality, he uses the affordances of print text to unearth and reveal those layers within the broader historical trajectory of film itself. Many critics of *Running Dog* have understood this scene in terms of Baudrillardian simulation, seeing the revelation of the bunker film's true content as a moment of political foreclosure within the media culture DeLillo critiques in the novel. Scott Rettberg, for example, suggests that the "layered" simulacrum of the bunker film can be condensed to "[p]eople with an idea of Hitler watch[ing] a film of Hitler that is not Hitler but Hitler pretending to be someone pretending to be Hitler."[66] Similarly, Patrick O'Donnell claims that, "[l]ike Baudrillard, DeLillo conceives of contemporary reality as a palimpsest of representations," while Tim Engels says of the scene that, "[a]s in *White Noise* . . . DeLillo continually depicts a looping, blurred interplay between people and cinematic performance."[67] As suggested by Engels's reference, these interpretations of the bunker film largely read the media-historical context of DeLillo's later and better-known novel back onto *Running Dog*, anachronistically approaching it through the lens of Baudrillardian electronic media culture. In doing so, they simplify the transitional media-historical moment it exists within and depicts. This moment is still deeply informed by analog media culture, as shown everywhere from the singular cinematic object of the bunker film to the novel's art house revival of *The Great Dictator*, which seemingly takes its origins from DeLillo's notes on an actual celluloid screening of the film.

Taking into account the technological context of this moment makes clear that the palimpsest O'Donnell describes is best understood as one composed not of dematerialized representations but rather of objects that exist within various forms and formats of analog storage. Thus by using form to register the material specificities of the bunker film as a singular celluloid object, DeLillo puts those specificities in play as the granular elements by which the novel as a format might rethink the material historicity of celluloid film. Admittedly, the political capacity present within such a rethinking is deeply qualified: as Deleuze suggests in his discussion of Hitler's cinematic history, there exists at best only a partial potential to go beyond the media information produced by and in the image of the Third Reich. Yet to the extent that DeLillo makes such an opening possible in *Running Dog*, he does so precisely by means of close attention to the materiality of images and media objects, and whatever possibilities he does imagine correspondingly appear in terms of that materiality.

DeLillo introduces the screening of the bunker film within the novel in a manner that closely echoes Pynchon's treatment of film in the closing moments of *Gravity's Rainbow*. Waiting for the screening to begin, Moll reflects on "that special kind of anticipation she'd enjoyed since childhood—a life in the movies."[68] Through this personal cinematic history, DeLillo marks Moll as one of the "old fans who've always been at the movies (haven't we?)" that Pynchon imagines in the theater about to be destroyed by Rocket 00000. Like those fans, Moll understands the two-dimensionality of film "so readily and well. They connect to us, all the city's spatial and temporal codes, as though from a place we knew before."[69] In much of his rendition of the bunker film, DeLillo uses form to register this familiarity, as in some of the scene's early moments:

> Plaster is cracked in places. On other parts of the wall it is missing completely. The lights in the room flicker.
>
> Three children appear. A girl, perhaps eleven, carries a chair. Two younger children, a boy and a very small girl, drag in a second chair between them.
>
> The children set the chairs on the floor and walk out of camera range.
>
> There is a disturbance. The picture jumps as though the camera has been jarred by some brief violent action.[70]

Here the images of the film appear almost as if they were simply observed and rendered in the language of conventional narration; the description is flat in tone, reflective of the banality of the scene, but it is not fragmented or explicitly mediated in and of itself. In this sense, this mode differs from much of the language in the *Great Dictator* passage, as well as from much of the novel proper outside of these cinematic moments. Indeed, when the camera does explicitly appear within these initial observational moments, it registers as a marker for something like the trappings of documentary realism. While the camera occasionally jumps and shakes from the shelling outside the bunker, lending an air of urgency to the passage, most of the time it "*is immobile. It does not select. People pass in and out of its viewing field.*"[71] To the extent that the camera (and thus the scene's language) serve plainly to record such moments from a fixed position rather than to serve as a means by which a cameraperson (or author) might intervene explicitly or directly, this portion of the text seems like a strange temporal palimpsest of cinematic technologies.

On the one hand, as DeLillo notes when Lightborne acquires the film in an earlier scene, it is "[s]ixteen millimeter . . . [c]onsidered an amateur film gauge at the time this footage was shot."[72] Yet it also seems to capture and store arbitrary events in a manner that resonates with the role of the stationary security camera prevalent in the contemporary moment of the novel, as described in an earlier exchange between Lightborne and Moll:

> "Go into a bank, you're filmed," [Lightborne] said. "Go into a department store, you're filmed. Increasingly we see this." . . .
> "The camera's everywhere. . . . Even in the bunker," [Moll] said.[73]

Presenting a home movie that is at once both midcentury and contemporary in its aesthetics, DeLillo draws a similarly nonlinear and nonteleological line of affiliation between the technologies of these moments: the late twentieth-century electronic video apparatus that allows for constant surveillance in the bank, the department store, and the changing room is perhaps less different from the celluloid apparatus of the 1930s and 1940s than it initially seems. Layering this history of documentation into the bunker film, he undercuts the seeming newness of the contemporary technology that saturates the world of *Running Dog*. In this sense these sections of the bunker film constitute a kind of counterhistorical detour, a moment in which the seeming anachrony of the home movie in the mid-twentieth century yields to a complexly compacted, recursive mediality between the old and new media of the novel's moment.

In the other mode that dominates the bunker film passage, DeLillo aligns his language with the operations and apparatus of cinematic recording as a means of thinking between the alphabetic and the cinematic in historical and mediatic terms. In their formal dimensions, the sentences in this category point up the technological status of the film as a whole as it appears on the page: DeLillo uses fragments to disrupt and cut against the banal, flat flow of information that characterizes the rest of the passage's text, situating these moments within his writing as an explicitly media-historical intervention. These divergences from the relative narrative transparency I discuss above demonstrate the extent to which the transcriptive methodologies of the *Great Dictator* passage shape DeLillo's writing here. A number of fragmentary phrases serve to establish the scene and location of the film as well as to foreground the passage's mediatic status within the novel: the first line of the text, for example, is the cryptic "*A bare room/black and white.*"[74] This juxtaposition of two descriptions of circumstance—one having to do with the physical situation of the room, one having to do with the technological situation of the film—forms a unit of text that is at once both fragmentary and overloaded, as if gesturing toward the sedimentary layers of mediation and information that accumulate beneath this single "bare" textual image. Other sequences of text, such as

> *A blank interval.*
> *Again the room. The camera setup is the same.*

or the paragraph that consists only of the words "*[v]isual static. Flash frames,*" similarly keep the scene's essence as a product of cinematic technology at the foreground—in these moments, DeLillo describes the film itself rather than the events it records.[75]

The description of Hitler's entrance shows this perhaps most substantively and radically:

For the first time the camera is active.

In a long slow panning movement, it focuses eventually on a figure just beyond the doorway. A man in costume. After an interval of distortion, the camera, starting at the man's feet, moves slowly up his body.

Oversized shoes, turned up slightly at the points.

Baggy pants.

Vest and tight-fitting cutaway.

A dark narrow tie.

A wing collar, askew.

A battered derby.

A white boutonniere in the lapel of the cutaway.

A cane hooked over his wrist. . . .

Flaccid mouth.

Smoothly curved jaw.

The famous moustache.[76]

In this passage, DeLillo uses the space of the page to make a claim on the reproductive material in play that is considerably more far-reaching than that made by the contextualizing fragments I discuss above. As with the transcriptive aesthetics of the *Great Dictator* notebook, the single-image lines used here register as a series of single-shot close-ups in language. However, DeLillo's use of this effect problematizes the material conditions of the bunker film in several ways. Firstly, unlike in the case of *The Great Dictator*, there is no actual real-world film from which this passage might be transcribed. In effect, the passage is a transcript of a film that does not exist beyond the world of the novel: thus the passage reads paradoxically both as transcription in the mold of the *Great Dictator* passage and as new authorial production, as a moment of both "copied" narration and editorial recombination. Secondly, the staccato sequence of discrete text-images both directly contradicts the unbroken continuity of the camera's "slow panning movement" that the passage alludes to and also scrambles the stated upward path of that movement, cutting at first from Hitler's collar to his derby and back down to his lapel and then wrist, and later from his mouth down to his jaw and back up to his iconically "famous moustache."

Thus this portion of the bunker film uses the architecture of the page as a multidimensional substrate to realize within text the "aberrant movements and false continuity shots" that Deleuze describes as buried within modern cinema. Time is out of joint at the most fundamental level of the shot within the film itself as well as with respect to its position within the authorial and historical temporality of the novel. Posing an internally contradictory record of the cinematic text in question, the formal divergences and discontinuities in this passage break up the image of Hitler's body and rearrange the resulting components on the surface of the page. This false continuity—a formal quality that Deleuze sees as central to film—resembles what he, writing with Félix Guattari, describes as "démontage," one of several related concepts that invoke and bear on the cinematic, but also extend beyond it in scope: as Lippit writes, "The assemblage—Deleuze and Guattari's figure of an irreducible but functioning heterogeneity—resembles an emulsion, by working only through dismantling, through *démontage*, which generates an asynthetic order."[77] Démontage, asynthesis, emulsion: these terms suggest a conception of cinema as defined not by connection between frames, images, or moments, but rather by disconnection, incommensurability, and parataxis. DeLillo adapts these cinematic aesthetics to the media poetics of the novel in this moment: simultaneously utilizing and subverting the transcriptive strategies he developed in the *Great Dictator* passage earlier in the novel, he uses form to produce a kind of textual démontage.

DeLillo's formal strategy here also serves as the means for a larger speculative inquiry about the historicity of this film and of film more broadly. In the middle of Hitler's entrance as Chaplin, he breaks from the form of shots quoted above to comment, "*This footage has the mysterious aura of an event that cuts across time. This is because the man, standing beyond the doorway, is not yet visible to the audience of adults and children in the immediate vicinity. The other audience, watching in a dark room in New York in the 1970s, is aware of this, and they feel a curious sense of preview. They are seeing the man 'first.'*"[78] This sense of preview, this "firstness," so to speak, is paradoxically a firstness rooted the past, in the uncanny sensation of the novel's 1970s characters' being the first people ever to see a movie from the 1940s, before any audience from its time, much less the people who filmed and were filmed within it. Some commentators on the novel have seen DeLillo's presentation of this element of the bunker film as a gesture of social critique on his part: Mark Osteen, for example, claims, "We readers of *Running Dog*, engaged as we are in observing the observers [of the film], are thus also implicated in its exploitative ideology."[79] Yet rather than collapsing the two temporalities in question, as such a reading seems to attempt to do, I would suggest that this sense of preview taking place both across the individual shots within the film and across the two historical moments inheres most fundamentally in the way in which it destabilizes time, suspending various moments in a kind of nonlinear parataxis. In this sense, the "cut" across time is not a vector of contact or connection but rather an démontagic cinematic cut, putting the two audiences in an unresolved temporal relation to one another.

The bunker film's microscopic engagement with cinematic form also resonates with the microscopic scale of film technology. The discontinuity of démontage finds its analogue in the "synthesis without synthesis" of emulsion, the chemical process that produces photographic and cinematic film.[80] In photographic emulsion, light-sensitive silver gelatin is coated onto a transparent substrate of film base to produce the film stock that is used to capture moving images. Lippit says of this process, "The notion of an immiscible mixture suggests a paradox, a synthesis that remains, in the end, unsynthesized. . . . As a chemical action, the principle of emulsion facilitated the advent of photography in the early nineteenth century. . . . [T]he material, chemical, and fantastical properties of an emulsion infuse the photographic and filmic unconscious."[81] Lippit's claim here suggests that just as the disordered shots of démontage produce a film that resists coherence into a normalized whole, the "immiscible mixture" of chemicals that constitutes film itself similarly exists in constant suspension, connected in disconnection. Thus within the fundamental elements Lippit notes, film displays paradox within paradox, fractally layered higher and lower orders of a shared situation of parataxis—the unsynthesized chemical components of the substrate storing the unsynthesized formal elements of the moving image. Moreover, given that the most common substrate material in the first half of the twentieth century was nitrocellulose—the highly flammable material DeLillo researched in his preparation for writing *Running Dog*—we can imagine that this chemical suspension characterizes the bunker film itself as well. Thus the formal paradox of the film's démontage and the material paradox of its unsynthesized layers are collectively inseparable from its combustible, dangerous, destructive condition. They mark it as a singular object of the archive that tends inexorably toward the incineration and remembered oblivion of the shadow archive.

Perhaps, then, it is for these historical and material reasons, as well as more immediate narrative ones, that DeLillo stages the bunker film as such an anticlimax. Lightborne describes it as "a disaster," "no good," suitable only for the museum rather than for the market, and with one reel left almost entirely unseen, a hired gun from the mob arrives to steal it from him.[82] Thus DeLillo presents it within the novel only for it to disappear again almost as quickly and arbitrarily as it appeared, pulled back into a shadow archive of a different sort. Through this failure of the film—its failure to live up to the expectations, pornographic or otherwise, of the novel's characters; to circulate publicly beyond this initial screening; to reveal somehow the history of film, or any history, for that matter—he circumvents any life for it within the world of the novel. At one level, this anticlimax functions as a kind of critique of media consumption, implicating the novel's readers in the disappointment its characters feel. Yet DeLillo's larger work here comes in using this circumvention to shed light on the afterlife of film that Deleuze considers in *Cinema 2*, unfolding the bunker film as a media-historical palimpsest. Formally discontinuous, materially contingent, oscillating in and out of time, the bunker film is an unstable document within an unstable history of visual media; it pushes that history off of its axis, layering it and reorienting it. Buried in the shadow archive of the 1940s only to reemerge briefly in the world of the 1970s, it circulates in the world of the novel undead, possessing and signifying for nothing more and nothing less than this afterlife.

This liminal status is as much a reflection on the format of the literary print novel as it is on the bunker film or on film more broadly. In the *Great Dictator* section of the novel, DeLillo uses the aesthetics of transcription in a kind of rescue mission, imagining a media poetics of preservation, while in the case of the bunker film he uses those same techniques to imaginatively dismantle the film. Yet these seemingly opposing processes are ultimately two sides of the same formal, mediatic, and historical coin—two faces of an archival poetics in the novel that is defined by the irreducible vulnerability and ephemerality of film, yet also recursively defines film itself through those same terms. The unstable media objects of *Running Dog* serve not only as the contents of a microscopic film archive imagined within alphabetic text but also more broadly as points of constellation in a revisionary media history, within which film stock and paper pages persist as substrates capable of invoking and reconfiguring one another through material and formal experimentation. To adopt Deleuze's language, DeLillo's strategy offers a vision of the afterlife of the novel in the face of the emergent saturation of visual media, framing it as a format engaged with the poetics of the archive rather than with the poetics of narrative or affect. By making visible the stratigraphic material sedimentation within the novel as a media format, he also traces its position within the larger sedimentation of the media technology of the last quarter of the twentieth century. In attempting to turn over the cinematic image through textual means—retrieving it, preserving it, revising it, fragmenting it, and returning it to the shadows—DeLillo turns over the image of text as well.

Coda: Digital Shadows

On the Internet, the bunker film is everywhere, and nowhere, and everywhere again. Yet this ephemeral permanence is no longer primarily a condition linked to the camera's being everywhere, as DeLillo suggests through Moll in *Running Dog*, but rather the result of a different kind of ubiquity— that of the apparatus of digital technology itself. Indeed, rather than marking the multilayered vulnerability of celluloid as it did in the 1970s, the most salient representation of Hitler's bunker in the digital landscape of the twenty-first century marks instead the constantly shifting circulation of information across the granular distribution of the Web.

In September 2004, the German film production company Constantin Film released *Downfall*, a fictionalized account of the last days in the Führerbunker.[83] The film earned an Academy Award nomination for Best Foreign Language Film, grossed over $90 million worldwide, and incited a debate about the ethics of humanizing Hitler that spanned both German and American journalism and film criticism. Yet *Downfall* will likely be best remembered for the deformations and parodic versionings it has inspired and provided the source material for: beginning with "Sim Heil," first uploaded to the Internet on August 10, 2006, a near-constant stream of *Downfall* parodies has appeared on YouTube and various other websites.[84] The vast majority of these parodies draws on a single piece of source text, a crux scene from late in the film where Hitler's high-ranking generals must reveal to him that the German army has not been able to hold off Soviet troops, and that thus Berlin and the Reich will fall. Hitler's reaction, a rant of nearly four minutes, moves from rage and indignation to melancholic, detached acceptance of the inevitable future. In the most common and widely known strain of parodies, YouTube users superimpose alternate subtitles onto the images of this scene, rewriting Hitler's dialogue to address a wide sweep of pop culture ephemera: celebrity breakups and deaths, sporting news, the tics and gaffes of politicians, and of course the inevitable metaparodies—Hitler ranting about the popularity of the *Downfall* meme itself, or about the fair use debates that arose around the videos. Taken together, these videos comprise a hall-of-mirrors reflection of the cultural rhetoric of the bunker film. In both cases, what looks at first to be grim and harrowing, the figurative if not the literal pornography of the bunker, gives way to absurdity and banality.

The crucial difference between the bunker film and the *Downfall* videos lies in the question of authorship: whereas in the case of *Running Dog*, DeLillo's singular authorship seems to address the audience of the film and the readers of his novel, deflating their expectations about the film being shown, in the case of the *Downfall* videos ordinary people themselves perform this deflation, applying it as a means to reflect on cultural issues not directly tied to the content or concerns of the original. In this sense, it exemplifies the aesthetics of reappropriation central to the memetic logic underlying a great deal of contemporary digital culture. Grounding a critical theory of reappropriation in the work of Michel de Certeau, Ryan M. Milner cites the practice as one of "five fundamental logics evident in the creation, circulation, and transformation of memetic media[.] . . . Without reappropriation there would be no memetic media. Digitization allows texts to intertwine with regularity and ease[.] . . . Memetic media are stitched together by the creative reappropriation of multiple modes of communication."[85]

As with the debate around the ethics of representation in the original film, the *Downfall* videos have themselves raised a number of ethical questions. Initially, the primary conversation around the videos closely paralleled the debates around the film itself, with critics concerned that the comedic tactics of the videos served to dilute the horrors of the Holocaust. As in DeLillo's novel, these videos shift approach from mocking Hitler himself (as Chaplin did) to using Hitler to mock something, indeed perhaps anything, else (as in the actual bunker film); as Mark Dery puts it, "In the viral videos, Hitler often seems less like the smacked-ass object of the joke than an actor named Adolf who is in on the joke, doing some weird strain of improv that, again, makes him more sympathetic."[86] Over time, the ethical conversation around the *Downfall* videos shifted from these issues of representation and implication to a debate over fair use and intellectual property that brought into view questions of materiality and circulation that also dovetail with those in and around DeLillo's novel. In April 2010, Constantin issued a Digital Millennium Copyright Act request for removal of their content from YouTube on copyright grounds.[87] Despite *Downfall* director Oliver Hirschbiegel's public approval of the *Downfall* meme and numerous countertactics by a growing community of *Downfall* parodists, Constantin's efforts were initially successful, resulting in the disappearance of many videos; since this initial clash, the studio has subsequently shifted course and chosen to monetize the parodies through advertising rather than wholly forbidding them.

This battle over possession and circulation of the parodies results in a complex online terrain that is constantly fluctuating between visibility and invisibility, presence and absence, the duplication of material and the removal of that same material. The culture of *Downfall* parodies is large enough to spawn its own subgenres, terminology, and ancillary dramatis personae (all preserved and historicized on the Hitler Parody Wiki), and yet this culture exists precisely in spite of and because of the granular ephemerality of the material of the parodies, a state that Dery describes as the result of an ongoing "cat-and-mouse game [between parodists and] authorities, rendering pointless the citation of any URLs for the videos."[88] This tension often produces complex paradoxes at the level of storage, access, and materiality. For example, "Sim Heil," the earliest known *Downfall* parody, has been repeatedly removed and uploaded in alternate forms, under alternate names, and on alternate sites. While the original is no longer accessible, a version with English subtitles was uploaded to YouTube by the Russian website ruknowyourmeme (a minor entity seemingly unrelated to the widely known meme culture repository Know Your Meme) on June 12, 2011, and was still accessible as of July 2021; the global, multilingual history of this media object attests to the complex layering such a digital object acquires as it circulates across the Web through various different modes and moments of accessibility and inaccessibility. The humor of "Sim Heil" derives from Hitler's complaining about the technical shortcomings of Microsoft's *Flight Simulator X* (the "sim" of the clip's title): "Everything is stuttered . . .

8 fucking FPS [frames per second]! ¿¡That's what I bought a Dual Core for!?
... There are bugs even in the installer."[89] Although this subject matter is
coincidental, more likely a function of the meme's emergence from gamer
subculture than of anything else, the centrality of technical dysfunction to
the humor here is striking; even and especially in the depths of the bunker,
it seems, horror and humor emerge from the irreducible errors and disso-
nances of technology.

Taken collectively, the *Downfall* videos resemble the bunker film multiplied, reworked, distributed and redistributed, the subtitles across Hitler's
image blinking in and out of the most visible and most invisible places of
the Web, repeatedly posted, blocked, mirrored, reposted, never gone but
never stably accessible. This constantly shifting corpus makes clear that the
technological and material questions of DeLillo's novel are not erased or
bracketed by the shift to digital storage and circulation but rather themselves multiplied, refracted, and restaged many times across the space of
the Web. As Matthew Kirschenbaum notes, "[T]he network itself, as a
redundantly distributed hard drive, function[s] as an agent of preservation"
in the case of these clips, a social domain that captures disappearances and
absences as well as instances of stability and permanence.[90] Writing of the
complex history of *Agrippa*, the multimedia collaboration between Dennis
Ashbaugh, William Gibson, and Kevin Begos, Jr., he argues, "No model of
digital inscription that rests upon the new medium's supposedly radically
unstable ontology can be taken seriously so long as innumerable copies
of this particular text remain only a search query away."[91] This corrective
provides a valuable critique of the medial ideology that assumes the digital
to be immaterial and evanescent. Yet Kirschenbaum's own argument—as
well as his thick technical description of the transformission of the poetic
text of "Agrippa"—makes clear that radical instability need not only mean
the binary (pun fully intended) opposition between wholesale presence
and disappearance. If we acknowledge that nothing is ever permanent on
the Web, but also that nothing is ever permanently gone, we must also
acknowledge that every artifact is shot through with instability at every
level, in every version, and at every moment. In acknowledging this, we
make possible a productive expansion of media's material instability on
a more granularly negotiated scale, so as to take account of the aleatory
circulations, reappearances, and reproductions of digital objects like the

Downfall videos or the text of "Agrippa." Conversely, DeLillo's use of form to trace an impressionistic contour of the cinematic archive of the 1970s in *Running Dog* testifies to the complexly granular instability inherent in the analog as well as in the digital—in celluloid film, plastic reels, and aluminum canisters as well as in binary files and electromagnetic impulses. In chapters 4 and 5, I consider the instability of the digital more fully, turning from the literary history of the analog that I have traced so far to consider how the literary as a format might advance a media poetics for mapping, indexing, and historicizing the contingent, shifting materiality of digital information across the spatial and technological landscape of the Web.

CHAPTER FOUR
Digital Materiality on Paper

Literary Form and Network Circulation in Hari Kunzru's
Transmission

If computer memory is like anything,

it is like erasable writing;

but if a penciled word can be erased because graphite is soft,

a computer's memory can be rewritten because its surface constantly fades.

—Wendy Chun, "The Enduring Ephemeral, or, The Future Is a Memory"

Vapor, Paper, and the Underwater History of the Internet

How does the book write the history of the Internet—not merely through narrative means, but through formal ones as well? How does print text on paper render the history of digital impulses stored on magnetic hard drives and circulating through fiber-optic cables? In the first three chapters of *Archival Fictions*, I considered how print literary writing might reckon with a series of analog technologies, showing how authors use form to think the materiality of those technologies—the typewriter, the phonograph, and celluloid film—as a way of thinking in turn about the larger arc of media history. In comparison to those analog technologies, the realm of the digital seems at first to present a different question of materiality and tangibility, and thus a different question of relation to the paper materiality of print literature. While typescripts, phonographic discs, and film canisters are all deeply visible and tangible as analog media formats, scholars and corporations alike have cloaked digital media to varying degrees in a rhetoric of ethereal invisibility and intangibility since its emergence into mainstream culture in the mid-1990s. Of course, digital technology and digital information are in fact as deeply and complexly material as analog and print media. Yet the materiality of the digital is often still thought of as profoundly *elsewhere*. In part precisely because they are so atmospherically omnipresent within the workaday operations of neoliberal technocracy, the inner workings of the digital seem out of sight and out of mind, untouchable behind the screen, in perpetual motion on the Web, vaporously everywhere and nowhere in the cloud. Understood as weightless and immaterial, these elements of digital infrastructure risk also being understood as outside of the historical and the social.[1]

The first three chapters of *Archival Fictions* sought new histories of analog media technologies through moments of formal and material breakdown within the literary as a media format. Over these chapters, I traced how authors reckon with analog media's instability and ephemerality—its susceptibility to material ends such as error, erasure, distortion, and combustion. I argued that these authors represent and exploit these vulnerabilities as a means of leverage for producing moments of formal experimentation that in turn serve as crux points for imagining trajectories of media history that are newly reflexive with regard to the medium and materiality of both the print codex and the other media in question. Digital media presents a different problematic of materiality and storage than analog media, which raises a correspondingly different set of issues for print literature. Wendy Chun notes, "Digital media, through the memory at their core, were supposed to solve, if not dissolve, archival problems such as degrading celluloid or scratched vinyl, not create archival problems of their own."[2]

Yet of course those new problems emerged nonetheless. As I suggested via Matthew Kirschenbaum at the end of chapter 3, digital storage media exist in complex and constant tension between ephemerality and permanence. As Chun puts it, "[T]he enduring is also the ephemeral. . . . [E]ven if data storage devices can be read forensically after they fail they still eventually fail."[3] Even data that can be reliably retrieved or recalled, Chun suggests, is always recalled with a difference. Thus, as in the case of analog formats such as the wax cylinder, the vinyl disc, and the celluloid strip, deterioration and preservation, ephemerality and endurance, and absence and presence are opposing sides of the same coin in the case of digital media, dramatically different states that exist in parataxis rather than in sequence or binary opposition. Fittingly, then, I delay discussion of how the staying power of the digital takes shape over the Web until chapter 5; here in chapter 4 I want to begin my discussion of print literature and the history of the digital by focusing first on literary representation of digital absence, corruption, and unreadability across the global space of the Web. As Lisa Gitelman suggests, focusing on "errors or pitfalls" in the workings of the digital offers a fuller, more layered perspective on its workings than any focus on specific sites or texts: "Considering groups of Web sites stands to offer a suggestive sense of the Web as a synchronic form, existing more in moments of access. By hinting at process, however, the study of errors offers the Web as it exists more certainly across time and amid the temporality of labor: the work of accessing and searching, yes, but also the differently capitalized work of scanning, programming, cabling, linking, writing, designing, and so on."[4] If access and retrieval show us momentary synchrony, then, error shows us history and diachrony: both the constant toggling between function and dysfunction and the longer, uneven temporalities of development and decay. Thus my sequencing here is intended to be strategic and evocative, privileging vulnerability and breakdown over stability and endurance as foundations of digital textuality: before we use literature to consider how the digital persists, we need to understand how and why it disappears and disintegrates.

Discussing digital media as the enduring ephemeral, Chun argues that it "is not always there (accessible), even when it is (somewhere)."[5] Her use of the parenthetical in this sentence establishes a complex, multilayered schema of presence, materiality, and location. Reading across the possibilities this schema poses, mixing and matching the parenthetical terms "accessible" and "somewhere" along with their respective antecedents "there" and the intransitive "is," we see that the digital is not always there even when it is, and that it is not always accessible, even when it is *somewhere*. Place, presence, and accessibility are crucially interdeterminate here, yet in an always unresolved manner: even when digital information is "there" in the immediate context of the user's screen, it is often somewhere else in addition or instead, stored and retrieved from the remote locations of the cloud. This spatial and geographic multiplicity is further complicated by

digital information's temporal multiplicity. For Chun, the digital's conflation of the ephemeral and the enduring inheres in computers' conflation of
memory, a process characterized by repetition and pastness, with storage,
a process characterized by forward-looking futurity: "By bringing memory and storage together," she argues, "we bring together the past and the
future," in turn situating information as "'undead': neither alive nor dead,
neither quite present nor absent."[6] Undeadness in this sense inheres at the
microscopic level of data. Each unit of information, each electromagnetic
pulse or fiber-optic pattern moving through circuits, across storage surfaces, or down long-distance cables constitutes a kind of undead return
of the informational past into a present that is always already flattened
against the speculated future. Each calling on the digital archive, then, each
invisible moment of digital reading and writing, is itself both historical
and historiographic—the retrieval of an object that is the same, but also
different, simultaneously a remembering and a forgetting.

How, then, might literature engage the mediality of the digital—how
might it pose, but not resolve, the question of the history of the Web?
Given the billions of circulations of information on computers and across
networks each moment of each day, such a task seems effectively impossible,
particularly through the considerably more finite affordances and trappings
of the print codex. Moreover, what complications arise for such a potential
history when digital material disappears—inevitably, sporadically, and often
irretrievably? How to historicize the materiality of the digital in a manner
that accounts not only for its presence and endurance but also—perhaps
even more importantly—for its discontinuity and disappearance? There is
a profound paradox in literary representation of the unstable storage and
circulation of information, in making the ephemeral seem to endure through
other means. This paradox is particularly rich for the novel. Gitelman sees
a productive convergence between the two media, quoting Leah Price's
thinking on the novel as a framework for understanding the network: "Like
an assiduous anthologist, the Web critic's presumptive 'ambition to represent a whole through its parts is always undermined by readers' awareness
that the parts have been chosen for their difference from those left out.' . . .
[T]he sheer size and diversity of the World Wide Web suggests that in this
case, balance might be a rank impossibility."[7] In a footnote to her citation
of Price, Gitelman acknowledges that "Price is writing about the novel, not

the Web, but her point still stands," suggesting that the same framework of incomplete synecdoche that characterizes the anthologized novel might also characterize analysis of the Web.[8] In both instances, the part stands in for the whole, but in doing so, it at the same time necessarily points toward the impossibility of the whole, the ways in which its scope resists containment through representation. If novelistic representation and representation of the Web are analogous in these similar problems of scale, scope, and selection, then the novel that seeks to represent the Web on paper redoubles these problems, taking on a task that is the exponential product of two different representational processes.[9] In this chapter, I pursue these problems through Hari Kunzru's *Transmission* (2004), a novel that centers on Arjun Mehta, a twenty-three-year-old computer programmer born and raised in New Delhi, who is fired from his job at an antivirus corporation in Washington State and responds by unleashing a computer virus with devastating effects worldwide.[10]

We might think of a number of symbolic locations as central to mapping and historicizing such a global network effect: perhaps Bletchley Park, where British mathematician Alan Turing did the World War II code-breaking work that would lead to the development of the computer, or the California garage where Apple cofounders Steve Jobs and Steve Wozniak pioneered personal computing and the graphic user interface in the late 1970s. However, rather than these singular sites of innovation and development, I suggest instead that perhaps Porthcurno, England, is an exemplary capital of the network history that undergirds and surrounds *Transmission*, a key node in a larger global network of information, labor, and capital. I acknowledge that this claim is tendentious and perhaps tangential (in both the rhetorical and spatial senses of the term): Kunzru never uses Porthcurno as a setting or even mentions it in passing, and I will not return to it in depth after this introductory framing. Yet this is precisely the point. Porthcurno is a capital en passant, so to speak, a crucial node in the decentralized geography and temporality of the World Wide Web. Beginning with the Falmouth, Gibraltar and Malta Telegraph Company's Indo-European cable in 1870, it has served as a landing point for numerous international and eventually intercontinental telecommunications cables. Six fiber-optic cables currently come ashore at Porthcurno, including RIOJA-1 and RIOJA-2, which connected the United Kingdom, Belgium, and Spain until 2006; Gemini, which connects the United Kingdom and the United States; TAT-12/13, the twelfth and thirteenth transatlantic telephone cables; and the Atlantic and Euro-Asian segments of FLAG, the Fibre-optic Link Around the Globe.

Nicole Starosielski sees the infrastructural contours of undersea cables as crucial markers of digital materiality:

> Locating the technologies that carry [digital signals] and documenting their pathways contributes to a politics of infrastructural visibility—the effort to reveal the hidden systems underlying our network society.... By following the routes of these transmissions we might better understand how cables are intertwined with the industries that use them, the content that is transmitted over them, and the everyday practices media users engage in. Moreover, tracking media flows as they extend underwater draws our attention to the ways that seemingly nebulous digital circulations are always anchored in material coordinates. While infrastructure sites do not determine the direction of the flows they carry, they nonetheless contort and deform the media landscape.[11]

Several of the cables that come ashore at Porthcurno—RIOJA-1, RIOJA-2, and TAT-12/13—are no longer in service. Yet they remain buried in the sea and underground, enduring channels for ephemeral transmissions, infrastructure that speaks volumes about global mediation precisely in no longer conducting actual information. If, as Starosielski suggests, attending to often-invisible features of digital infrastructure helps to reveal the geopolitics of the digital economy—a profoundly material, buried counternarrative to the vapor rhetoric of the cloud—then approaching *Transmission* with the history and materiality of this infrastructure as a critical framework allows us to see how Kunzru gestures at it through form.

FLAG, one of the cables that reaches ground at Porthcurno, plays a central role in an earlier narrative of digital materiality and history, namely Neal Stephenson's "Mother Earth Mother Board," a lengthy travelogue published in *Wired* magazine in 1996. Stephenson describes "Mother Earth Mother Board" as a narrative of "hacker tourism," in which he visits various landing points for FLAG, which was still under construction at the time of publication, interweaving his reportage and reflection with a history of the construction of the world's earliest transatlantic cable, begun in 1854 and first used in 1858.[12] Early in the essay, in a section titled "FLAG facts," Stephenson offers up an extensive catalog of the cable's route and landing points. I quote this catalog in its paragraph-long entirety to convey both its content and its formal, rhetorical effect—the way in which it captures the global sweep of FLAG as simultaneously arbitrary and seemingly incalculable in scope:

> The FLAG system, that mother of all wires, starts at Porthcurno, England, and proceeds to Estepona, Spain; through the Strait of Gibraltar to Palermo, Sicily; across the Mediterranean to Alexandria and Port Said, Egypt; overland from those two cities to Suez, Egypt; down the Gulf of Suez and the Red Sea, with a potential branching unit to Jedda, Saudi Arabia; around the Arabian Peninsula to Dubai, site of the FLAG Network Operations Center; across the Indian Ocean to Bombay; around the tip of India and across the Bay of Bengal and the Andaman Sea to Ban Pak Bara, Thailand, with a branch down to Penang, Malaysia; overland across Thailand to Songkhla; up through the South China Sea to Lan Tao Island in Hong Kong; up the coast of China to a branch in the East China Sea where one fork goes to Shanghai and the other to Kojedo Island in Korea, and finally to two separate landings in Japan—Ninomiya and Miura, which are owned by rival carriers.[13]

Although some of these locations have larger global significance, in many cases they are relatively anonymous, undistinguished, selected by cable-laying corporations largely for topographical and geographical reasons rather than for cultural, economic, or political ones. They are capitals of nothing more and nothing less than the global map of information delivery, indiscriminate nodes in an irregular network. Stephenson's catalogic prose is notable here as a strategy for reckoning on one hand with the scope, dispersal, and asymmetry of the route he traces, and on the other with the uncanny way in which global telecommunications links these sites invisibly.

I turn to the network poetics of the catalog as a formal device in greater depth below in my discussion of Kunzru's novel; here it is important simply to note that such an approach highlights both Porthcurno and FLAG itself as effectively arbitrary reference points for a literary history of the digital network, which is precisely why I have chosen them as framing signifiers of its enduring ephemerality. The crucial quality at stake here is not the specific geography of these or any physical elements of the network, but rather their physicality itself. In their obsolescence, disuse, and submerged invisibility, they serve as points of resonance for the paper materiality of print literature. As Gitelman says of electronic documents, these infrastructural sites and the cables that stretch between them do not resist history, but rather "compel attention to themselves as differently—often dubiously—historical, where history always happens at the levels of—at least—data, metadata, program, and platform," a list to which we might, in this context, add the level of network.[14] Attending to the dubious, different historicity of this infrastructure, condensing the vaporous rhetoric of the cloud down into the oceanic depths of global connection and transmission, allows for a thick media poetics of the digital within the literary. If we see the buried infrastructure of the present, we see at the same time the persistence of the gaps in communication that both disrupt and define digital transmission: bits, impulses, and characters that are not vaporized in the cloud but rather always already buried in (and emerging from) the spaces and times of the sea and the page.

What does it mean, then, to render the poetics of the network—dispersion, disappearance, invisibility—through the format of the literary page? In a number of passages in the novel, Kunzru represents the circulation of this virus in ways that place pressure on the affordances of the page as a substrate and on the literary novel as a format. In doing so, I argue, he imagines an approach to narrative and literary form that takes its inspiration from the operations of the virus. The novel's central concern is not aesthetic material in the sense of *what* is transmitted, but rather the titular process of transmission itself at all levels of scale, and the ways in which it at once both resists representation and shapes any potential representations in its image. By using the virus as both a plot device and a formal model for the novel's media poetics, Kunzru introduces the possibility of an otherwise invisible glimpse of the system of global telecommunications at the extreme, of that system actively working against its own constitutive conditions and its own outer limits. In order to represent this destructive circulation, Kunzru imagines the destructive nature of the virus *as* representative—not as the entity that destroys or dismantles the network, but rather as the entity that makes the network visible, bringing into view structures and working principles that would otherwise be invisible amid the noise of data.

Indeed, the work of the virus in *Transmission* illustrates Jussi Parikka's vision of the virus as a defining figure of late technocapital rather than an aberration: its seeming dysfunction is what both produces and defines the limits of the network with regard to both geographical space and historical time. For Parikka, the virus is an apocalyptic agent, not in the destructive sense of the term but rather in its original etymological sense of revelation: "Machines reveal their logic as they break down, and this state of accidentality bears in itself important epistemological and ontological repercussions. . . . Apocalypses reveal new temporalities."[15] Thus the disruptions of linearity and causality by the seeming accidents of viral contagion serve as the point of departure for a history of digital culture defined not only through "trac[ing] 'what happened'" but ultimately extending toward "a minoritarian archive, or a memory, of digital culture."[16] In *Transmission*, such an archive is minoritarian in geoeconomic and geopolitical terms, with the novel encapsulating Arjun's migratory trajectory from India to the United States and beyond in search of labor within a global neoliberal technology industry and his eventual status as a fugitive and assumed enemy of the state. Yet it is also deeply minoritarian at a material level, a history that, like the digital materiality it remembers, is not always there, defined by and composed of what is invisible, lost, deleted. Thus the formal techniques that Kunzru uses to describe the virus over the course of *Transmission* press against the limits of the novel in ways that reveal the material discontinuities inherent in representing the structure and circulation of the Web in textual form—the ways in which the architecture of the page changes shape in attempting to capture mediality, what it records and what it loses, as it sketches the shape and history of the digital.

Lyric, Novel, Network: Discontinuity and Digital Writing

Before plunging into the empty, lost, submerged gaps of the network, we first need to look more closely at the information that circulates across the surface world of *Transmission*. The prologue to *Transmission* ends with a moment of divergence from conventional narrative prose that performs the discontinuity of digital global culture at its widest scope, establishing an initial framework for the novel's critical consideration of digital information. I quote this passage, somewhere between prose and lyric poetry, in its entirety below in order to consider fully the ways in which it raises questions of global connection and discontinuity through form and structure rather than content:

> Morning through venetian blinds.
> A cinema crowd watches a tear roll down a giant face.
> The beep of an alarm. Groans and slow disengagement of limbs.
> She shuts down her machine and
> They sit together in a taxi
> A curvature. A stoop.
> She swivels her chair toward the window and
> Someone in the stalls makes loud kissing noises
> poor posture
> between the two of them a five-inch gap
> she takes another bite of her sandwich.
> laughter
> the posture of a young man standing outside a New Delhi
> office tower.
> An arbitrary leap into the system.
> Round-shouldered, he stands for a moment and pokes a finger
> inside the collar of his new polycotton shirt. It is too tight.[17]

Kunzru's use of this formal feature in the novel is telling, considering the place of poetry in the history of computer viruses. As Parikka notes, the Elk Cloner virus, which was created and circulated by Richard Skrenta in 1981–82 and is the earliest known example of a computer virus circulating publicly on personal computers, was designed as a "harmless prank" involving poetry.[18] Spread by floppy disk, Elk Cloner was attached to a computer game; after a computer infected with the virus was booted for the fiftieth time, it displayed a short poem announcing itself. Skrenta's use of poetry draws a striking, foundational line of affiliation between literary poetics and digital function, marking viruses as a profoundly textual and literary network intervention in both content and form.

Transmission's prose poem operates similarly: here, as at several other crucial moments in the novel (a number of which I discuss over the course of this chapter), Kunzru juxtaposes a formal tracing of the circulatory patterns of connection and disconnection against the aesthetic content of literary text as two approaches to thinking the structures of global digital culture. For example, the lines "A curvature. A stoop. . . . poor posture . . . the posture of a young man standing outside a New Delhi office tower. . . . Round-shouldered, he stands for a moment and pokes a finger inside the collar of his new polycotton shirt. It is too tight" form a thread describing the novel's protagonist Arjun as he prepares to enter the office tower in question for a job interview that will set in motion the events of the novel. Similarly, the lines "A cinema crowd watches a tear roll down a giant face. . . . Someone in the stalls makes loud kissing noises . . . laughter" describe a scene in a movie theater showing a film starring the Bollywood actress Leela Zahir, whose image is attached to the virus Arjun circulates and who has a plotline of her own in the novel, while "Morning through venetian blinds. The beep of an alarm. Groans and slow disengagement of limbs. / She shuts down her machine and / They sit together in a taxi . . . She swivels her chair toward the window and . . . between the two of them a five-inch gap" provides a typical morning in the troubled relationship of the central characters of the novel's third plotline, the London-based global branding executive Guy Swift and the Swiss film-industry publicist Gabrielle Caro.

Each of these strings of lines provides a characteristic thumbnail representation of the characters—Arjun as the stereotypically awkward techie, Leela as the larger-than-life icon, Guy and Gabrielle as the global power couple in a troubled relationship. Yet the contents of these lines themselves are effectively arbitrary: none of the moments these lines depict has any direct connection in and of itself with the events of the novel, and Kunzru makes no direct references to the poem or the moments it narrates over the course of the novel. Instead, these flashbulb moments provide Kunzru with arbitrary representational material for tracing the overarching structures and patterns (rather than scenes) of global connectivity. Indeed, the poem's content is banal in a manner that becomes virtually ineffectual and blank in and of itself, serving instead as the context through which Kunzru makes the workings of global technocapital alternately visible and invisible. The structure of this prose poem represents the global sweep of digital culture as impossibly closely connected across space and time, each character's plotline literally woven into those of the other characters. Yet this promise is disingenuous as well—the poem compels the reader to make sense of its connections (and to read the novel that follows it in order to do so), while at the same time deferring and even altogether blocking those connections. Indeed, the characters in *Transmission* are connected not by common traits such as shared political interest or mutual longing for human contact in the chaos of the global world system, but rather by the figure of the computer virus that is at the heart of the novel. In addition, many of the poem's lines—for example, "laughter," "she takes another bite of her sandwich," or the almost anticlimactically self-referential "An arbitrary leap into the system"—are vague enough to make it difficult to attribute them to any scene or character with much certainty. This lack of coherence is not a solely writerly effect per se, but rather a function of Kunzru's attempting to represent global networking as subject matter, appropriating the structures and operations of networking as the poem's own in order to stage a critical rethinking of those structures and operations: while the poem is a "network poem," so to speak, it assumes this status not because of the unexpected, indirect, complex connections it reveals but rather precisely because of the opposite effect, namely the discontinuities and blank, opaque relations it reveals. Kunzru asks us to read for gaps in this global macronarrative, for empty spaces that span the distances between seemingly connected agents and events in the global network.

This approach speaks to a self-conscious concern with structure on Kunzru's part—the structure of the novel, of the network, and of the novel in the age of the network. In a keynote address at The Literary Consultancy's 2012 conference "Writing in a Digital Age," he argues for the unique capability of literary fiction to understand networks by concretizing the abstract, fixing and naming the evanescent and the fleeting.[19] Kunzru claims that while this work of mapping has a long literary history (parts of which I trace below), it has never been more relevant or important than in the twenty-first-century moment of network distribution. In *Transmission*, he engages network structure as a material, technological question within digital culture prior to any particular teleology or instance of coherence, and indeed precisely in opposition to them. As the opening prose poem suggests, the novel presents a collection of overlapping, complementary, and contestatory systems of informational flow, which are themselves connected, outlined, and made visible by the operations of the computer virus. As literary form makes visible technological form, and with it both technological function and dysfunction, it also opens up fragments of the nonhuman time of the Web, using text on the page to gesture toward the spaces of the Web where the time and history of digital circulation crystallize in incomplete, lost communications.

From Digital Bodies to Viral Bodies: The Global Traffic in Information

Before Kunzru fully turns toward the scope of the network, the main text of *Transmission* begins on a more human scale with Arjun's narrative. Thus before turning to a discussion of the virus and the history of network absence and ephemerality it traces, in this section I consider how the novel treats digital circulation at the narrative level so as to establish a context against which its formal techniques operate later in the novel. In order to fulfill his dream of coming to America to land a top job, Arjun signs a contract with the Databodies information technology consultancy corporation and finds himself on a plane to California in a matter of days. Before leaving home, Arjun imagines a stereotypical fantasy of America as the land of hard work and opportunity in the global idiom of technologized play: "Silicon Valley . . . so exciting that like Lara Croft you had to rappel down a cliff-face to get in. One up. Player Mehta, proceed."[20] Staged at the level of the virtual—taking place literally inside a video game, as it were—Arjun's fantasy embodies the neoliberal rhetoric of subjectivity within the digital as fluid and mobile, free from the obstructions of nationhood, race, or capitalism. However, the reality of Arjun's life in America is far less transparently negotiable, in both economic and cultural terms. He finds himself without work for long stretches of time, sharing a house with three other nonresident Indian information technology workers and experimenting in what Kunzru describes as American "[l]inguistic glamour. Examples: when he watched TV, it was the 'tube,' when he thought of his parents, he didn't think of them as his parents, but as 'the folks back home.' The others did it too; little experiments with slang, tentative new accents."[21] Through these "experiments"—which he condenses into the list-like one-line paragraph "The folks. The bench. Man, good"—Kunzru marks Arjun and his housemates as out of place within the global market's uneven systems of language.[22] Global telecommunications brings them into the linguistic, cultural, and economic sphere of the United States, but it is also the very force that makes them outsiders within that sphere.

Kunzru also embeds digital communication more directly within the flow of *Transmission*'s text, illustrating the integral ways in which Arjun's narrative is itself an instance of global information circulation as well as a circumstantial product of it. The language of an e-mail Arjun sends to his friend Amir back in India exemplifies this synthesis in the way that it articulates the complex linguistic, cultural, and technological dimensions of his condition in America:

> From: arjunm@netulator.com
> To: lovegod2000@singhshack.com
> Subject: RE: small pants?
>
> hello aamir thank you for your message how are you yes i am all american now even eating beef pork products that is between you and me someone just gave bacon cheeseburger this is how it starts things ok here yes lots of girls wear short pants yes it is nice no have not spoken to many yet or seen p anderson or bv slayer busy got to go—
> arjunm[23]

Lacking the demarcations of capitalization or punctuation like an exaggerated version of text-message grammar avant la lettre, Arjun's e-mail echoes the streaming, boundless abstraction of digital code, almost as if stripped down to the bare informational minimum in order to convey its message with maximum efficiency, occupying as little bandwidth as possible within the undersea cables connecting California to New Delhi. In this context, digital communication's promise of seemingly liberating efficiency and speed becomes an imperative at the level of language: Arjun must "talk fast" in his e-mail precisely because the information he sends moves so quickly itself. Even the content of the message takes shape in the image of the binary ones and zeros of code, disingenuously excising the ambiguities of cross-cultural experience: yes, he is already all-American; yes, lots of girls wear short pants in America; no, he has not spoken to many of them; no, he has not seen Pamela Anderson or Buffy the Vampire Slayer. Yet the simplicity of Arjun's responses to his friend's questions paradoxically produces a complex, irreducibly polyvalent state of semantic overload, as the clauses and phrases of the message exceed their bounds and mix with one another: does Arjun mean to say that he is "all-American now—even eating beef, pork products, that is" or that he is "eating beef, pork products. That is between you and me [i.e., him and Amir]?" Or is it between him and his friend Amir that "someone just gave bacon cheeseburger?" The potential meanings within Arjun's text overlap and circulate indiscriminately between disclosure and secrecy, refusing to offer a transparent communication. The ambiguity around "between" is particularly pertinent—the entity that is most in-between, after all, is Arjun himself, caught within and across the network in both body and data.

As these multiple contradictory messages paratactically resonate within and against one another, Kunzru suggests that binary code and digital communication cannot accommodate the complexities of lived cultural experience, and also that they structurally produce their own specific complexities and moments of dissonance independent of the content they contain. Form, format, and content intertwine and bend back on one another here: the informational dissonance of e-mail as a globally circulating, instantaneous mode of electronic communication operates not just as a rhetorical means for transmitting the expression of the cultural disjuncture Arjun is experiencing but also as a key constitutive element of that disjuncture in and of itself. Indeed, the very codes that have structured Arjun's movement to America subsequently corrupt his channel of communication back home, producing a dissonance that affects him as well as the reader. Just as Arjun exists within America but can neither read nor write its cultural material with any clarity (and indeed can only write its lack of clarity), Kunzru presents the reader with the material of Arjun's e-mail, yet the way in which its form speaks to both its cultural location and its underlying technological structure makes it impossible to parse as a stable communication. We can read it only for its irreducible, indexical gloss on the instabilities of global digital circulation.

The computer virus that Arjun produces and disseminates further underscores these instabilities. As the two key agents within the novel's narrative, Arjun and the Leela virus move through similar circuits (figurative and literal ones, respectively) of global technocapital, yet they do so on radically different scales and with radically different stakes. Like the biological forces from which they take their name, computer viruses pass from site to site, carrier to carrier, in a manner that is rapidly and rampantly expansive yet at the same time effectively devoid of any agency or intentionality. Although viruses lack consciousness or will in the humanist sense, their underlying project is to exploit the structures of global connectivity in order to be distributed as widely as possible, in as many places at once as possible. By contrast, Arjun circulates through the network of global technocapital precisely because he does not control his place within the information economy, regardless of his will. Effectively indentured to Databodies, Arjun moves from India to California to Maine and back to California again in pursuit of short-term contract work, pursuing a closed path of circulation in which he relies on the instabilities of the information economy for his subsistence rather than decisively intervening within or manipulating that economy. By contrast, the virus he creates is capable of reproducing and circulating itself within the global network in a way that he never can. This dichotomy is a new version of an old problem, an emergent posthuman subject circumscribed within and wholly dwarfed by a fully posthuman network.[24] Yet Kunzru's use of the virus is geared toward a more focused and strategic task than mapping global posthuman subjectivity. In centering his novel on the virus, he brackets these broader issues in order to turn to an extreme case of how digital information circulates through the global reaches of the Internet.

In an inevitable market downturn in the second act of the novel, Arjun is laid off from his position at Virugenix and consequently faces having to return home to his life in India. His response to this turn of fortune is to unleash the Leela virus. While this action ultimately has destructive results, it is not a vengeful hacker intervention or a deliberate disruption of the larger global network for its own sake. On the contrary, Arjun's reason for unleashing the virus is almost tautologically naïve and self-contained: he figures that if there is a virus that only he can combat, he will be able to prove his worth to his employer, regain his job, and remain in America. In this sense, his motive further underscores his status as an ephemeral body in the IT industry, vastly inferior to the virus's capabilities of movement and self-preservation through reproduction. Circulating widely, the virus also has an aesthetic and cultural dimension in its attachment to the image of Leela Zahir. The Western characters in the novel are at first almost uniformly ignorant of the figure taking over and crippling their computers, a cultural blind spot that becomes something of a running joke. As such, the attachment of Leela's image to the virus functions as an indexical mark of the differences in global scope and visibility between Western, Anglo-American popular media and the massive, yet comparatively far less visible and lucrative, world of Bollywood. In an extreme case of the old maxim that any publicity is good publicity, Leela-as-virus circulates much wider than Leela-as-film-star could have ever previously hoped to, exponentially increasing the global profile of the previously regional actress. Moreover, the appropriative gesture that Arjun performs in attaching a computer virus to a video loop of Leela might be said to thematize a number of key issues about global digital culture: it functions as a highly abstracted form of fan art, with Arjun as a kind of protostan for the actress, and it catalyzes a global mystique around her image that presciently anticipates the widespread popularity of YouTube and viral video shortly after the publication of the novel.

Yet Kunzru seems more concerned with the structural and operational question posed by the technological materiality of the virus and the networked relays of connection and circulation that it illuminates than with these cultural issues as such. Indeed, the visibility of Leela is itself a dramatically unresolved question within the novel. While the human Leela gains increased cultural visibility as a result of the virus, the Leela-image attached to the virus appears tantalizingly little within the text. When it does appear, it does so in a fashion that is fairly oblique given the centrality of the virus to the plot of the novel. In the opening lines of the novel, for example, Kunzru refers to Leela "dancing in jerky QuickTime in a pop-up window on your screen. Even at that size you could see she was beautiful, this little pixelated dancer."[25] Later he tellingly writes that Arjun's thrill from watching the "jerky five-second loop" of Leela spread across multiple computers is, tellingly, "indescribable. Leela, widening her eyes and making a flirtatious ticking-off gesture at the viewer, London's West End briefly visible in the background."[26] Still further into the novel, the loop is simply "a little pixelated woman and a snatch of screeching violins," and by the novel's end, it is nothing more than "a tinny blast of Indian music and a depressingly familiar little dancing figure."[27] Kunzru makes a deliberate rhetorical move in limiting both the depth and the frequency of these descriptions over the course of the novel—while the circulatory reach of the Leela-image is global, the image itself is effectively illegible, for both the novel's characters and its readers. Kunzru frequently turns to the language of technological limitation in these descriptions, a gesture visible in the repeated references to pixelation and the "jerky" quality of the footage, the "tinny" sound of music on computer speakers, and perhaps most dramatically the notion of the image itself as "indescribable" in its technologically replicated nature. As the effects of the virus begin to spread, this limitation manifests across other technologies as well. Numerous phone conversations in the novel are plagued by noise and static, such as one Guy places from Dubai to Gabriella in Scotland, in which the sound of her voice seems to him "mixed in with . . . some artifact of the telephone system, a strange electronic rushing noise. It sounded like splintering information, communication space," the dissonance of data being corrupted and decaying as it travels unknown routings across the intercontinental network.[28]

In their accumulation, these markers of limitation collectively suggest that the seductive image of a young dancing woman becomes a stand-in for something far less comprehensible to the human eye. Indeed, Kunzru draws the reader's attention to the familiar site of the image as a point of aesthetically produced affective and semiotic exchange, the lingua franca of global media culture, only to reroute that attention below the surface of the image, toward the often-unseen machinery of digital culture: its overwhelming streams of code, its opaque networks, nodes, and pipelines sponsoring the circulation of information. As Kunzru himself states it at the outset of the novel, the looping video clip of "the girl with the red shoes, cursed to dance on until her feet bled or the screen froze" is ultimately "a surface effect. The real action [is] taking place in the guts of the code . . . an invisible contagion of ones and zeroes. . . . [H]er clinging sari divert[s] attention from the machinery at work under her skin."[29] These minimal descriptions of the Leela-image over the course of the text deliver on this initial promise of invisibility, performing it within the text in a manner that mimics the actual effects of the virus: at these moments, Kunzru offers a provocative glimpse of this enigmatic figure, only to "crash" this textual display, returning to the main narrative. Thus the appearance of Leela Zahir as attached to the virus rapidly and repeatedly gives way to the enactment of the virus's dysfunction and informational loss for both the novel's readers and its characters. The actual virus, pervasive and promiscuous at the level of narrative, is virtually nowhere at the level of the text, a paradoxical kind of ubiquitous invisibility within the novel. What endures, if anything, in this slippage from representation to function is the further paradox of the repeated losses and absences of information that are gestured toward by the virus's flickering appearance; these disappearances themselves gesture in turn toward the otherwise invisible materiality of the digital network.

"Gaps That Have Never Been Filled": Network Discontinuity, Catalog Aesthetics, and the Blank Form of the Digital

By deliberately employing omission as a rhetorical and formal strategy, Kunzru shifts the focus of the novel from the cultural question of how Bollywood's cinematic aesthetics circulates as a metonym for Indian experience within a globalized world to the material, infrastructural question of how raw digital information circulates, appearing and disappearing across the global telecommunications network. Kunzru's gesture brings to the fore a complex process of semantic absenting, through which meaning and information are consistently and abruptly secreted away. This absenting produces an extreme instance of Chun's concept of the undeadness and enduring ephemerality of information, reflecting in turn on the stakes of the print novel as a form and a format: how can it tell the story of an entity that is constantly disappearing, much less gloss the larger media history that surrounds that entity?

This representational aporia stands in stark contrast to the coherence and closure of *Transmission*'s narrative. Kunzru uses this narrative closure, which is all the more notable for its hyperbolic complexity, as a counterpoint against which to stage his representations of the virus's circulation and its impact on global connectivity and communication. Up to this point in my discussion I have focused predominantly on the plotline involving Arjun rather than on those involving the real-life Leela or Guy and Gabrielle. Thus I offer here a brief encapsulation of the rest of the novel, delivered for the aesthetic effect of narrative density and compression as much as for context: while shooting her latest film in Scotland, Leela faces an onslaught of media attention as a result of the virus and goes into hiding. Meanwhile, Guy travels throughout Europe and the Middle East in a seemingly futile effort to keep his failing branding company afloat, while Gabriella is hired by Leela's managers to spin the virus story. She travels to Scotland, sleeps with Leela's costar, and develops a close personal bond with Leela, who ultimately flees the film location and goes into hiding. Guy's work on a branding proposal for the new EU border patrol fails in a marvelously ironic fashion when, as a result of the "shuffling" action of a variant of the Leela virus that "randomly reassociates database attributes," he is mistaken for an Albanian national illegally seeking asylum in Germany and promptly deported. Arjun, who has been following the media coverage of the virus's spread, is eventually named as a suspect and goes on the run, hoping to escape to Mexico.[30] In an epilogue to the novel, we learn that after helping Leela disappear, Gabriella leaves Guy for a global media magnate, only to die in an apparent suicide. Although Guy eventually finds his way home, he turns his back on the world of transnational capital and becomes a rural recluse. Arjun successfully escapes to Mexico, and the closing lines of the novel suggest that he and Leela are in a romantic relationship, undercover and happily on the lam together.

The novel's epilogue makes clear (as I hope my recapitulation of its larger narrative arc does as well) that its high degree of connection and closure is at least in part hyperbolic, an exaggerated narrative manifestation of the interconnectedness often attributed to the global digital network.[31] For Kunzru, this hyperbole serves both as a critique of the neoliberal rhetoric of the digital and as a self-reflexive commentary on practices of literary authorship and readership in the late twentieth and early twenty-first centuries. His narrative strategy in the epilogue to *Transmission* appropriates the structuring, connective principles of the global network (and of narrative representations of the network) precisely in order to subvert, exaggerate, and deform them. Both the tone and content of this section convey a sort of metapastiche of the postmodern paranoia of earlier authors such as Thomas Pynchon and Don DeLillo, as the circumstances of Arjun's disappearance become the subject of intense, obsessive analysis by groups ranging from the federal authorities to the mass media to a group of conspiracy theorists who come to be known as "Mehtologists." Detailing Arjun's last known movements through a mall near the US-Mexico border, Kunzru writes, "Like the Zapruder footage or the Watergate tapes, the mall's surveillance record of Arjun Mehta's seemingly aimless amble from the Timberland store to Starbucks has been pored over, debated, and scrutinized[.] . . . Attention has focused on the $8.99 yellow-rimmed 'Freebird' plastic sunglasses purchased by Mehta during the so-called coffee walk. Their conspicuousness invites speculation that they were some kind of signal."[32] Through the parodic tones of this excess, Kunzru simultaneously makes visible the impossibility and absurdity of such coherence within a complex global system and implicates readers in a paranoid conspiracy regarding that coherence at the level of literary narrative and interpretation. In tying things up in such an overly airtight manner, he offers a critical response to two seemingly diametrically opposed worldviews, namely the neoliberal rhetoric of connectivity and the paranoid patterns that Pynchon and DeLillo trace as a gesture of political intervention and critique in encyclopedic network novels such as *Gravity's Rainbow* and *Underworld*.[33]

The epilogue of *Transmission* echoes texts such as these in order to upend the assumptions about networking that they convey. For Kunzru, conspiratorial speculation about Arjun's place in the global system, from the consumer detritus that clutters his escape in the passage quoted above to news reports that place him "one day at an antiglobalization demo in Paris and the next coming onto the pitch in a hockey game match in rural Gujarat," constitutes both the zenith and the nadir of the sorts of paranoid frameworks traced by Pynchon and DeLillo.[34] Only the completely naïve and the completely paranoid, he seems to suggest, imagine a necessary pattern, meaning, or message within the operations of digital networks. In order to map the global digital system, it is instead imperative to include absence, disappearance, emptiness, interstice—the blank spaces that appear between and at times even in place of the nodes we are trained to see as multiply and perpetually connected.

In place of the connection imagined by novelists such as Pynchon and DeLillo, Kunzru offers the conditions of Grayday, "the period when there was most noise in the global system" as a result of the Leela virus, a time of "appalling losses, drop-outs, crashes and absences of every kind." In contrast to the conviction of narratives of global closure and connection, "Grayday names a moment of maximal uncertainty, a time of peaking doubt. We have records of events that may not have taken place. Other events took place but left no record. All that can be said with honesty is that afterward there were absences, gaps that have never been filled."[35] Here the digital archive becomes fundamentally unreconcilable, with event and record at odds with one another both materially and historically. The historicity of the Web, its capacity as a self-recording repository of data, collapses on itself, leaving a string of aporias in its place: how to verify a digital record when there is no offline evidence pertaining to it? How can we verify, remember, or even begin to know an event that lacks a record? Gitelman says of the reflexivity of media history, "Our sense of history—of facticity in relation to the past—is inextricable from our experience of inscription, of writing, print, photography, sound recording, cinema, and now (one must wonder) digital media that save text, image, and sound. . . . Inquiring into the history of a medium that helped to construct that inquiring itself is sort of like attempting to stand in the same river twice."[36] This problematic, which I first raised in the introduction, is also particularly, urgently in play in the case of the history of gaps and disappearances that Kunzru imagines here. As Gitelman suggests in the passage I quoted earlier, the history of the Web, dubious and different as it is, spreads across platforms, networks, servers, cables, and clouds. When that history is *only* on the Web itself, and the Web fails, where does that history go? Where (if anywhere) does it exist and persist, other than in the antipersistence of absence, deletion, loss, and forgetting? Here the Web raises the question of history precisely through the disappearance of history, framing an archival media poetics that is inseparable from and co-constitutive with the enduring ephemeral of the digital.

Yet Kunzru's most provocative representation of this paradoxical media poetics of circulation and absence appears not at the level of narrative—in the way in which the uncertainty of Grayday makes visible the self-parodic hyperbole of the novel's concluding plot turns—but rather in the novel's moments of radical formal divergence. In these moments, form sits uneasily alongside narrative on the surface of the page, as Kunzru traces the spread of the Leela virus, juxtaposing linguistic dysfunction against the novel's excessive function at the level of plot. Through a series of catalogic formal techniques that diverge from the narrative trajectory of the rest of the novel, he offers a representation of the movement of information through global digital networks as intensely disconnected and discontinuous; using the architecture of the page to register the digital gaps and "crashes and absences" of Grayday, these gestures resist assimilation into a larger network of meaning beyond discrete data. Kunzru's turns to catalogic form within the novel constitute a complexly and self-consciously hedged consideration of the effectively impossible task of representing digital information as raw material within the space of a printed paper text. Through them, he reflects on both the narrative structure of his own novel and the affordances of the print novel more generally as a media format in dialogue with digital information. These moments constitute a kind of mediatic limit-game of print textuality in the context of digital information, a deliberately futile attempt to catalog the totality of digital material within the affordances of the paper page. Much as the narrative omission of the Leela-image draws attention not only to the absence of that image but also to the irreducibility of absence itself within the operations of digital technology, Kunzru uses these catalogic figures to gesture at the totality of the virus—its underlying code, its processes of deletion, its global circulation and spread—in a manner that also deliberately figures the impossibility of comprehensively representing or recording its spread due to both the global scale and the global ephemerality of digital information.

Indeed, the format of the literary cannot rationally reproduce the full circulation and contagion of the virus, nor can it fully fill in the interstices between the discrete units and data points that collectively constitute these movements. Thus in using the catalog's deceptive air of totality and inclusion in these moments, Kunzru nonetheless refuses to impose a stable continuity or coherence on digital information through narrative. By listing discrete data points—locations, agents, calculations—without articulating any connection between these points, he offers an appropriative representation of the operations of digital information that at the same time consequently acknowledges the impossibility of accurately or fully representing those operations within the format of the print novel. These moments in the text constitute records of digital history written simultaneously in miniature and at the global scale, at once seemingly totalizing and visibly incomplete.

In one description of the virus's movement, Kunzru turns to the encoded language of transmission itself, linguistically tracing the virus through the pipelines of the Internet, "through MAE-West and East, into hubs and rings in Chicago and Atlanta and Dallas and New York, out of others in London and Tokyo, through the vast SEA-ME-WE 3 cable under the Pacific and its siblings on the seabed of the Atlantic."[37] This passage imagines the virus's movement as nonphysical, nonlinear, and multiple, pursuing several pathways in a manner unbound by the constraints of material efficiency. Thus at the level of sequencing and event, it becomes difficult to discern how these multiple pathways—through American "hubs and rings," through London and Tokyo, across the Pacific and the Atlantic—relate to one another. Are they sequential, simultaneous, overlapping? Compressed into densely acronymic language, the history of the virus's spread becomes at once both readable and unparseable; the "politics of infrastructural visibility" Starosielski calls for in relation to the pathways of digital transmissions reveals itself as related to a media poetics characterized by linguistic compaction and encoding. In registering this infrastructure, Kunzru's list-like recording of the virus's movement offers connection without causality or order. Yet for all of this nonlinearity, the relations in the passage are relatively clear in semantic terms. Much of the challenge of parsing the passage takes place instead at the level of technical, infrastructural code: to comprehend the passage fully, to make visible the movement of the virus within the text, it is necessary either to know or to decode the meanings of the acronyms that bookend the passage. For example, in order to know that "SEA-ME-WE" stands for South East Asia–Middle East–Western Europe, we either need to know the code in play or break it (or, of course, look up the acronym on the Web). Yet that answer itself yields no higher knowledge about the geopolitics of information flow in this or any other instance. What criterion could coherently connect the massive span of those three regions other than the cable itself to which Kunzru alludes, and—more importantly—what could make that connection distinctly visible other than the paralyzing movement of a computer virus through that cable? Infrastructural visibility here hinges paradoxically on error, collapse, the apocalyptically revelatory dynamics of technological dysfunction.

In another, more visible formal break, Kunzru also represents the transmission of the Leela virus through an eclectic listing of people who click on the e-mail attachment that triggers the virus:

Kelly Degrassi, insomniac, mother, receptionist at the offices of
the Holy Mount Zion Church in Fort Scott, Kansas, opens and
clicks.

Darren Pinkney (dairy farmer, Ballarat, Australia) clicks.

Altaaf Malik (student, Leela Zahir fan, Hyderabad, India) clicks.[38]

The language in this second passage is relatively transparent at the surface
level, yet its narrative form (or lack thereof) poses a much more explicit
and dramatic challenge to reading than in the previous passage. Recalling
the poem in the novel's prologue in terms of both form and thematics, this
passage imagines a "topological curiosity" of information flow that is so
multiply and chaotically determined as to be effectively random, impossible
to parse in terms of readerly linearity or causality.[39] Kunzru's decontextu-
alized, paratactic listing shifts from the macroscopic, global scale of the
passage discussed above to the microscopic, global scale of individual users,
performing what Chun describes as *tracing the moments of connection—the
ways in which the local unfolds to the global*" and back again.[40] Yet while this
passage shrewdly shuttles between the local and the global, the question
of whether it traces connection, and if so, what connections, and how, is
more complex and less resolved. Kunzru offers no indication of whether
these "characters"—who do not appear in the novel before or after these
passing mentions—exist in a chain following the sequence of the text, with
each one passing the virus to the next, or in some other disjointed and
indirect configuration, with all the characters clicking on the Leela e-mail
simultaneously (or in some other order entirely) rather than sequentially.

Faced with this unexplained list, we must hover between two possible
readings of the passage, opposing extremes that each carry their own set
of implications regarding global technological connectivity and how print
literature represents that connectivity: either these characters exist "in
sequence," forwarding an e-mail with the Leela virus to one another in a
manner that would necessitate some unstated connection over vast global
distance, or—precisely the opposite—they have no connection, direct or
indirect, beyond being common victims of (and participants in) the random movement of information. As with the gaps between nodes within
a network, it is difficult to measure or quantify the gaps between items

in this list. Within the architecture of the page, these gaps are at once both regularized and negligible. Kunzru's succinctness in describing these noncharacters and the regularized formatting of text on the page together foreground the massive differential in scale between the materialities of bound paper and of undersea cabling; these two formats of storage and transmission reverberate in complex commensurability in the white space of the novel. Likewise, on the physical spaces of the map to which these gaps refer, they are arbitrary and irregular in size, and as spaces between points along the pathway of the virus as information, their sizes and relations are indeterminate, a condition foregrounded by the directness with which Kunzru lists them. In presenting this list, he delivers information to be charted and computed, but refuses to take up those processes himself. Here we see the dissonant interdependence of paper and fiber: the disjunctures and differences between this printed list and the global diffusion it disingenuously seems to stand in for are thus partly a function of the inherent material differences between the two storage media at stake and partly a function of Kunzru's willful, deliberate refusal to assimilate and domesticate the digital to the constraints of paper.

In an earlier section of the novel, a set of log information is interspersed within a description of the virus:

> Legitimate programs were doing legitimate things. Until they stopped. Until she took over.
>
> *Release +3 hrs: 17,360 hosts*
> *Release +4 hrs: 85,598 hosts*
> *Release +5 hrs: 254,217. . . .*
>
> So when Arjun appeared at work the next morning, haggard and drawn from a night without sleep, despite the infection raging around the world, not one sample had come into Virugenix for analysis. Leela was in the wild, and for the moment totally invisible.[41]

Like the passage listing the computer users who "click" on the Leela attachment and unwittingly further its transmission, this passage offers the blank disjuncture of information in place of clearly articulated connectivity, posing multiple unanswerable questions as to the spread of the virus: what happens between hours three and four, or four and five? What patterns and logarithms (if any) determine the virus's rates of increase over time? Perhaps most importantly of all, what subsequent data is missing from this abruptly truncated listing—what transpires within the compressed, synecdochical space of the ellipse? What fills the temporal and informational gap between this middle-of-the-night dispersion and Arjun's arrival at work the next morning? By juxtaposing this log against the mundane events of Arjun's workday, Kunzru uses this defamiliarizing technical text to foreground the simultaneously expansive and ephemeral status of the virus, with the seizure of the narrative by data precluding a more easily accessible or intelligible description of the virus's circulation.

This technique exemplifies N. Katherine Hayles's notion of narrative and aesthetic flexibility as predicated on the restricted meaning inherent in code: "Flexibility and the resulting mobilization of narrative ambiguities at a high level depend upon rigidity and precision at a low level. The lower the level, the closer the language comes to the reductive simplicity of ones and zeros, and yet it is precisely the ability to build up from this reductive base that enables high-level literariness to be achieved."[42] As the text tends toward the semantic minimalism of discrete data points, these points become increasingly difficult to read as integrated elements within the narrative with any sense of fixity or closure because of both their impact on the events of the narrative and their status on the space of the page. These data points constitute a cognitive map of *Transmission*'s world that is strikingly nonhuman, pivoting on the strange tension between information's ubiquity and its invisibility. At the same time that he records the virus's spread in direct, precise terms, Kunzru also self-consciously records how that spread escapes the page into blankness and lost history: the more the virus spreads over time as recorded in these data points, the more activity takes place in the gaps between data points, outside of the detection or comprehension of either the novel's readers or the antivirus computers at Virugenix. The passage of clicking characters produces a similar effect: compared to the complex, overlapping relationships that occupy the bulk of the novel, Kunzru's unembellished list of the virus's victims and transmitters registers as fractured and lacking in connectivity in any sense beyond the technological materiality of immediate, momentary transmission of the virus. The flatness of the "clicks" that ends each line of the list hammers home the opacity and the detachment that hold it together, and in this sense it undoes the exaggerated global eclecticism of the list—the Australian dairy farmer, the insomniac working mother, the obligatory Leela Zahir fan. In these moments of formal divergence, then, Kunzru crashes the function of the novel in an even more dramatic fashion than with the minimal, momentary glimpses of the Leela-image—after all, the truncation of the log file has the effect of an interrupted message itself, and the sound of a computerized "click" can denote system failure as well as activation. These passages present us with microscopic records of global technological events, arbitrarily selected points that cannot help but fail to stand in for a larger lost history of expansion, corruption, and dysfunction.

In using form to trace a media poetics of transmission—one defined by incompleteness, absence, disappearance, dysfunction, and above all the impossibility of history within the digital—Kunzru offers an immanent critique of the catalogic impulse as a means of reckoning with the scale of global networking. This shift resonates with a phenomenon that Brad Evans describes as "circulation with gaps," a process marked by "circulation as itself embedded in objects that pop up on us unawares, again and again, in different contexts, and in ways that appear, somehow, to escape the regimes regulating our everyday commerce with objects."[43] For Evans, this "aesthetic delight in the incongruity of multiple iterations" of texts, images, and other "things . . . circulated out of place" derives from "that ephemeral space—that lost time—between the [object's] appearance at point A or point B (as well as from the space left between items X and Y on the list)."[44] In their creation of "gaps that have never been filled" in the historical record of the novel, computer viruses as Kunzru represents them serve as a sort of ne plus ultra case of circulation with gaps, exemplifying this production of ephemeral space and lost time through both their circulatory operation and their technological impact. Viruses are nothing if not unpredictably mobile, pursuing pathways that are—if we take Kunzru at his word in relation to these catalogic passages—so far from the regimes of everyday commerce and circulation as to be virtually arbitrary. Indeed, both the "aesthetic delight" of these passages and the theoretical provocation they provide derive from following out their implications to the farthest horizon of Evans's formulation: What, if anything, exists in the "space left between" the lines, people, and data points in these lists? Can there be any "out of place" in a network so widely distributed as to cover individuals as different as Kelly Degrassi,

Darren Pinkney, and Altaaf Malik? What and where would such an "out of place" be, and how might its inclusion within this mapping shift the overall map of global digital circulation? What takes place during the lost time between each hourly count, and what possibilities are there—if any— for reconstructing such a lost history? In the absence of any suggestion of such a reconstruction, the gaps on the page between items on these lists become blank geopolitical and geotechnological spaces that limn the shape of a minoritarian geography and history of global telecommunications, to which I turn in the following section.

Toward a History of Destruction

Using Evans's model to consider how Kunzru problematizes catalogic form in response to network technology raises a complex set of ideological and ethical questions produced by the virus's central role in the novel. How are we to imagine the ethics of network circulation—as well as the ethics of literary engagement with this issue—when the virus and Kunzru's formal evocation of its ruptures produce aesthetic pleasure of the sort Evans describes? Any readerly identification with Arjun as an antihero, an everyman of global capital mistaken for a rogue cyberterrorist, presents an ethical dilemma at the narrative and thematic level—what we might call, following Craig Dworkin's taxonomy of politics and form, the politics in the text. Yet this dilemma extends beyond this level to the fabric of the text and our experience of reading it—the politics of the text inherent in "what is signified by its form, enacted by its structures, implicit in its philosophy of language."[45] The virus is the generative force of the novel, the operant agent that makes possible the text's narrative structure, its development, and its most distinctive aesthetic effects. Yet is also a profoundly destructive force at the levels of narrative and information: it produces blankness, throwing the narrative into chaos and disconnection and presenting itself to us as readers through the relative obscurity of raw data. The gaps of its circulation are gaps of foreclosure as well as of movement; in taking pleasure in these gaps, we necessarily take pleasure in the devastating, literally deleterious paralysis the virus imposes on the entirety of the Web, the indiscriminate loss of continuity, and, moreover, of accessible information itself, that we both witness and experience on the page.

In this sense, then, Kunzru presents a formal manifestation of the "destructive creation" that Alan Liu considers to be the "new sublime" and the "most extreme verge" of "new media aesthetics." For Liu, destructive creation—or, as he refers to it more frequently, destructive creativity—is "the critical inverse of the mainstream ideology of creative destruction" by which global capital perpetuates and extends itself.[46] He traces the roots of destructive creativity to the autoiconoclasm of the twentieth-century avant-garde, and finds its logical extreme in the aesthetics of the viral, which he describes as "a destructivity that attacks knowledge work through technologies and techniques internal to such work. The genius of contemporary viral aesthetics is to introject destructivity within informationalism."[47] Kunzru's narrative of a virus that cripples the circulatory capacity of the Web by exploiting that same capacity shares the operational design of Liu's model, yet resists its recourse to broader ideological intentionality. The exemplars of destructive creativity that Liu discusses are digital artists and activists passionately committed to a radical left politics, whereas Arjun is simply a cubicle drone in crisis, a worker trying to retain his livelihood within the global digital economy rather than subvert it. Of course, at one level, this position makes him the purest incarnation of the engaged knowledge work that Liu calls for in his critical study. Stripped of political abstraction or generalization, Arjun's actions employ destructive creativity in a manner that is focused and conscious in order to enact localized, functional change. Yet at the same time, he exhibits less direct agency than almost anyone or anything else in the novel, including and especially the Leela virus itself. Destruction is a practical means for him as opposed to an explicitly aesthetic or political end; ironically, it is an attempt to remain productive within the system of global digital capital rather than deliberately to critique or destroy that system as such.

What, then, is creative about the destruction of the Leela virus in and of itself? Here the difference between Kunzru's approach and Evans's model becomes an urgently relevant criterion, as the paradoxical status of the virus within the novel makes it necessary to consider it in terms of both pleasure and destruction. If, as Evans's model would seem to suggest, the act of tracing the destruction of the virus through the unreadable gaps of its circulation produces a kind of pleasure, and if that destruction has no overarchingly intentional human agent within the bounds of the text, what larger end result emerges from the impact of the virus? Liu, in his discussion of destructive creativity, makes a strong case for the critical power that art attains by taking on a viral form—in what ways might a virus conversely be artistic or communicative? Similarly, Evans suggests that across different instances and patterns of circulation, "content is equivalent to iteration"— what happens when content is iteration that destroys content?[48] Viewed through the lens of these paradoxes and reversals, Kunzru's novel shares common ground with Warhol's *a* in its predication on and attention to this "extreme verge" of a given media system. Each author simultaneously throws the affordances of the systems they consider—the network and the typing pool, respectively—and the internally destructive capacities of those systems into relief through formal play. Much as the disruptions and errors of *a* served to set the typing pool and the material mechanics of the typewriter into relief, tracing a critical outline of its vectors of power and information, Kunzru's attempts to trace the composition and destructive movement of the Leela virus similarly gesture at the shape of the global digital network through which the virus circulates, revealing as much about this network through the inevitable failure to represent it fully as through the gesture itself.

Despite outlining these tensions between creation and destruction, between complicity with Arjun's actions and critique of them, Kunzru's formal work in *Transmission* ultimately functions not in terms of critique as such but rather in terms of juxtaposition and delimitation along spatial, temporal, material, and mediatic axes. Rather than positioning print literature in a particular ideological relation to the digital, he uses form to trace a media poetics rooted in the material incompatibilities between these different media formats. On one hand, *Transmission*'s instances of catalogic incompleteness lay bare the capacities and limitations of paper as a substrate and the novel as a format against the context of a massive digital event and its subsequent record. Yet conversely, as the inability of paper to record the totality of such an event echoes back on the comparable inability of the digital to provide its own failsafe record, the limitations of the digital are intimately close at hand in these moments as well. As Chun suggests, neither format solves the problems of the other; on the contrary, caught in complex interdependency, each one sheds light on the other's boundaries and limitations.

Thus the novel's formal representation of the destructivity of the virus is most creative in what it reveals about the relations between paper and digital media—the differing temporalities and materialities of inscription, storage, dispersion, and deletion that these technologies make possible and visible (and at times invisible) when facing one another. Within the space of the novel as an object, Kunzru captures the losses of Grayday in the narrative development of *Transmission*'s main text, but also in the blank gaps within the poetic, catalogic, and logarithmic formal breaks that populate and interrupt its pages. The undersea cables that carry the Leela virus flicker into view momentarily in these gaps, invoked through blankness within the infrastructural landscape of the novel's world. My use of the term "flicker" here draws on Hayles's concept of the "*flickering signifiers*, characterized by their tendency toward unexpected metamorphoses, attenuations, and dispersions," that characterize the materiality of digital information.[49] While Hayles draws her formulation from the microscopic scale of binary code, perhaps the macroscopic scale of the network flickers as well. Indeed, Kunzru thrusts these cables into the history of the digital, and thrusts that history itself into view on the page, precisely as that history seems to disappear into thin air and blank, white space. These cables, like the information they transmit, are always somewhere but almost never accessible. Hidden in the plain sight of the novel's gaps and breaks, they constitute a phantom map of the digital global system, an alternate geography demanding a history that is as literal and physical as it is theoretical and critical.

Yet as in the case of the combustible film stock I discussed in chapter 3, the very possibility and necessity of such a history hinges on an inevitable, uneven obsolescence. Undersea cables have a working life of several decades, yet they are outstripped by faster, newer cables far before this time ends. Still functional yet blank, devoid of transmissions, they become yet another phantom layer, another undead, palimpsestic accretion in the unseen digital topography of the global system. Perhaps Kunzru captures this evanescent future in the gaps of *Transmission* as much as any ephemeral past: while the cables will remain, the creative destruction that drives capitalism's march forward in time virtually demands that their circulations end, supplanted by the next constellation of immanent, contingent routings. The infrastructure so central to the current moment of the digital is always already slipping from the new and the now into the old and the obsolete. In raising this question of history—media history, digital history, network history—through the breakdown of the Web on paper, the empty spaces of *Transmission* point both backward and forward in time. The blank whiteness of the page opens out onto a sunken past of lost data and forgotten infrastructure, but also toward the immanent, impending future that defines and delimits every medium and every technological object, whether analog or digital, paper or fiber: the revelatory moment when the device ceases to hold information, when the network ceases to transmit, when the somewhere—the elsewhere—of the digital ceases to be anywhere at all.

Coda: Borderless Printing and Paper Monuments

If we consider paper's relation to the global digital network in its fullest scope, perhaps we need to think of it as having not two sides, but six—as fully occupying width, height, and an infinitesimal yet crucial depth. As being three-dimensional in its objecthood, its accumulation, its historicity.

Aleksandra Domanović's *Grobari* (2009) stands a little over a foot tall, the height of 3,500 sheets of paper. An early example of the artist's "paper stacks," or "printable monuments," it derives from a single 180-megabyte PDF file.[50] To generate the work, Domanović created a ten-thousand-page PDF, each page displaying markings around its edges; when a user—whether a viewer, a gallerist, a collector, or Domanović herself—prints out the document in its entirety using the "borderless printing" setting on their printer and stacks it in the order of printing, these edge markings combine to constitute images on each side of the fully formed stack. *Grobari*, like a number of Domanović's early monuments, displays images of smoke from fires set by members of the Grobari, extremist nationalist fans of the Serbian football club FK Partizan.

The individual pages of *Grobari* range from being nearly blank on the recto and verso to being (in the case of pages higher in the stack) entirely so. Each of these categories destabilizes the page as an inscriptive surface in its own way. The pages that have markings push those markings to the outer margins so as to be positioned to accumulate on the sides; here the architecture of the page transforms from that of a two-dimensional, horizontal inscriptive surface to that of a three-dimensional, vertical one. The unmarked pages, by contrast, add height and scale to the work, but not—at least in any visible sense—the inscriptive mark of the image. Taken as a material whole, then, the work straddles the fulcrum between substrate and sculpture, mobilizing paper in differing ways at different microthin slices of the stack. Viewing the printed work in the space of the gallery, we cannot contemplate the infinitesimal three-dimensionality of a single sheet and the monumental three-dimensionality of the stack as a whole separately from one another.[51]

Likewise, we cannot contemplate either of these extremes without also thinking of the oblique materiality of the PDF that produces them both. Lisa Gitelman crystallizes the PDF's representational paradox as a format straddling digital and print media: PDFs are, Gitelman writes, "documents that may be said to conjure themselves . . . documents [that] are experienced as pictures of themselves . . . an image and/of a text, a text that is somehow also an image of itself."[52] *Grobari* unfolds this complex reverberation between text and image to a third dimension: the work is a document that becomes, through printing, a sculpture of itself—a sculpture and/of an image, an image and/of a sculpture. This play across format, substrate, and dimensionality becomes particularly rich in the context of Domanović's later work with actual three-dimensional printing. If 3D printing transforms a digital object into a physical object, a file into a sculpture, *Grobari* at once both anticipates that transformation and short-circuits it, asking what it might mean to 3D print a sculpture made only of paper, the prevailing—indeed the only—printed material throughout most of the digital age. Seen most expansively, Domanović's stacks suggest that all printing is three-dimensional and sculptural, even and perhaps especially the materially mundane, infinitesimally thin output of paper-based laser, inkjet, and dot matrix printers. These works materialize the digital through the materiality of paper, making clear the complex, dissonant resonances between a file on a hard drive or in the cloud and the physical output of that file.

All of these provocations point toward the project's larger intertwined questions of historiography through media and the historiography of media: if Kunzru's lists figure the lost global history of the Web through blank, "unbuilt" space on the two-dimensional architecture of the page, *Grobari* does so through the three-dimensional monumentality of the paper stack. Domanović describes the piece as a memorial to the .yu Internet domain, the country code top-level domain for the Socialist Federal Republic of

Yugoslavia.[53] The .yu domain was established in 1989; while Yugoslavia ceased to exist as a nation in 1992, the domain was still in operation serving Serbia and Montenegro for nearly two decades, slated for termination in 2009 and finally terminated in March 2010. Thus it occupies a strange, uncanny history, its existence as a virtual simulacrum of nationhood long outdating the actual nation in its political, physical incarnation.[54] In memorializing the .yu domain rather than the actual nation of Yugoslavia, Domanović makes clear that at some level, the domain's residuality was itself already a memorial to the disappeared country, an undead claiming of virtual space for a nation with no physical space.

In *Grobari*, then, Domanović uses printed paper to memorialize the evanescent digital and the already vanished national. The project exists across three states (a term I use here in the material sense, but which certainly has geopolitical resonances as well): the digital file, the individuated paper sheets, and the installed sculpture. Across these, stability and statehood are both constantly mobile and fugitive, perpetually out of reach—a condition accentuated by the work's near-blankness and the contingency and ephemerality it invokes in what relatively little inscription it does contain. Indeed, the project's use of the borderless printing setting is a practical strategy to push the work's inscriptive visual content to the margin of each page, producing a visible image on the side of the overall stack. Yet it is also of course a meditation by way of this method on the idea of the border itself as a geopolitical demarcation: always already virtual and unstable, and made all the more so by the globalizing impact of the Internet. The fact that these images accumulate to reveal smoke from fires set by nationalist vandals is itself another cross-media pun—the image of a force that would consume and destroy the work's paper material captured and preserved on that paper material, forming a tight circuit between the enduring and the ephemeral that in turn indexes the material instability of lived politics within the public sphere. Interweaving the visual, the physical, and the ideological, these material metaphors draw our attention to a geopolitical problem that is inextricable from the global digital network.

Grobari uses paper to frame that problem through blankness, but this is not the same as silence or absence. Here blankness has presence, manifesting as both literally and figuratively monumental. Stacked neatly on the gallery floor, yet vulnerable to collapsing from a single touch or a gust of wind, blankness in *Grobari* holds history, has history, is history—a history of digital infrastructure that is itself vulnerable, evanescent, mediated through and superseded by the uncanny time of the digital network. If, as Gitelman suggests, "[i]nquiring into the history of a medium that helped to construct that inquiring itself is sort of like attempting to stand in the same river twice," and if Kunzru's catalogic gaps in *Transmission* trace that history through blankness, Domanović's stack of paper materializes it as blankness—not the moment when the foot of the historian steps into the river, but rather the moment just before the water rushes in to fill the void left behind.[55]

CHAPTER FIVE
Page Shredding
Digital Textuality and Paper Cinema

Paper Theory, Vapor Theory

Chapter 4 asked how paper—whether in the bound codex form of Hari Kunzru's novel or the rectangular sculpture of Aleksandra Domanović's stacks—might figure the materiality, form, and history of the digital through its own form. As in the preceding chapters, this question sought to open up the material excesses and limitations of the media archive as a theoretical concept: of what can and cannot be represented, fixed, and stored from other media formats within the architecture of the printed page; and of what those representations, preservations, disappearances, and obsolescences might have to tell us about the history of media technology from the twentieth century onward. In this final chapter, I approach these issues through a question from the opposite orientation: how does the digital render paper—how does it figure its materiality and trace its history?

This is a deliberately backward question. Figuring the materiality of the digital—or indeed of any of the other new(er) media forms I have considered thus far—on paper is an authorial intervention that hinges on adaptation, innovation, and the historiographic project of unevenly imagining the new within the affordances of the old. Figuring paper within the digital poses crucial questions through its inversion of the model I have employed in the first four chapters of *Archival Fictions*: Why mobilize the new in ways that accommodate and recuperate the old, the (seemingly) obsolescent? What is at stake in using digital inscription as a way of reaching back in time and technology to think through the materiality and historicity of print and paper? Jessica Pressman's work on bookishness is a useful framework here for its theorization of a print literary aesthetic that "appropriates characteristics of digital technologies and Web 2.0 reading practices into the book-bound novel in order to enhance the book's status as an innovative medium." For Pressman, "bookishness present a serious reflection on the book—and the literary book in particular—through experimentation with the media-specific properties of print illuminated by the light of the digital."[1] What might it mean, then, to imagine the digital as richly (if unevenly) bookish—as reflecting on the book and the paper inside it through the media-specific properties of digital technology?

Much as with the case of the greatly exaggerated death of the book I outlined in the introduction to *Archival Fictions*, paper is likewise still everywhere within the moment of the digital. Despite the explosion of sales in e-readers and digital texts around the turn of the 2010s and the utopian rhetoric of the paperless office that has characterized corporate and bureaucratic discourse since at least the mid-1970s (if not since the time of Edison's introduction of the phonograph in 1877), paper still persists within the digital in numerous ways.[2] It circulates as input to be scanned and as substrate to be printed on, but also as metaphor and skeuomorph, in the documents, file folders, and desktops of the contemporary computer's graphical user interface. Yet it is far from stable, whether in comparison to the digital or otherwise. On the contrary, paper is mobile, fragile, vulnerable, and mutable, both in terms of its individual materiality and in terms of its larger historicity; the experimentations that define bookishness for Pressman exemplify this quality. Thus I argue in this chapter that we need a poetics of digital inscription that imagines both the digital and its print antecedents as interdependent and in flux, materially and historically. Such a poetics turns our attention to the ways in which elements of print materiality persist as undead within digital information, not merely as abstraction or as skeuomorph but rather as a kind of mediatic specter, troubling how we understand lines of technological transition, innovation, and obsolescence. What happens, then, when we theorize digital textuality through its relation to paper materiality? To return to Wendy Chun's terms from chapter 4, what happens when paper's own ephemerality and vulnerability become not only the metaphor through which we imagine the enduring ephemeral of the digital but also the deep history through which we understand it? What questions—of literary and artistic practice, of aesthetics, of materiality, of media history—emerge through such an understanding? In order to unfold these questions in the sections that follow, I read the work of the electronic literature collective Young-hae Chang Heavy Industries (YHCHI) through the lens of the early computing practice known as page shredding, an approach that illuminates the mediatic conditions and concerns of both the group's own work and the larger culture of networked storage in which they reside. My reading of YHCHI hinges not only on paper as such but also more specifically on paper's place within the material landscape of early cinema around the turn of the twentieth century: tracing how the digital form of YHCHI's *Dakota* remediates the paper cinematic technologies of the 1890s, I argue for a poetics of new media that takes account of the spectral, undead persistence of paper within digital art.

The Machine, Way Back: Digital History on Shredded Paper

In order to understand how early twenty-first-century digital art remediates late nineteenth-century paper art, we first need to understand how early computer networking remediated paper. Early networking began in the corporate sector: the terminals attached to the mainframe computers used in the 1980s by financial services companies and investment banks, some of the first corporations to adopt networked computing on a large scale, could neither process data on their own nor communicate with other computers. Capable only of displaying static data stored on the mainframe, they were—to use a multiply resonant term—terminal indeed. So much so, in fact, that users often dubbed them "glass Teletypes" or "virtual Teletypes" due to their ability to present information but not transform it. These anachronistic terms conveyed the impression of the machines as already obsolete and retrograde even in the first years of widespread computing, as if perpetuating the static nature of a paper printout within the seemingly dynamic domain of the computer.[3]

The computer terminal had previously solved a material problem haunting the financial services industry. Michael Bloomberg describes the Salomon Brothers office of the 1960s as a space in which

> [p]iles of papers crammed with facts about the companies behind . . .
> securities littered our desks. Each night, a clerk would painstakingly
> go through the day's transactions and, like Bob Cratchit, manually

> update all of our trade history records. This mid-twentieth-century
> information-gathering operation was in the tradition of the Dickensian,
> quill-pen nineteenth century but it was the only way we could get
> the information we needed to conduct our trading business. . . . Near
> the end of the "go-go" market of the 1960s, the paper deluge became
> so difficult to manage that the New York Stock Exchange shortened
> its workweek; for a while, it actually closed on Wednesdays. . . . A
> solution existed, however. From what I had read, computers were
> good at storing information.[4]

While early computer terminals indeed solved this problem in terms of
storage, they did so only to reinstantiate the problem at the level of interaction and inscription. Humans could read the screens of terminals eventually
introduced at Solomon Brothers and elsewhere, but only in the limited way
in which they could read the paper output of the Teletype rather than being
able to write on it or rewrite its contents in any meaningful way. Mainframe
data was not directly, immediately accessible to these terminals, a status
that effectively rendered them one-directional display machines, devoid
of any interactive capacity. As David Leinweber, author of a 1988 article
"Knowledge-Based Systems for Financial Applications," puts it, earlier
"computer-like screens watched by traders were simply that, *like* computers.
Traders' screens resembled computers, but had the soul of cable TV. The
underlying technology was video distribution and switching," "pictures of
data transmitted over video channels" rather than "true digital data feeds."[5]

How, then, to make this data malleable, accessible, and actionable so as
to be able to exploit it in trading calculations and actions? How to give it,
to use Leinweber's terms, a more fully digital soul? Bound to legacy mainframe systems at the dawn of the age of the personal computer and thus
faced with the formidable technical challenge of making terminals speak
and think, corporate computer users opted instead for a workaround that
made these machines at least seem as if they were fully interactive. Rather
than taking on the arduous process of retyping static data stored in the
mainframe into the more easily executable environment of a trading console—a transcriptive practice that, like the faux-corporate work of Warhol's
a, would have raised its own array of fascinating textual and technological
questions—these corporations devised a practice that eventually came to

be known as "screen scraping." Within screen scraping, another computer would effectively read the static display of information on a mainframe terminal and extract and reproduce it within a different, PC-based context for use by analysts and traders, transforming a fixed image of data into a readily manipulable database.

As early as 1988, financial professionals had begun referring to this practice as "page shredding": in an article from that year, Leinweber notes that because "[t]he first digital market feeds emulated video systems, transmitting page images rather than logical record data[, e]laborate page-shredding was required to transform data into machine-usable format."[6] Page shredding provides a richly material metaphor for the manipulation of data at play in early networking, signaling a shift away from conceptualizing that manipulation as a solely screen-based operation and toward acknowledging its antecedents in the disorderly materiality of paper evoked in Bloomberg's memories quoted above. To traders and analysts working at consoles populated with data scraped from fixed-image screens, that data arrived in a mess. This scraped information appeared like thin strips of shredded paper that desperately needed to be read and made sense of, to be pieced together in the interstice between stasis and dynamism, between the then-new surface of the personal screen and the phantom vestige of the Teletype's paper strip echoed in the older mainframe terminal. Indeed, the metaphor locates the precise juncture in the process at which materiality matters most urgently, as information in digital form becomes at once both differentiated from and dependent on information in paper form: in order to arrive at the messy, yet manipulable, state of the console screen, it was necessary to shred the fixed output of the glass Teletype.

With this material history in mind, digital page shredding serves as a metaphor and point of departure for my consideration of the poetics of the digital archive in this chapter. Page shredding hinges on the constant fluctuation in early networked communication between paper and pixel, between the block fixity of the screen and the granular mobility of individual units of text. As such, it offers a powerful historiographic framework for how new and old technologies intertwine with, communicate with, and remediate one another—how the cutting edge of any moment always builds from and is haunted by the seemingly obsolete. In chapter 4, I used Kunzru's *Transmission* as a groundwork for considering how print literature appropriates and approximates the materiality of the Internet as a way of tracing its historicity. In this chapter, I both extend that consideration and rotate its axis, using Google Cache, Flash authoring software, Flash decompilers, and other digital tools alongside a thick history of protocinematic artifacts such as the Mutoscope and the paper print in order to consider how a work of electronic literature invokes the workings of earlier paper-based technologies. In using page shredding as a metaphor and framework, my intent is to engage closely, critically, and deformatively with the materiality of an electronic literary text as a way of considering how it resonates with the materiality of earlier textual forms. Thus I argue here that a rigorously material media poetics of digital textuality—one that shreds its imagined pages in conceptual terms, if not actual physical ones—sheds light not only on that textuality in and of itself but also on its complex interdependence with the always already unstable paper that precedes it. Contextualizing the digital within media history and understanding the digital itself as a means of media-historical investigation thus constitute two intertwined strands of a larger inquiry into the relations among mediality, form, format, and history. Pursuing this inquiry through YHCHI's *Dakota*—exploring a number of media-historical antecedents for *Dakota* and closely reading its digital materiality—I argue for this work as a text that multiply invokes paper materiality and print textuality in order to imagine a complexly historical media poetics.

On the Digital History of Paper, Part I: Materiality and Metaphor

YHCHI is a group composed of two individuals, CEO Young-hae Chang and CIO Marc Voge, who use Flash to produce primarily black-and-white, text-only animations set to music: in much of the group's work, blocks of black, all-capital text in Monaco font vibrate, expand, blink, and scroll in multiple directions across a white background to a soundtrack that includes postwar jazz, bossa nova, and rhythm and blues across various different pieces. These animations have been shown in art exhibitions and in film festivals, and also appear on the group's website, yhchang.com. YHCHI's work, and *Dakota* in particular, provides fertile ground for thinking the material historicity of electronic literature for several reasons. Some of these are simply canonical and institutional: the group is one of relatively few artists from what N. Katherine Hayles has described as a "second generation" of electronic literary practitioners to generate not only an extensive, widely published and exhibited body of work but also a cohesive critical conversation among scholars, particularly those working in literary studies.[7] In addition, their own play with preexisting cultural texts and forms—for example, their simultaneous appropriation of the text of Ezra Pound's first *Canto,* the visual aesthetics of modernist film, and the sounds of hard bop jazz in *Dakota*—shares many strategies and concerns with works I have discussed in preceding chapters.[8] More broadly important, however, are the ways in which the textual multiplicities of YHCHI's work invite us to consider the larger question of text-based literature as a format in relation to the history of digital information and media technology more broadly. This is a question of how alphabetic writing changes shape across the space and time of the web, but also a question of how those transformations body forth the historicity of the digital—a historicity that, I will argue here, loops back recursively to analog print textuality.

As Rebecca Walkowitz notes, most critical studies of YHCHI have focused on situating the group's work in the context of either literary and cinematic modernism or the emergence of electronic literature, a pairing to which she adds a focus on political, cultural, and economic exchange between the Western and Eastern Hemispheres.[9] In order to both add to and depart from these frameworks, this chapter attends to other moments and materialities across technological and cultural history, using those moments to trace a genealogy of YHCHI's work. What emerges from this differently focused reading of that work? What new forms and iterations might come into view through a critical framework focused on the shifting materialities of the page, and what do they suggest about the relations between digital technology as a medium and literary writing as a format, and about media history more broadly through those relations? I turn to a number of these forms and iterations in the fifth section below. First, however, I establish a foundation for that analysis through several media-historical explorations of *Dakota*.

Building on Pressman's thinking, Walkowitz argues, "While it might seem perverse to call Chang and Voge's project 'bookish' since their works are not produced on paper, there is something purposefully old fashioned about their emphasis on the bodies of readers, authors, and texts and their reluctance to engage in a celebration of universal mobility. . . . Chang and Voge register the friction of medium" in invoking both the analog and the digital, the page and the screen.[10] This friction manifests as a provocative metaconsciousness about media. Viewed through the lens of Hayles's medium-specific analysis, YHCHI's digital bookishness takes shape not only as similar to books but also as about books, invoking the historicity and materiality of print in ways that are variously intentional and contextual. As digital objects, these works present a bookishness that is uncanny and uneven, serving as the crux of a media poetics that sheds light on the exceptionalities and irregularities of print materiality. This slant history of print materiality by way of the digital intersects with Walkowitz's thinking on the bookish state of postdigital print publishing. Writing of digital creators such as YHCHI alongside deeply bookish small press print publishers releasing works in the wake of digital media—for example, Visual Editions, "which has designed, in both paper and digital formats, medium-specific, even medium distinctive editions of a single book"—Walkowitz notes that "the born digital and the post-digital may seem like parallel but separate developments, but that's not really the case."[11] Extending and redoubling terms of Walkowitz's thinking here, YHCHI presents a case in which these developments are not only connected but one and the same, part of a complexly recursive historical dynamic; their born-digital art is postdigital avant la lettre (pun fully intended) precisely because of its invocation of predigital print. Born digital, postdigital, predigital: rather than these temporalized terms cancelling one another out to simply show us a representative digital work, they accumulate like sedimentary layers, past and present coexistent, reverberating back and forth across time and technology.

YHCHI's bookishness is uncanny by way of this layered nonlinearity, using the technology of digital animation (quite new at the time of the creation of *Dakota* and other of the group's early works) to register a paper materiality that is paradoxically at the heart of the moving image's indeterminate, incunabular origins. While I focus below on how paper in particular permeates the media poetics of *Dakota*, I understand this permeation as existing in the work alongside the more immediate cinematic precedents it invokes, rather than in opposition to or instead of them; indeed, these different genealogies are all equally present and latent within the work, coexisting in its mediatic imaginary.[12] Yet when we leap over the work's references to mainline cinematic modernism toward the earlier substrate of paper, we find not only a different set of historical reference points but also a fuller and more syncretic window onto *Dakota*'s engagement with media history and media poetics. Writing of the postcinematic aesthetics of digital imaging and animation, Tom Gunning suggests that "a serious consideration of post-cinema should open up a new conception of pre-cinema."[13] As *Dakota* illustrates, the inverse is true as well: thinking seriously about the precinematic origins of YHCHI's postcinematic work allows us to see that work in a new way—one that is determined precisely by how it imagines the artifacts and methodologies of precinema.[14]

At the heart of this exchange between present and past is the force of metaphor, a term I use here both in its common representational sense and in a sense closer to the strictly etymological, connoting the transferring or bringing across time I discuss above. Writing with Pressman and Jeremy Douglass about William Poundstone's *Project for Tachistoscope {Bottomless Pit}*, another foundational work of Flash art, Mark C. Marino notes that "programming in Flash is not just about code, data, and technology. It is about metaphors. The force of these metaphors is that they turn the act of programming into an act of symbolic manipulation: algorithms represented as analogies."[15] Extending Marino's claim a step further, we might say that if Flash on the whole is about metaphors, *Dakota* is a Flash work about Flash itself as a metaphor. While every Flash work metaphorizes other technologies, *Dakota* is unique in its self-conscious reflection on this metaphorization through its testing and engaging with the medium specificity of Flash, thinking about the ways in which it both remediates and deforms the workings of earlier moving-image technologies.

Flash operates on two governing metaphors—film and depth—each of which has its own media-historical resonances and implications. The application's filmic dimensions appear most explicitly in the structuring of a Flash animation in a timeline of frames, drawing on the vocabulary and materiality of celluloid film. Depth, Flash's dominant, "operational metaphor" according to Marino, inheres in the division of the timeline into multiple layers that allow multiple streams of visual information to be manipulated and displayed at once; for example, a figure in the foreground in one layer of a Flash file might walk from left to right onscreen while a plant in the background in another layer might wave back and forth to connote wind in the same scene.[16] Thus depth invokes the cinematic as well, although by way of celluloid animation rather than live-action filming: just as a frame of a hand-drawn animation might consist of different layers, so does the Flash authoring environment allow for multiple layers. Given this imagined depth, perhaps the most pertinent media metaphor for the form of Flash is thus not the recorded shots of film per se but rather the more specifically inscribed surfaces and layers of animation.[17] Yet as Marino notes, these metaphors begin to break down as soon as they come into play. Whereas a frame in celluloid cinema—essentially a single photograph in a series of rapidly displayed photographs—occupies a fixed duration, a frame in Flash is a container of information that can be shown for any length of time. Moreover, "[u]nlike film, images in Flash are not indexical signs; the images are data objects," representations of information that foundationally exists as code rather than as drawing or capture.[18]

While the layered, sedimented condition of Flash is true for the application as a whole, and thus pertains to any file, YHCHI's use of textual form exploits, reveals, and deconstructs this condition in unique ways; as the metaphor of the frame breaks down in *Dakota*, it gives way to the metaphor of the page. In a manner that is closely intertwined with its textual nature, *Dakota* contains very little spatial movement within the screen in any given duration of time. On rare occasions, a word or group of words will move or change size onscreen, but in most cases, each textual unit is simply replaced either by the next unit or by a brief blank white screen before the next unit.[19] Faced with this textual *détournement* of Flash's filmic metaphor, we must shuttle between watching—an action predicated on a moving image onscreen—and reading, an action predicated on static text, here located on the surface of what we might see as an imagined page. Populated only by alphabetic characters, *Dakota* is not a moving-image work but rather a moving-text work residing uncomfortably within the metaphors and contexts of the image. Its conceit of an all-text film paradoxically invites us to think in terms of cinematic frames precisely by disrupting their usual flow, challenging us to pay close attention to the discrete segmentation of visual information in a manner that interrupts the illusion of motion we traditionally associate with film, whether live-action or animated; we begin to see the work's frames, in a conceptual sense, only when their workings are disrupted (to say nothing of being evacuated altogether). Yet through this disruption, the very same system of textual substitution—black characters replacing one another against a white background—inevitably invites us to see *Dakota* not just as a written text in the broad sense of those terms but more specifically as a printed one: what if this digital film were sheets of paper? Raising questions of format and substrate, this speculative possibility woven into the form of the piece imagines a corresponding speculative media history for it. I turn to this history in the following sections of this chapter, discussing the paper print and the Mutoscope, two cinematic technologies from the turn of the twentieth century, as media-historical antecedents and metaphors for *Dakota* and Flash more broadly. Both individually and collectively, they reveal a shadow history of paper within the contemporary history of the moving image, allowing us to see how YHCHI cuts bookishly across media and time, excavating earlier media technologies through its aesthetic form.

On the Digital History of Paper, Part II: When Cinema Was Paper

Perhaps the most basic metaphoric antecedent for *Dakota* is the paper print. Beginning in 1894, the kinetoscope—a projection-based motion picture viewing technology invented by Thomas Edison and designed for individual viewing—became a popular attraction in motion picture houses and amusement parks, setting in motion the age of film as a mass medium. However, prior to 1912, the Library of Congress provided no copyright provisions for the then-new medium of film. As a result, piracy and intellectual property theft ran rampant in the nascent film industry. In 1894, in an effort to maintain control of the Edison laboratory's intellectual property, Edison's assistant, William K. L. Dickson, submitted a copyright application for one of the studio's earliest films, *Edison Kinetoscopic Record of a Sneeze*, more commonly known as *Fred Ott's Sneeze* in reference to the Edison employee it depicted. Because the existing copyright law did not recognize film as such, Dickson submitted the film as a kind of de facto photograph, printing out its forty-five frames in sequence on paper and affixing them to a single card, in the process producing what came to be known as the paper print. Dickson's workaround set a standard for film copyrighting until the Library of Congress established actual provisions for film nearly twenty years later.[20] The lack of any explicit protocol in this intervening time opened the submission process to a diverse range of formats, all of which have been retroactively grouped under the descriptor of the paper print: while some filmmakers and studios submitted full sheets of their films as Dickson did, others submitted rolls of paper printed with all the film's frames in a single strip, while still others submitted a kind of skeletal outline of their film, comprised of a few frames from each scene.

Across all of these formats, paper prints pose a strange instance of film as a medium without film as a material. Paper scrapings of celluloid information that anticipate the intermedia page shreddings of 1980s computing, they are themselves both historically liminal—a unique instance of "Motion Picture Incunabula," as Howard Walls describes them—and liminal with regard to mediality, raising a number of crucial theoretical and material questions around the status of film and moving-image media more broadly.[21] Perhaps the most evident and immediate of these questions stems from the pressure they place on the medium specificity of film and the moving-image: Is a film that has been broken down to its composite parts, presented in its entirety as still photographs, still a film? When does it become a photograph, or a series of photographs? How do material substrates play into these questions—if we can comfortably acknowledge that photographic paper is a part of the larger apparatus of photography, what does it mean to imagine that paper as part of film as well? Put more pointedly, what does it mean to have a film as an object without film as a substrate? The physical dimensions of an entire film printed out—even a relatively short one, as *Fred Ott's Sneeze* was, or even as a sheet rather than a long roll—stretch the definition of the form (both literally and figuratively) to its extreme. Paper prints are also at the heart of an archival irony within film history. The vast majority of films produced in the early years of the medium—as much as 90 percent, according to Charles Grimm's estimate—no longer exist.[22] Many of the films that do remain from this early era remain because they were incidentally preserved as paper. In considering the disappearance of nitrate film and the cinematic archive in chapter 3, I discussed Paolo Cherchi Usai's provocation, "It is the destruction of moving images that makes film history possible."[23] Revisiting this idea in the historical and material context of paper prints, we might extend Cherchi Usai's claim to say that we have early film history, yet for the most part we do not have early films—only their recreations, filtered and mediated through paper.

The making-paper of film in its earliest years also raises a number of questions around the materiality of the film object itself. As film became more materially durable in becoming paper, it became more opaque as well. The image to be seen, then, was not the projection of light through the object as in the case of celluloid film, but rather the object itself, whether a sheet or a roll—a difference in dimensionality, planarity, and perspective that in turn opened up a different mode of visual consumption.[24] To return to the language of depth I introduced in the previous section of this chapter, if we might say that a celluloid strip has depth by way of its translucency and projectability—indeed, perhaps such affordances are the essence of celluloid film as a format—the paper print, by contrast, has none. These qualities make viewing a paper print a strange visual experiment. In contrast to the mechanized linear progression of projected film, the display format of the paper print is nonlinear, offering a more open, almost random access to its frames. On a single sheet of forty-five frames constituting the approximately five seconds of *Fred Ott's Sneeze*, which image to look at first? The rules of the Western codex would seem to suggest a left-to-right, top-to-bottom sequence, paralleling the temporal sequence of the projected film itself. But the wholly visual, all-at-once architecture of this page means that such an approach is only one possibility, hardly a given. Even a rolled print presents this dilemma, almost inevitably revealing more than one frame at once, and continuing to display each frame after its initial appearance rather than simply replacing it; such a format resembles the random-access capabilities of the scroll more closely than the linearity of the projected film. Laid out across the space of the paper print, stripped of the onscreen illusion of movement, cinema steps outside of time, its sequence replaced by simultaneity, visible as an uncanny kind of print text. Cinema is not necessarily textual in the sense of alphabetic inscription—indeed, the primary formal effect of YHCHI's work hinges on the fact that alphabetic textuality is the exception rather than the rule within the medium. However, paper prints suggest that we might nonetheless understand cinema, at least in the case of celluloid film, as rooted in the affordances of printed objects, its origins bodying forth the materiality and opacity we more commonly associate with paper.

If the paper print shows us a history of the moving image as bound to paper, the Mutoscope and its immediate predecessor, the flip-book, show us a history of the moving image as more specifically and explicitly bookish. The object that came to be colloquially known as the flip-book was first developed as the folioscope in France in 1860 by Pierre-Hubert Desvignes, and later patented as the kineograph by British printer John Barnes Linnett in 1860.[25] Among the many moving-image technologies that emerged in the mid- to late nineteenth century—the zoetrope, the thaumatrope, the phenakistoscope, and numerous others—the flip-book was the first that functioned based on images moving in a linear, rather than circular or spherical, fashion.[26] As described in Linnett's 1868 patent application for "Producing Optical Illusions," this linearity was rooted in the affordances of the codex as a media object. Linnett described his innovations as follows: "I print or otherwise produce on separate leaves of paper or card or other flexible material a series of different pictures, in which the object or portion of the object which it is intended shall have the appearance of moving is represented in different positions.... These leaves or cards are secured at or near one edge so as to bind them together in a series similar to the leaves of a book."[27] By holding the secured edge of this booklike object in one hand and flicking the leaves on the opposite edge with the thumb or finger of the opposite hand, a user could produce the illusion of movement on the page. In 1882, Henry Van Hoevenbergh was the first American to patent a similar device, followed by Dickson and Herman Casler's invention of the Mutoscope in 1894.[28]

The Mutoscope was essentially a mechanized flip-book: the movement of its leaves was powered by a hand crank, and its leaves and other moving parts were encased in a box for individual viewing in commercial amusement contexts. In this sense it was broadly similar to Edison's kinetoscope. However, where the kinetoscope relied on a strip of celluloid film to create the illusion of motion, the Mutoscope utilized a series of paper cards printed with photographic images, all attached to a circular reel not unlike the twentieth-century technology of the Rolodex in form. Even though the images and moving parts of the Mutoscope were untouchable to audiences, contemporary reactions to this new technology nonetheless framed it in terms of the book as a hand-held media object. An 1897 article in the *New York Herald* noted of its mechanics that when the device's cylinder holding the photographic prints "is slowly revolved, the picture cards being held back by a stop, and allowed to snap past the eye one by one, as one thumbs the leaves of a book, an apparently moving picture is the result, and it is difficult to realize that the picture is not endowed with life"[29] A *Scientific American* article of the same year similarly noted how the Mutoscope's stop "allows the pictures to slip by in much the same way as the thumb is used upon the leaves of a book," while an article from 1901 returned to the language of the *Herald* nearly verbatim, as well as describing the photographs inside the device as "set up in circular book form."[30]

The Mutoscope's use of paper images made it more durable in comparison to Edison's kinetoscope, which used celluloid film, but also made it less lucrative, as the kinetoscope's use of celluloid allowed it to be adapted into technology suitable for projected mass viewings, eventually leading to the Mutoscope's obsolescence amid the rapidly developing cinematic culture of the early twentieth century. Writing of the residual persistence of the Mutoscope "in penny arcades and at community fairs" into the early 1970s, Laurence Kardish notes of the two technologies, "Although the Mutoscope has had a longer life than its competitor, it is the Kinetoscope that is the more important in the growth of motion pictures because it used film."[31] Kardish is certainly correct here with regard to market share and longevity. Yet we might also see another, less teleological history of the moving image alongside the narrative he points to, attending to the presence and disappearance of paper cinema in a way that resonates with and provides context for YHCHI's textual animation. Tom Gunning sees the possibility of such an alternate history in the writing of experimental filmmaker and commercial artist Douglass Crockwell, quoting Crockwell's program notes for a 1966 Museum of Modern Art exhibition on the Mutoscope: "Visually the motion picture is sequential art. . . . Motion is but one of the incidental byproducts. In essence the Mutoscope reel presents one image after another, after another, after another——. Timing of the interval has no basic importance. The raw material of this art is the topological arrangement in time of a given set of images."[32] "Crockwell," Gunning writes, "provides a radical definition of the origins of film art, against the grain of the traditional interpretation of the essence of film as the reproduction of motion . . . motion pictures become a sort of serial art based on the temporal permutations of images."[33] Understanding cinema in this fashion—as based on sequence and seriality rather than on movement, speed, or time—dismantles the centrality of the celluloid strip and its linear motion, and in doing so opens cinema to other formats, substrates, and forms. The printed photographs of the Mutoscope flying by the viewer's peephole to create the illusion of motion clearly constitute a film, yet the same set of photographs sitting in a stack next to the Mutoscope might constitute a film as well; indeed, so might the flip-book and the book itself. Indeed, the alternate possibilities posed by Gunning and Crockwell through the technological dead end of the Mutoscope suggest that we might reimagine film to include the affordances of print and paper as well as those of celluloid. In doing so, we excavate a media poetics and history across which text and image—writing, drawing, and showing—circulate in recursive, interdependent ways.

Source, Cache, File, Layer: Shredding *Dakota*, or, Toward a Poetics of Bookish Film

How might we conduct this excavation, and what insights might it yield about the intertwined histories of literature and film, text and image? How can we see *Dakota* anew by seeing it as a rediscovery of paper within film—a digital Flash file that presents itself like a celluloid film that presents itself like a Mutoscope reel that presents itself like a book? This chain of remediation invites inquiry through the framework of page shredding I discussed earlier: if we can see that *Dakota* consists of virtual pages, then what do the conceptual vocabulary and technical protocols of page shredding have to tell us about how the work's technological materiality imagines media history? What would it mean to see the frames and words of *Dakota* not just as imagined, virtual paper, as it were, but as imaginatively shredded pages—to thus see their invocation of the paper of early cinema as informed by early networking's invocation of paper? How might we see this work as triangulating among the digital screens of the early twenty-first century, the digital paper of the late twentieth century, and the paper cinema of the late nineteenth century? Jessica Pressman notes of *Dakota* that attending to its "retroaesthetic" focus on the mass media of modernism "provides a way to reading between text, film, and digital art" in the work by drawing on Eisensteinian montage and Ezra Pound's poetic method of "super-position . . . one idea set on top of another."[34] Yet her analysis that follows from this foundation approaches the mediality of text, film, and the digital largely at the thematic level, leaving the material relations among those different media largely untouched, particularly with regard to text itself and the paper substrates it invokes. I argue that superposition in the case of *Dakota* is not merely conceptual or spatial, as in Pound's famous "In a Station of the Metro," but also material as well, a point of entry into thinking the thickness of paper itself. In the analysis that follows, I expand Pressman's attention to the retroaesthetic dimensions of *Dakota* to focus on the work's engagement with the material poetics of paper.

Like the financial computers of the early 1980s, *Dakota* is, at a surface level, noninteractive. It offers no objects to manipulate, no paths to choose from, no choices to make. These absences stand in diametric opposition to the dominant discourse of electronic literature.[35] Perhaps the most immediate instance of this noninteractivity is the fact that—at least seemingly—a viewer of *Dakota* cannot pause, rewind, or reverse the work as it is being played. This absence of functionality resembles the properties of both the paper teletype, which "prints one line at a time [and] cannot erase what it has already typed or go back to retype earlier lines," and the digital terminal known as a glass teletype, where "material which has scrolled off the top of the screen often cannot be retrieved."[36] *Dakota*'s surface purports to be defined by this inexorable movement of the glass teletype, with its professed noninteractivity announcing the piece as irreversible, inexorably moving forward on a linear timeline. And in many instances, such as when the work is displayed in an art gallery or museum, this is indeed the case. However, just as programmers and financial workers in the 1980s shredded the digital output of the glass teletype as if it were paper—distorting, fragmenting, and reproducing text onscreen in a manner that at once both concealed and revealed the historicity of the paper teletype—*Dakota*'s digital form figures a corresponding textuality that resonates with paper's manipulable materiality. As I show below, its seemingly impermeable digital surface ultimately gives way to figure the analog, bodying forth a mess of printed text. Tracing *Dakota*'s digital materiality and its circulation online resurrects the technological workings of the page-shredded terminal as well as of early paper cinema. Moreover, scholars of digital literature might themselves do something similar *with* this work: shredding the materiality of *Dakota*'s Flash file, opening it up to imagine alternate ways of reading its poetics, we reveal manifestations of its text that both diverge from and overlap with the piece as traditionally presented, illuminating multiple media-historical temporalities across page and screen.[37]

In the pages that follow, I trace several of these deformative inter-actions and the manifestations of the text that they produce, beginning with user interactions that depart from the original playback of *Dakota* on YHCHI's website. The shifting form of YHCHI's site complicates the work of tracing and exemplifying these deformations, posing its own questions of the archive, the artifact, and the media history in and of the text. When I first began examining the code of their site in the early 2010s, viewing the page that holds *Dakota* in the version stored in Google Cache revealed a rhythmically repetitive iteration of the piece's text. This iteration, which I discuss below, was presumably scraped from the frames of the original Flash file by Google's Web-crawling tools. By the mid-2010s, Google Cache returned only the Flash file itself, playing in time in the same way as on the actual page, and thus providing relatively little insight as to the work's infrastructure in code. As I complete this manuscript in 2021, yhchang.com presents all of the group's work as Vimeo and YouTube files, hermetically sealed corporate formats whose privacy settings make it impossible to access the actual Flash file altogether.[38] As of the end of 2020, Adobe, Inc.—the software corporation that has sup-ported Flash since its 2005 acquisition of Macromedia, the corporation that introduced Flash in 1996—no longer supports Flash, rendering the format altogether obsolete.[39] In this sense, *Dakota* has moved progressively closer to a glass Teletype textuality over time. Thus while many of the textual dimensions of *Dakota* I discuss below are no longer technically accessible as of this writing, I nonetheless treat them as extant possibilities. Indeed, because of the historiographic stakes of these material transformations, the obsolescence of these forms of the text makes them more relevant rather than less so—these lost objects offer a counternarrative, however inaccessible, to the positivist and futurist ideologies that might other-wise shape how we see the development of the digital moving image and digital textuality more generally. Like afterimages or traces of an image that is no longer present or accessible, the interactions with *Dakota* that I trace here constitute a series of attempts at a kind of fugitive history of the work's material dimensions: these deformative unfoldings sketch a history of the work that parallels its own history of earlier digital and cinematic media.

The first and most basic of these interactions with *Dakota* in its initial form is to right-click on the piece as it is playing, bringing up a contextual menu that allows the user to pause playback at any point. While this option may not have been available on all (or any) browsers when YHCHI first released *Dakota* around the year 2000, it was built into at least one browser as early as 2010, when I first attempted to deform the work this way, and presumably remained present as a possibility until the page's conversion to its current state sometime between 2017 and 2018. The ability to pause the work in this way dramatically changes its materiality and meaning, situating it somewhere between the material affordances of celluloid film and digital video. The web browser's contextual menu also allows a user to view the page's source code, which in its earlier incarnations would yield a minimal shell page of sorts holding the actual Flash file of *Dakota*, which could then be downloaded. Such a possibility profoundly changes the terms of control, interactivity, and manipulability around the work, shifting from a dynamic defined by access to one defined by ownership and making a text that was previously effectively untouchable—viewable only on a gallery wall or in the evanescent connective space of a web browser—suddenly subject to close contact and examination. Here the digital becomes interactive not because of artistic choice or intent but rather because of the affordances of code, file structure, and the tools embedded in the modern web browser.

This Flash file, which I discuss in greater depth below, finds its counterpart in the scraped textual version I note above, also available in the 2010s. While this version is no longer accessible in Google Cache, it can be accessed by viewing the source code of any archived version of *Dakota*'s page dating from before its current Vimeo-based state on the Internet Archive's Wayback Machine.[40] Within this source code resides a purely text-based version of the film extracted from its construction in frames within the Flash environment. Because each unit of text appears within *Dakota* for multiple frames, this version of the film contains numerous repetitions of each unit. For example, the early passage in the film in which the speaker states that he and his companions "waltzed out to the car, leaned in and turned on the ignition," appears as

```
WALTZED WALTZED WALTZED WALTZED WALTZED WALTZED ØUT ØUT
ØUT ØUT TØ THE CAR, TØ THE CAR, TØ THE CAR, TØ THE CAR,
TØ THE CAR, TØ THE CAR, TØ THE CAR, TØ THE CAR, TØ THE
CAR, TØ THE CAR, TØ THE CAR, TØ THE CAR, TØ THE CAR, TØ
THE CAR, TØ THE CAR, TØ THE CAR, TØ THE CAR, TØ THE CAR,
TØ THE CAR, TØ THE CAR, TØ THE CAR, TØ THE CAR, TØ THE
CAR, TØ THE CAR, TØ THE CAR, TØ THE CAR, TØ THE CAR, TØ
THE CAR, LEANED IN LEANED IN LEANED IN LEANED IN LEANED
IN LEANED IN LEANED IN AND TURNED ØN AND TURNED ØN AND
TURNED ØN AND TURNED ØN AND TURNED ØN AND TURNED ØN
THE IGNITIØN, THE IGNITIØN, THE IGNITIØN, THE IGNITIØN,
THE IGNITIØN, THE IGNITIØN, THE IGNITIØN, THE IGNITIØN,
THE IGNITIØN, THE IGNITIØN, THE IGNITIØN, THE IGNITIØN,
THE IGNITIØN, THE IGNITIØN, THE IGNITIØN, THE IGNITIØN,
THE IGNITIØN, THE IGNITIØN, THE IGNITIØN, THE IGNITIØN,
THE IGNITIØN, THE IGNITIØN, THE IGNITIØN, THE IGNITIØN,
THE IGNITIØN, THE IGNITIØN, THE IGNITIØN, THE IGNITIØN,
THE IGNITIØN, THE IGNITIØN, THE IGNITIØN, THE IGNITIØN,
THE IGNITIØN, THE IGNITIØN, THE IGNITIØN, THE IGNITIØN,
THE IGNITIØN[41]
```

Taken as a whole, the resulting text becomes a strangely monotonous kind of prose poem version of *Dakota*, extruding the Flash text's core of fewer than 1,000 words to nearly 7,500. Yet as I suggest below, this scraped text is not simply an elongated transcription of the Flash piece, nor is the Flash piece the realization of the scraped text in motion. Rather than one serving as a means to understand the other, the two are inseparably intertwined and interdeterminate.

In tracing *Dakota*'s text across these two different artifacts, we see how intensely it relies on and invokes paper as a material metaphor—not merely as a digital animation but also as a corpus of text, offering up a media poetics of alphabetic inscription by way of unstable figures on the screen and the page. Indeed, both of these objects are doubly cinematic and textual at once. The scraped text version functions like a paper print of the Flash animation, showing us all the iterations of its word-images—each unit of text a frame alongside others—while the Flash file, decompiled as I discuss it below, presents a Mutoscopic version of the work, with textually inscribed paper cards (in digital form) that can be moved through under the viewer's control. If the Flash file, then, is a film made of pure text, the scraped text as quoted above is text rendered cinematic. Hinging on repetition, it shapes the consumption of *Dakota* as an experience of duration. Stretched and repeated in still text, the often-discussed velocity of the piece inverts: its central question becomes not how fast it moves but rather how slow, how many times each unit of text repeats.[42] Faced with this incarnation of the work, we must wonder not whether we can keep up with it, but rather how long to linger on it—how much we should read its repetitions, and indeed whether we should read them at all. At a basic functional level, these repetitions serve as indices of duration: six repetitions of "WALTZED" in the passage above representing six frames, four of "OUT" for four frames, twenty-eight of "TO THE CAR" for twenty-eight frames, and so on. Yet this incremental quantitative equivalence is only the most literal element of what these repetitions connote. Beyond their invocation of the local duration of a particular word or phrase, they serve as a more global index for the uneven mediatic commensurability and formal friction that coalesces across these forms of *Dakota* between text and image, among paper, celluloid, and screen. The repetition of a word or phrase as text in space both can and cannot stand in for its persistence as an image in time. How can the monotony and boredom of reading a single textual unit sometimes dozens of times correlate to its presence onscreen for a few short instants? How do we have to imagine the relations of text, image, reading, seeing, motion, stillness, and time in order to calculate such a correlation? Taking into account the speed of the film that Pressman and others focus on, what would the scraped text of a moving version of *Dakota* that was slowed down enough to read in real time look like, and how long would it be?

Durational questions such as these speak to part of the uncanny nature of this text, but they also open onto larger questions of mediality and materiality. If the analog screen scraping performed by the production of a paper print captures and records every frame of a film, what happens when that film is purely textual—how does our engagement with the resulting corpus shuttle between reading and watching, and what would it mean to *watch* a static alphabetic text? Seeing cinematic text on paper as in a paper print seems not only anachronistic to the twenty-first-century eye, but also confusing, with the visual protocols of time-based media becoming difficult to parse when transported into another medium. For example, the Edison studio's paper print for *Fred Ott's Sneeze* suggests that as much as a sequence of frames in a filmic paper print might look largely the same to the naked eye, each one is different from those before and after it, capturing a different instant. Can we say the same of the series of "WALTZED"s early in the scraped text of *Dakota*? To see each of those words—identical in spelling, font, and other characteristics—as different is to profoundly reconceptualize the process that produced this document. Understood in this way, these units of text stand not as transcription or even as repetition as such, but rather as a kind of slow, infinitesimally gradual shredding of the Flash file's frames set in motion by the Internet Archive's scraping of that file and the page on which it is stored, each iteration a thin slice of space and time sheared from the moving text of *Dakota*. Presenting difference as repetition, this uncanny, elongated counterpart to YHCHI's compressed, rapid film documents a textual poetics of the digital image—a poetics that in turn reveals the deeper poetics of paper as an always already unstable media-historical origin with the digital.

If the scraped textual version of *Dakota* bodies forth its genealogy in the paper print, the film itself resonates with the Mutoscope's repeated substitutions of opaque photographic prints rather than the linear mechanical movement of the translucent celluloid reel.[43] This resonance appears within the perceptible aesthetics of the piece as well as at the level of the file itself. Both traditional and digital animation are defined by key frames, frames that represent the beginning and ending of a particular onscreen movement or transformation: in the classic example of a bouncing ball, key frames would depict the ball at an initial height about to fall, making impact with the ground, and then in the air again after having risen back up. In traditional animation, these key frames were usually drawn by a lead animator, while the work of drawing the intermediate frames, known as in-betweening or tweening, was done by a less senior artist. The digital environment of Flash divides this labor technologically, with the animator designing and designating key frames and the software itself calculating and creating the tweening. As a solely textual work, *Dakota* relies almost entirely on key frames alone rather than tweening between key frames. Each word is introduced on a key frame, remains onscreen for a particular duration, and is replaced by another word on a key frame. This process of short-circuiting the workings of Flash (indeed perhaps of animation itself), using it to produce repeated, instantaneous substitution rather than continuous linear movement, is central to the media poetics of the piece. Exemplifying the sequential, topological arrangement of images imagined by Gunning and Crockwell—motion is not only incidental here but effectively absent nearly altogether—YHCHI distorts the parameters of new media to meet the affordances of old media.

The first word of *Dakota*, "FUCKING," illustrates this technologically deformative work. First appearing in frame 425, it vibrates slightly at the center of the screen, moving diagonally in space in what is a rare instance of onscreen movement in the piece.[44] After briefly remaining still, it recedes into the center of the screen, becoming progressively smaller until it disappears. Each increment in these changes—each movement, each change in size—is its own key frame. Thus these actions, which seem like the continuous movement we conventionally understand as the "essence of film" and animation, are instead discrete substitutions. What appears to be the movement of a single word in the space of the screen is, at the level of the file, the replacement of that word with a different version of the same word—sometimes at a different place, sometimes a different size, but always on a new key frame, just as every subsequent word replaces the one that preceded it. This series of replacements suggests that *Dakota* is Mutoscopic rather than kinetoscopic, displaying change and substitution rather than movement, and that it consequently draws on a differential, deeper history of the moving image that includes type, text, and paper as well as image and celluloid. Thus as the digital form of the piece distorts the filmic metaphor of Flash, that metaphor takes shape anew not within the dominant history of film as we have come to know it but rather in the history of paper.

Indeed, the historical presence of paper within *Dakota* troubles the dominant metaphor of depth within Flash as a technology. In a conventionally image-based animation, whether analog or digital, depth within the image would emerge as a function of the "composite of layers" that comprise it.[45] In a hand-drawn analog animation of the sort that dominated most of the twentieth century, these layers would exist on multiple transparent sheets of celluloid, while in a digital animation these layers are metaphorical, serving as structuring tools of the user interface of Flash authoring software. *Dakota* distorts Flash's depth metaphor in a number of ways. The first and most immediate of these is the work's simulation of black ink on white paper, itself a metaphor that is at odds with the transparency of the celluloid sheet. Onscreen, the whiteness of *Dakota*'s background signifies for both the transparency of the cel as an inscription surface for the work's black text and the opacity of the paper as an inscription surface. Thus the screen here signifies as a screen, but also as celluloid and as paper, invoking three different surfaces that are materially at odds with one another. The question of depth and layering, then, becomes not actual as it is in celluloid animation, nor metaphorical as in digital animation, but rather historical—a question of invocation and reference as these different imagined surfaces become visible both through and against each other, visually bodying forth the inscriptive genealogy of *Dakota* across multiple media formats and historical moments.

The movement of words across layers within *Dakota* further distorts and transforms its use of depth. The Flash file of *Dakota* consists of four visual layers and a sound layer that contains a sound file for Art Blakey's "Tobi Ilu," the hard-bop composition that serves as the work's soundtrack. Within the four visual layers, the vast majority of the work's text appears on layer 1, with layers 2 through 4 primarily containing text when the piece displays multiple words or phrases. For example, the initial title sequence accumulates text across all four layers over time: the word "YOUNG-HAE" appears on layer 1 at frame 332, the word "CHANG" on layer 2 at frame 340, the phrase "HEAVY INDUSTRIES" on layer 3 at frame 348, and the word "PRESENTS" on layer 4 at frame 356. At frame 364, layers 2 through 4 go blank, and the title "DAKOTA" replaces "YOUNG-HAE," occupying layer 1.[46] This use of layers within the file is relatively rational, based on a logic of accumulation that allows the viewer to read the title text as it appears over time. Other moments in the piece employ layering in less linear, rational ways, shifting words and phrases between layers across consecutive frames without any clear reason. In these moments, the file's layers and Flash's metaphor of depth seem at once both essential to such a movement and also wholly arbitrary. Why move a word from one layer to another, only to have it immediately disappear? Why do the file's layers matter at all as a structuring metaphor when the piece seems designed to connote flatness and depthlessness? Simultaneously thematizing and subverting Flash's presentation of depth, YHCHI draws a recursive circuit of visual, material parallels among the file, the cel, and the illusionary, depthless depth of the printed page, staging *Dakota* as a bookish digital film with a media history that is itself complexly layered.

This play with layering becomes even more complex in the instance of the one word in *Dakota* that engages all four of the Flash file's visual layers. This word, "BURP," appears early in the work, as the narrator describes how he and his companion "DRANK—AND/ INSULTED—EACH/0THER'S—M0THERS.—BEER—IN—0NE—HAND,—B0URB0N—IN—THE—0THER,—WE—DRANK—AGAIN,—THEN—ATE—S0ME—HAM—AND—CHEESE—SANDWICHES.—THEN—I—SP0KE—A—GASSY—SPEECH—AB0UT—DYING—Y0UNG.—(BURP.)."[47] The final frame of this passage, 1288, occupies all four layers of the file as follows: layer 1 contains a visual symbol, a semiopaque gray block that fills the playback screen, making the text momentarily less visible and thus visually accenting this frame; layer 2 contains "(BURP"; layer 3 contains the closed parenthesis, ")"; and layer 4 contains the period, "." This division of such a small unit of text across multiple layers is unusual and uneven, with the key word—an onomatopoetic expulsion, at that—on one layer and the punctuation around it on two others, a construction that explicitly draws attention to the metaphorical and material work of layering itself. As the onomatopoetic sound of "burp" suggests, layering here becomes a way of taking text beyond the constraints of language. Indeed, the configuration of layers here suggests multiple inscriptive metaphors: the piece's black text on a white background invokes a single opaque sheet of paper, while the structure of the Flash file also invokes four transparent celluloid sheets. Yet these together also invoke another imagined object, a stack of four sheets of paper, seemingly at once both transparent and opaque. The increased number of layers to this word suggests the possibility of moving through its textual material not horizontally, from word to word across the timeline in keeping with the movement of the work during playback, but rather vertically, putting its imagined depth into play within this single frame. Through such a reading, we literally descend into the text's metaphorical layers, moving simultaneously deeper in space and further in time through an opening parenthesis, an expulsion, a closing parenthesis, and concluding punctuation.

Rather than shredding this unit of text horizontally or vertically, such a reading divides the infinitesimal depth of its imaginary paper toward even thinner layers. The Poundian superposition Pressman discusses, then, occurs materially as well as spatially and textually, at the most microscopic of scales. To understand *Dakota* in this way demands that we excavate a three-dimensional architecture of the page as a metaphor for its structure, reading in order to tease out the stratifications of print materiality concealed by the seeming flatness and depthlessness of the screen. Shifting in planarity and perspective not only brings the spectral presence of paper within *Dakota* into relief but also reveals that paper itself as materially dynamic—a substrate that moves, separates, and recombines across time and space. Couched in the context of *Dakota*'s moving text, the depth-based metaphor of animation's layering and the time-based metaphor of the flip-book and the Mutoscope twist and turn against each other; the spectral digital sheets of the work move in time and in space at once, revealing in their flickerings a glimpse at the layers of inscription and textual materiality underlying the glass screen.

I have suggested over the course of this chapter that *Dakota* invokes many metaphors and antecedents from across the history of visual and textual media: celluloid film, to be sure, but also the glass Teletype, the Mutoscope, the paper print, and the flip-book. While I have traced the lines of affiliation between their materiality and historicity and that of *Dakota*, it is crucial to underscore that none of these metaphors is exact, nor is it totalizing; each applies partially, irregularly, and unevenly, much like the persistence of paper itself in the digital era. Indeed, these material metaphors shed light on the persistence of paper in the digital precisely in their inexactitude, capturing the inexactitude of that persistence itself. Just as print authors such as Don DeLillo and Kevin Young represent and respond to technological change in deliberately disjunctive ways, throwing into relief what print writing can and cannot render about other media as a way of tracing and reimagining the contours of media history, YHCHI conversely offers a theory of paper that emerges from a theory of the digital as the skew intersection of multiple historical paths, the paper past and the digital present feeding back into one another. *Dakota*'s articulation of paper is textual and visual, flat and layered, metaphorical and material, digital and analog—at turns alive, dead, and undead. Secreted in black and white across the surface of the screen, paper is at once everywhere and nowhere in *Dakota*. Persistent in its fragility, transparent in its opacity, it serves—here as throughout *Archival Fictions*—as the uncanny surface for the writing of a speculative media history defined by irregularity, residue, and reconfiguration.

Coda: Discards

and the last fantastic book flung out of the tenement window, and the last door closed at 4
A.M. and the last telephone slammed at the wall in reply and the last furnished room emptied
down to the last piece of mental furniture, a yellow paper rose twisted on a wire hanger in
the closet, and even that imaginary, nothing but a hopeful little bit of hallucination—
—Allen Ginsberg, "Howl"

Right as the music starts, the camera pulls back to reveal him, standing
in the alley next to the Savoy Hotel in London. Shown in the right-hand
side of the frame in a medium-long shot, he holds a stack of rectangular
cards up toward the camera, waist high—the first reads "BASEMENT," in
all caps, black ink on white paper. As the lyrics begin to stream out on the
soundtrack, he drops each card in time with the music, revealing another
word or phrase, written in varying, uneven hands. Midway through each
verse, it seems, he falls behind the soundtrack, rushing to drop card after
card in order to keep up. The camera never cuts or moves, and the whole
thing is over in just over two minutes: the lyrics completed, he holds up
and drops the last card, "What??," unspoken in the song, and walks forward
off-screen, gingerly stepping either around the pile of discards or directly
onto it, we cannot tell which. We never see the pile.

D. A. Pennebaker's 1967 film *Dont Look Back* [*sic*] documents Bob Dylan's
1965 tour of England, recording Dylan's promotion of his album *Bringing
It All Back Home* and his transition from acoustic folk music to an electric,
more rock-oriented style.[48] *Dont Look Back* begins with this scene, a kind
of music video for "Subterranean Homesick Blues," the first track on the
album (the video also served as a promotional trailer for the film). This
video is a transitional, pivotal text in multiple ways. In addition to announcing Dylan's new sonic and lyrical style and the changed persona that will
accompany that style, it also announces a new relation between popular
music and moving images: according to Dylan's tour manager and fellow
musician Bob Neuwirth, who appears in the far-left of the frame alongside
Allen Ginsberg, Dylan devised the conceit for the video with the intent to
feature it on the Scopitone.[49] An early video jukebox, the Scopitone first
appeared in nightclubs and bars in France in the late 1950s, expanding to

the United States in the early 1960s. For the price of a few coins, Scopitone patrons could watch a short 16mm film featuring a vocal and dance performance of a popular song, complete with lip-synced music on a magnetic soundtrack. An early antecedent of the late twentieth-century music video, the Scopitone disappeared from the market before ever catching on in the United States: while as many as 1,500 machines were produced for the U.S. market, the technology never captured mass interest, and was largely forgotten by the time Pennebaker's film appeared in theaters.[50] Not unlike the Mutoscope, the Scopitone occupies a liminal position within media history, the forgotten precursor of a form that would come to dominate the media landscape years later.

Similarly, Pennebaker's clip is often cited as the first music video, a reading of the text that foregrounds Dylan's broader attempt in *Dont Look Back* to put the rock music he was beginning to produce in dialogue with the circulation of the global moving image. Yet as David Yaffe notes, Dylan does not lip sync in the video, instead standing in the street motionless and "stone faced."[51] Thus we might see "Subterranean Homesick Blues" not as a prototypical music video *per se*—after all, it figures performance in a largely different manner than much of the genre, even in its other early instances—but rather as a kind of experimental media poem that both enacts and theorizes an experimental media poetics of textual materiality. Indeed, the film's central goal is less the representation, reproduction, or translation of Dylan's song than it is the mediation of it into another format; as Pennebaker notes in a commentary on the scene, the central impetus for it came when "Dylan came up with the idea of having a lot of things written down on pieces of paper. . . . he didn't, we didn't think about what you're going to do with them, but you had these things on cards and he said, 'Is that a good idea for the film?,' and I said, 'It's a terrific idea.'"[52] Dylan's idea was so "terrific" that numerous subsequent artists have reworked and referenced it: "Weird Al" Yankovic's "Bob" features the parodist dressed as Dylan on black-and-white video, raising and dropping cards that contain only palindromic phrases, as suggested by the song's palindromic title—"Madam, I'm Adam," "Too hot to hoot," "Oozy Rat in a Sanitary Zoo," and so on—while the Australian rock band INXS's "Mediate" applies the same approach to the song's lyrics, a string of words and phrases all ending in "-ate."[53] These riffs on the original clip attest to how intensely Pennebaker's film engages with the inscriptive shape of textual language and the ways in which that shape can be—to use INXS's titular term—mediated. Indeed, while Dylan's prescient intention to render his song as a film certainly makes it a historically and formally charged audiovisual text, the formulation of sound and image within "Subterranean Homesick Blues" cannot be fully understood without also understanding the complex ways in which the video relatedly deploys text as material, presenting and discarding pieces of the song's lyrics as visual, physical signifiers. As such, I want to close this chapter, and *Archival Fictions* as a whole, by considering how this video engages with the textual imaginary of the archive.

The textual aesthetic of "Subterranean Homesick Blues" closely resembles that of *Dakota* and much of the rest of YHCHI's oeuvre: short phrases, often only a single word, in black capital letters on a white background, appearing and disappearing in a linear manner, closely connected with a musical soundtrack. William Rothman notes that Dylan's words are "so vivid they stand out like neon signs," a claim that itself registers the technological signifying capacity of these paper inscriptions.[54] The words chosen by Dylan and his companions to write on the cards follow an inexact pattern. While the cards that accompany the first verse of the song uniformly display end-stopped rhyming words at the end of a lyrical line—"basement," "medicine," "pavement," "government"—cards for subsequent verses take on a less regularized pattern, with some presenting the beginning or middle of a line. Like the words of *Dakota*, they serve as key frames, marking movement through the highly visualized and materialized text of the song. Indeed, if we could lay out all the cards Dylan drops, resurrecting them from the trash heap of the 1960s and putting them in left-to-right reading order, we would have something like a paper print of the key frames of the song, textual anchors to a visual poem in motion.

But of course such a record could never be, can never be. Whether we watch the film on opening night in 1967 in a theater in San Francisco or frozen and preserved in time on YouTube in 2021, we have to know that Dylan's cards are destined for disposal, gone even before they appear. Falling to the ground almost instantly, they register the deformative effects of textual mediation and textual absence, constituting a shadow archive defined by its vulnerability and ephemerality. The critical conversation around this sequence situates it as a break from the prevailing documentary aesthetics of its moment. Keith Beattie, for example, argues that it "signals an emphasis on the performative which extends beyond the realms of the stage." The highly constructed status of the sequence, described by Beattie as an "abandonment of the pretence [sic] of naturalism," extends to the cards themselves.[55] As David Yaffe notes, Dylan "wants us to focus on the words—bad puns, clichés, and random maxims—but he also wants to give the impression that he couldn't care less about them."[56] Indeed, it is the silent dropping of paper that matters most here: as the pivotal prop in a performance of disposal, the cards are most crucial and central to the sequence precisely in their discardedness and disappearance, even more so than in their presence and appearance.

Thus materiality is at stake here precisely in its indeterminate nature. Pennebaker notes in his commentary on the scene that the lyrics were written on "shirt cardboards from the laundry," paper surfaces designed not for inscription but for one-time use and disposal, while numerous commentators on the sequence describe them as cue cards.[57] Cue cards for what, though, and for whom? Nobody is singing, after all. Dylan already knows the lyrics, and cannot see the inscribed surfaces of the cards. Rothman notes that while the cards "do nothing but point to the words and phrases being sung," those words and phrases themselves "already function as cue cards."[58] Indeed, the song's collection of deliberately "bad puns, clichés, and random maxims" proleptically anticipate the film's visual aesthetics of textual indexicality and material disposability, only to be themselves disposed of in visual, material form. Technology begets text begets image, modes and moments circulating paratactically across time out of joint.

With no visible singing or lip-syncing in the sequence, Dylan's cards function less as cues or reminders than as markers of time, frames of alphabetic film to be shown and then discarded. Dylan would later denigrate Warhol as "Napoleon in rags" in "Like a Rolling Stone," but here his working principle is strikingly close to Warhol's valuation of the inscriptive leftover; indeed, the leftover is not only the most important part of the work here, but in a very real sense the only part. Thus we can see in Dylan's repeated gesture of disposal a self-conscious claim not just about celebrity performance and persona but also about textual practice, pointing toward a latent critical potentiality for literary experimentation across the moment of modern and contemporary media. Textual gestures such as Dylan's that trace how inscription and storage share space with disruption, distortion, disappearance, disposal, and disintegration across different technologies have much to tell us about the history of media technology, and about how we might write that history in the image of the uncanny, fragmentary experimentations I have considered in *Archival Fictions*. N. Katherine Hayles argues in *How We Became Posthuman* that within the emergent digital moment at the turn of the twenty-first century, "even print texts cannot escape being effected by information technologies."[59] The texts I have explored here suggest that Hayles's claim about the relation between print and digital media might be expanded to include other technologies as well—Dylan's cinematic lyrics that become a textual animation, but also works that respond to and refigure themselves in the image of the typewriter, the vinyl record, the home movie, the Internet cable, and others. Of course, these texts thus also demonstrate that the vector of effect Hayles imagines has the potential to go in both directions, as they imaginatively reshape technologies on the surfaces of their pages.

As Hayles's claim suggests, no literary text written in the wake of these or countless other technologies can remain wholly impervious to or untouched by those technologies. All novels of the 1960s, for example, whether typewritten in draft form or merely typeset at some point in the production process, bear the mark of the typewriter in some way much as Warhol's *a* does. Similarly, given that "[a]ll but a handful of books printed in the United States and Europe [in the twenty-first century] will be digitized during some phase of their existence," all books have circulated through the global network that *Transmission* traces.[60] Yet relatively few texts foreground or explicitly attend to the mediations that surround and impact them in the formally radical manners of the ones I have discussed in *Archival Fictions*, and thus relatively few texts engage in the imaginative refigurations of mediality I have traced here; in most cases, the traces of these technologies are all but invisible, silent, hidden in the plain sight of the standardized architecture of the page. In this sense, the experimental operations pursued by the authors in *Archival Fictions* are the dramatic instances that testify to the rule Hayles posits. Through the radical formalism of their textual idiosyncrasies, irregularities, and extremities, they body forth the material and textual conditions that inform them as well as their more formally conventional counterparts. In doing so, these texts ask us to read for form as a way of reading for affordances, tracing how breaks in the material configuration of text on the page point to breaks within technological protocols across time.

Through these experimentations, literary writing bends around moments of media change but also imaginatively bends those moments themselves, thinking about the critical possibilities of alternate history through moments and modes of distortion. Figuring error, static, and loss on the page not only expands the realm of literary possibility but also brings into view new ways of imagining the history of media as itself catalyzed and energized by these forces. The resounding negativity and instability of those terms is, of course, precisely the point and precisely their greatest strength as tools for literary and media-historical analysis. Capturing localized technological breakdowns through their own localized textual breakdowns, archival fictions offer models for how contemporary media history might be rewritten—not around or through the print book, nor against it, but rather in the image of its complex, deeply intimate incompatibilities with the forms and formats that follow it in time. These incompatibilities constellate a multimedia archival imaginary that shifts and breaks across the page, never fully contained by its surface but always illuminating that surface and illuminated by it in return, pointing in multiple directions at once toward powerfully differential formulations and understandings of inscription, storage, materiality, and time.

CONCLUSION
Valeria Luiselli's Undocumentary Novel

The final two chapters of *Archival Fictions* considered how print and digital textual productions figure one another across the global space and time of the web. What happens, then, if we collapse this circuit—what of paper and the codex themselves within this network? What might print literature's self-conscious inquiry into its own substrate and its own format tell us about the larger poetics of mediality and media history within the current moment of global culture? Having traced the affordances and echoes of paper within the digital across chapters 4 and 5, I turn in this conclusion to consider how Valeria Luiselli's 2019 novel *Lost Children Archive* engages with the mediality, historicity, aesthetics, and ethics of paper as a substrate and the codex as an object in the contemporary moment.

Lost Children Archive focuses on a family of four virtually unnamed characters—a husband and a wife, each with a child from a previous relationship—on a car trip from New York City to Arizona. Both adults work in sound documentary, having met as part of a massive project to document the soundscape of New York, "to sample and collect all the keynotes and the soundmarks that were emblematic of the city," in the words of the female character, who narrates the first half of the novel.[1] Their trip is fraught with tension between the subsequent documentary projects each one proposes: the wife plans to study undocumented children on the United States–Mexico border in hopes of connecting with a friend's two daughters who have been detained by U.S. Border Patrol, while the husband sets out to assemble "an inventory of echoes" that documents the ghosts of Geronimo and the Apache nation, "captur[ing] their past presence in the world, and making it audible, despite their current absence, by sampling any echoes that still reverberate of them."[2] Luiselli's narrative is deeply concerned with the aesthetic and ethical relations among documentation, the concept of the archive, and the landscape; in tandem with these thematic investments, she structures *Lost Children Archive* around a series of seven finding aids interspersed across the novel. These moments of mediatic experimentation, archivally focused formal breaks from the narrative, catalog the banker's boxes the family brings with them on their trip: four for the husband and one for the wife, filled with research materials, and one each for the children, empty at the start of the trip. In the case of the husband, these breaks are wholly alphabetic, listing notebooks, books, maps, photocopies, folders, and other materials, while the sections for the mother and son's boxes each include documents themselves—or, rather, representations of documents: photographs, migrant mortality reports, and facsimiles of maps and publications in the case of the mother's box, and a collection of Polaroid images taken by the young boy on the trip in his box.

Luiselli's engagement with the media archive through these materials is neither wholly narrative—as, for example, in W. G. Sebald's use of illustrations—nor wholly invested in bookish materiality in the manner of Jonathan Safran Foer's *Tree of Codes* or Marc Saporta's *Composition No. 1*; indeed, *Lost Children Archive* is not a book in a box, as in the case of Saporta's unbound work, but rather a box (or a series of boxes) imagined within a book, a speculative engagement between the codex and the media archive.[3] Following the conclusion of the novel and her acknowledgments pages, Luiselli states in a section titled "Works Cited (Notes on Sources)" that she is "not interested in intertextuality as an outward, performative gesture but as a method or procedure of composition."[4] Composition here takes on a specific valence, signifying for both the novel's literary work of collecting, organizing, and juxtaposing textual references and its imagined engagement with the archival work of collecting, organizing, and juxtaposing documents; if Saporta composes pages, we might say in comparison that Luiselli composes both texts and artifacts. While some of the novel's intertexts appear in conventional terms at the level of language—through texts that Luiselli either quotes directly or alludes to and then documents in "Works Cited"—others are only imaginatively collected in the family's boxes and listed in their catalogs, intertextually present within the text in archival terms rather than discursive ones.

Understanding the poetics of intertextuality, of the archive, and of composition as intertwined, codeterminate fields of practice within the novel sheds light on its simultaneously metafictional and material strategies. As the narrative progresses, Luiselli gives more and more space to a book within the book, *Elegies for Lost Children* by Ella Camposanto; while the rest of the novel's intertexts exist as texts in the real world, documented and cited in various ways, *Elegies* is wholly Luiselli's invention. Perhaps the most densely allusive component of the novel, it draws on a range of authors (many of them highly allusive themselves), such as Ezra Pound, Joseph Conrad, and T. S. Eliot. Focused on the story of a group of children attempting to migrate to an unnamed land atop a freight train, the narrative of *Elegies* echoes both the migrations of the family in *Lost Children Archive* and the migrations of the children the mother hopes to document, and in the climactic moments of *Lost Children Archive*, the children of *Elegies* and the children of the couple in the main narrative come face to face in a collapse of the novel's fictional layers.

Yet what might otherwise register as a moment of primarily narrative experimentation, an exercise in postmodern metafiction for its own sake, becomes speculatively material in the context of Luiselli's novel, a meditation on the relation between the book as an object and the archive as a concept.[5] As the family travels further west, the son learns to use the Polaroid camera his mother has given him as a gift. Beginning with his first successful image, he stores the pictures he takes between the pages of *Elegies*, an act that Luiselli's narrator returns to several times over the novel: "[A]s soon as the picture slips out, he puts it in between the pages of the book, which I'm holding open for him. . . . Once the picture is spat out by the camera, he places it inside the little red book tucked under his arm. . . . I open the little red book, *Elegies for Lost Children*, ready to read for a while in silence. A couple of pictures slip out from between its pages— the book has been getting fatter and fatter with the boy's Polaroids. I pick them up and slide them between the pages toward the end, and then flip back carefully to the first pages of the book."[6] These images at the end of *Elegies for Lost Children* are, of course, the images at the end of *Lost Children Archive*. Figuring Camposanto's imagined novel-within-the-novel as a kind of archive, Luiselli's novel itself becomes its own kind of archive—her conceit produces not only a collapse between layers of fictional worlding but also a collapse between real and imagined codex objects. This collapse registers most compactly in the convergence between the two texts' titles and the questions that emerge from the uneasy fit between their two distinct terms: What shared ground can there be between archive and elegy? How can the archive be an elegy? Whom can it mourn, and how? What does it mean to store trauma, or loss? How can the book as a format do justice—to the archive, to mourning, to the loss and violence of removal and deportation?

In taking up these questions through metafictional engagement with archival materials, Luiselli triangulates among three dimensions of what might broadly be considered the discourse of the document and documentation. The first of these is the form of the documentary as practiced by the novel's central family, whether via sound, photography, or other media. As the son puts it in his narration in the second half of the novel, "Officially, Pa was a documentarist and Ma was a documentarian, and very few people know the difference. The difference is, just so you know, that a documentarian is like a librarian and a documentarist is like a chemist. But both of them did basically the same thing: they had to find sounds, record them, store them on tape, and then put them together in a way that they told a story."[7] Lisa Gitelman's concept of the document as a situated textual category sheds light on a second dimension of this discourse within the novel. Gitelman suggests that "documents help define and are mutually defined by the know-show function, since documenting is an epistemic practice: the kind of knowing that is all wrapped up with showing, and showing wrapped up with knowing."[8] Following Bruno Latour's interest in inscription, Gitelman focuses on the document in order to mediate critical attention between the mentalist extreme of the literary—"a category of imagined and imaginative works"—and the materialist extreme of the book, "a category of material goods, an object of commerce." "The document, in contrast," Gitelman writes, "lives at a larger, lower level"; it belongs "to that ubiquitous subcategory of texts that embraces the subjects and instruments of bureaucracy or of systematic knowledge generally."[9]

The items Luiselli incorporates and references in the experimental moments of *Lost Children Archive*—particularly those in the mother's box— live at this level. Engaged with both the literary and the book but fully at home in neither domain, they are epistemic to the point of being bureaucratic. Yet as I suggest below, this hardly means they are outside of ideology, but rather quite the opposite; as Gitelman notes, the knowing-showing function of the document "can never be disentangled from power—or, more properly, control."[10] While these documents interrupt the narrative and textual flow of the novel, they do so in a manner that is visually and materially banal, in sharp contrast to the typographic, architectural, and haptic experimentation of other bookish works. Luiselli uses these moments to figure a documentary materiality that is deeply bound up with the state and its discursive, textual, and political power, pushing the literary not only toward the documentary but also toward the document.

Yet of course the novel's literary investment in the archive and the paper document is inseparable from the absence and negation of those same discourses that define the undocumented populations, particularly children, circulating through its landscape. As Jacques Derrida suggests, "The history of politics is a history of paper, if not a paper history," and nowhere is the epistemic function of the document more co-constitutively entangled with power—particularly the power of the state—than in the presence and absence of the papers that confirm the nationality and citizenship of the individual.[11] For Derrida, these papers have what Gitelman would describe as a powerful epistemic function, at once both showing citizenship and allowing knowledge of that citizenship: "[T]he law is guaranteed by the holding of a 'paper' or document, an identity card (ID), by the bearing or carrying [*port*] of a driving permit or a *passport* that you keep on your person, that can be shown and that guarantees the 'self,' the juridical personality of 'here I am.'"[12] Yet such a document also serves as a condition of possibility for the very ideas of citizenship and statehood themselves: "[W]hen we fight on behalf of 'paperless people,' when we support them today in their struggle, we *still* demand that they be issued with papers. We have to remain within this logic. What else could we do? We are not—*at least in this context*, I stress—calling for the disqualification of identity papers or of the link between documentation and legality."[13] The state creates paper, and paper—both granted and refused—creates the state as an exclusionary institution; while people can exist without papers (albeit contingently and vulnerably), the state as a construct cannot. In light of this circuit, it is crucial to unfold (pun intended) the two key terms here, namely the English "undocumented" and the French *sans papiers* (without papers, or paperless, as Derrida uses it above). While these terms are broadly equivalent at the level of sense, the inexactitude of translation is revealing. To be undocumented is not, or not only, to be without documents or papers, as a literal translation from the French would suggest; it is also to be categorically and explicitly deprived of documents, deprived of being documented—subject to deliberate excision and restriction from the state by way of excision and restriction from the archive of the state.[14] A passport, then, is its own kind of archival fiction, simultaneously constructing the subject, imagining the state, and enacting the violence of the state through and as paper textuality.

Luiselli takes up this crucial friction between paperlessness and undocumentation at several points within the narrative of *Lost Children Archive*. Early in the novel, the mother attends a vigil for undocumented detainees and deportees at a Passport Agency building in lower Manhattan. Father Juan Carlos, the priest organizing the vigil, tells her that "the building, which occupied an entire block of the city's grid, was not actually just a place where you got a passport but also a place where people without passports were being held. It was a detention center, where Immigration and Customs Enforcement agents locked people away after detaining them on the streets or raiding their homes at night."[15] Here documentation and undocumentation are two sides of the same coin, circulating together within the same location. Derrida's etymological meditation on the archive as a site of control further illuminates the connections Luiselli sketches among paper, space, and biopower: "[T]he meaning of 'archive,' its only meaning, comes to it from the Greek *arkheion*: initially a house, a domicile, an address, the residence of the superior magistrates, the *archons*, those who commanded."[16] Here the archive produces and holds both papers and bodies, liberating and detaining, granting free movement and withholding access to that movement through the hinge of a single document. Another moment later in the novel amplifies this vibration. Some time after the family's trip is underway, Luiselli catalogs among the contents of the mother's box a "loose note," presumably written by the mother, listing euphemisms for atrocities wrought by settler colonialism and the U. S. government: "Euphemisms hide, erase, coat," the note begins. "Euphemisms lead us to tolerate the unacceptable." The list begins with "Term: *Our Peculiar Institution*. Meaning: slavery. (Epitome of all euphemisms.)," and concludes with "Term: *Undocumented*. Meaning: people who will be removed."[17] It is impossible, Luiselli suggests, to separate documentation from undocumentation, and undocumentation from the violence of removal, confinement, expulsion, deportation, and genocide; across these moments, she situates paper as the crux substrate of empire from early America to the contemporary setting of the novel.

Alongside the media poetics and politics in the novel that she develops through these narrative engagements, Luiselli takes up the question of paper and undocumentation similarly through the mediatic content that constitutes *Lost Children Archive*'s formal breaks, particularly the images in the mother's and boy's boxes. Thus I conclude here by briefly turning to the place of undocumentation and the undocument within the archival and media-historical poetics and politics of the novel. As in the case of the shadow archive or anarchive I discussed in chapter 3—a structure that, to return to Akira Mizuta Lippit's conception, archives *"otherwise . . . that, in the very archival task of preserving, seeks to repress, efface, and destine its own interiority into oblivion"*—we might see the poetics and politics of undocumentation in *Lost Children Archive* as concerned not with capture via audiovisual media or paper inscription but with loss and disappearance—with the failure of the substrate to record and bear witness, whether it be celluloid, silicon, or paper.[18]

The Polaroids the boy learns to take over the course of the family's trip, many of which appear in his box at the end of the book, are perhaps the pivotal manifestation of this poetics and politics within the novel. Occupying the last twenty-four pages of the novel, one to a page, these images are ambiguous, oblique, and recursive. Grainy, low-resolution, washed out and overexposed in certain spots, they collapse the chasm between the photographic affordances of actual Polaroid film and the early 2010s faux-Polaroid digital aesthetic of Instagram. Just as we cannot know their original format, their origin and provenance are similarly unclear and unstated. While numerous images clearly correlate to moments and locations in the novel, as if actually documenting the family's fictional journey, it seems likely that that they were taken on Luiselli's own cross-country family trip in 2014, an experience that served as the inspiration and framework for *Lost Children Archive*—thus the material and the metafictional converge again here at the end of the codex.[19] While the use of the Polaroid format here is a narrative convenience, allowing the images to appear instantaneously to characters in the narrative, this convenience is inseparable from the question of format and materiality. By grounding this dimension of the novel in analog old media (as opposed to the digital images that saturate the contemporary world in which the novel takes places), Luiselli situates these images as tangible objects with chemical and physical layers, thickness, and texture. Their objecthood cannot be immediately collapsed into the flatness of the page, even though this is precisely what the novel does. These images are undocuments: while they can reproduce and represent Polaroid images, they can never be or contain Polaroid objects. Much in the same way, Luiselli's novel underscores more broadly the material, ontological, and historical tension, which I have traced across *Archival Fictions*, between the literary codex's capacity for thinking the archive as a concept and its inability to be an archive, or an archives, in the literal sense of those terms.

Following from the implications of the document above, we might consider the undocumentary as not only an aesthetic category but also an archival and anarchival one. As such, the undocumentary poetics of the novel inhere even more dramatically (if paradoxically so) in the instance of the images that do not appear in this final box within the codex, the results of the boy's failed first few attempts to use the Polaroid camera after he receives it. His first attempt "comes out entirely creamy white," and the second "comes out blue and then slowly turns creamy white."[20] His mother hazards the explanation that "[p]erhaps they're coming out white not because the camera is broken or just a toy camera but because what you're photographing is not actually there. If there's no thing, there's no echo that can bounce off it. Like ghosts, I tell him, who don't appear in photos, or vampires, who don't appear in mirrors, because they're not actually there."[21] If the images that appear at the end of the novel document a cross-country trip—whether the fictional family's or Luiselli's—these absent images undocument, recording "*otherwise*," to use Lippit's term. In both their blankness and their disappearance, they testify to a history that cannot be contained or captured on photosensitive film, much less on paper. The specters the mother invokes point to the spectrality of the photographs themselves; the documentation of absence is inseparable here from the absence of documentation. What would it mean to include these images in the novel, these objects in the archive? We can never answer this question, never know; we have to imagine that they were thrown out, excised, forgotten. Here again, the conceit of the novel's narrative progression bears on the speculative media poetics of its formal and mediatic experimentation, which in turn bears on its geopolitical critique—after all, we might also imagine these media objects within the world of the novel simply as lost.

As part of the novel's title, "lost" is a rich term within the novel's network of meaning. It resonates alongside others I have traced here ("document," "undocumented," "archive," "paper," "euphemism"), and it takes on a particularly fraught meaning for the family at the center of the novel. Reflecting on their conversations about children at the border, the mother remarks that "[w]henever the boy and girl talk about child refugees, I realize now, they call them 'the lost children.' I suppose the word 'refugee' is more difficult to remember. And even if the term 'lost' is not precise, in our intimate family lexicon, the refugees become known to us as 'the lost children.' And in a way, I guess, they are lost children. They are children who have lost the right to a childhood.[22] Like the other terms within the mother's note in her box—removal, relocation, reservation, peculiar—"lost" is a strangely rich euphemism: it stands in for flight, separation, detainment, deportation; for death, as documented in the migrant mortality reports that sit alongside the list of euphemisms in her box and on the pages of the novel; for the loss of one's childhood and more. And of course it is also profoundly literal as well. What does it mean to imagine the codex as an archive for lost children, an archive of lost children? In their status as undocuments, the missing photos of *Lost Children Archive* speak—in their blankness, their absence, their status as lost—for the children who are also lost; here the novel, like the anarchive it invokes, offers elegy not through what it stores, but through what is not present within it.

The failure of paper to be a Polaroid—the irreducible friction of one substrate against another—is inseparable from the failure of the literary and the mimetic more broadly, two asymptotic curves running alongside one another. If the print literary codex cannot testify to the materiality of camera mechanics and photosensitive emulsion, how can it testify to family separation, displacement, detention? What marks are not mediations, what words are not euphemisms? These deficiencies are never simply deficiencies of representation, but always also of recording, mediation, format, inscription, substrate, documentation, and undocumentation. Touching the surface of the page, though, the image that is not really there, we feel this limitation, this absence, present and bodied forth for us. Even though the book cannot be an archive—especially because it cannot—it holds that which can never be archived.

Notes

Introduction: On the Undeath of the Book

1. *Oxford English Dictionary*, s.v. "kindle, v.1," accessed March 3, 2019.

2. For Edison's list, see Roland Gelatt, *The Fabulous Phonograph: From Edison to Stereo* (New York: Appleton-Century, 1966), 29. On the history of prophesies of the death of the book, see Leah Price, "The Death of the Book through the Ages," *New York Times*, August 10, 2012, https://www.nytimes.com/2012/08/12/books/review/the-death-of-the-book-through-the-ages.html. On the more recent wave of conversations regarding the death and life of the book, see Jessica Pressman, "The Aesthetic of Bookishness in Twenty-First-Century Literature," *Michigan Quarterly Review* 48, no. 4 (Fall 2009), http://hdl.handle.net/2027/spo.act2080.0048.402, which I discuss in greater depth below.

3. Price, "Death."

4. Andrew Piper, for example, suggests that the "bibliographic mourning" of the emergent digital age is largely a heightened instance of the "persistent sense of loss" and melancholy that has always accompanied the book as an object. Piper argues that across history, "The question is not one of 'versus,' of two single antagonists squaring off in a ring" but rather a matter of the book as perpetually "part of an ecosystem." Anthony Grafton sees a similar historical recurrence in the tension between print and digital information, one that "will result not in the infotopia that the prophets conjure up, but in one more in a series of new information ecologies." Andrew Piper, *Book Was There: Reading in Electronic Times* (Chicago: University of Chicago Press, 2013), 152–53, xi, 156. Anthony Grafton, *Codex in Crisis* (New York: The Crumpled Press, 2008), 9.

5. Of course, these print texts onscreen also have lives and afterlives beyond their original use, thanks to their embeddedness within the Internet itself. Thinking materially about the book as a digital object, Matthew Kirschenbaum notes that "the 'death of the book' was an exceptionalist fantasy," and that "in the networks of viral capital, books have proven as adaptive to the ontologies of the digital as anything else." Kirschenbaum, "Books after the Death of the Book," *Public Books* March 31, 2017, https://www.publicbooks.org/books-after-the-death-of-the-book/.

6. Marc Saporta, *Composition No. 1* (London: Visual Editions, 2011); Jonathan Safran Foer, *Tree of Codes* (London: Visual Editions, 2010); Mark Z. Danielewski, *House of Leaves* (New York: Pantheon, 2000).

7. Pressman, "Bookishness."

8. Bernhard Siegert, *Relays: Literature as an Epoch of the Postal System* (Stanford, CA: Stanford University Press, 1999), 246.

9. For these more fully structurally experimental texts, questions of category—the novel, the collection, the archive, and so on—are one crucial area of inquiry, as I discuss in their respective chapters below.

10. M. L. Caswell, "'The Archive' Is Not An Archives: Acknowledging the Intellectual Contributions of Archival Studies," *Reconstruction: Studies in Contemporary Culture* 16, no. 1 (August 2016), https://escholarship.org/uc/item/7bn4v1fk.

11. I turn more directly to the condition Derrida terms "archive fever" in chapter 3's discussion of film, incineration, and Akira Mizuta Lippit's concept of the shadow archive.

12. Kate Eichhorn, "Radical Archives: Introduction by Kate Eichhorn," *Archive Journal*, no. 5 (2015), https://www.archivejournal.net/essays/radical-archives/.

13. Matthew Kirschenbaum (mkirschenbaum), "With thanks to everyone who offered input! Here's the revised version: [attached image]," Twitter, July 24, 2018, https://twitter.com/mkirschenbaum/status/1021856568508391429.

14. Joseph Tabbi, *Postmodern Sublime: Technology and American Writing from Mailer to Cyberpunk* (Ithaca, NY: Cornell University Press, 1996). John Johnston, *Information Multiplicity: American Fiction in the Age of Media Saturation* (Baltimore, MD: Johns Hopkins University Press, 1998).

15. Caroline Levine, *Forms: Whole, Rhythm, Hierarchy, Network* (Princeton, NJ: Princeton University Press, 2015), 3.

16. Levine, *Forms*, 3.

17. Levine, *Forms*, 6.

18. Levine, *Forms*, 6–7; emphasis in source.

19. Levine, *Forms*, 19.

20. Matthew Kirschenbaum, *Mechanisms: New Media and the Forensic Imagination* (Cambridge, MA: MIT Press, 2008), 4, 32.

21. Lisa Gitelman, *Paper Knowledge: Toward a Media History of Documents* (Durham, NC: Duke University Press, 2014), 10.

22. Jonathan Sterne, *MP3: The Meaning of a Format* (Durham, NC: Duke University Press, 2013), 7–8.

23. Sterne, *MP3*, 8.

24. Bonnie Mak, *How the Page Matters* (Toronto: University of Toronto Press, 2012), 4.

25. Mak, *How the Page Matters*, 5.

26. To formulate the question differently, *Archival Fictions* seeks to perform for the page what Matthew Kirschenbaum and N. Katherine Hayles describe as media-specific analysis, an attention to materiality as "the interplay between a text's physical characteristics and its signifying strategies." N. Katherine Hayles, "Print Is Flat, Code Is Deep: The Importance of Media-Specific Analysis," *Poetics Today* 25, no. 1 (2004): 72.

27. Sterne, *MP3*, 9; emphasis in source.

28. I use Sterne's term here for its historical fluidity in comparison to other models of relations among media. Whereas earlier theories such as those of Marshall McLuhan or Jay David Bolter and Richard Grusin focus on linear historical progression dependent on the perpetual "'newness' of media," mediality emphasizes "a sense of cross-reference as routine." Sterne, *MP3*, 9. See Marshall McLuhan, *Understanding Media: The Extensions of Man* (1964; repr., Cambridge, MA: MIT Press, 1994); and Jay David Bolter and Richard Grusin, *Remediation: Understanding New Media* (Cambridge, MA: MIT Press, 1999).

29. Craig Dworkin, *Reading the Illegible* (Evanston, IL: Northwestern University Press, 2003), 4–5; emphasis in source.

30. Craig Dworkin, *No Medium* (Cambridge, MA: MIT Press, 2013), 7, 10.
31. Dworkin, *No Medium*, 9. Bill Brown notes, quoting Derrida, that "deconstruction could be coded as a kind of 'materialism without matter' . . . a figural materiality" attributed to texts in the abstract. Bill Brown, "Introduction: Textual Materialism," *PMLA* 125, no. 1 (January 2010): 24. Following Dworkin, my approach to archival fictions conversely suggests that the materiality of figures—inscriptions, alphanumerical and otherwise, real and imagined—sets the conditions of possibility for the sort of textual instability often associated with deconstruction and poststructuralism more broadly.
32. My use of the term document here draws on Lisa Gitelman's definition of the category; see Gitelman, *Paper Knowledge*.
33. Lisa Gitelman, *Always Already New: Media, History, and the Data of Culture* (Cambridge, MA: MIT Press, 2008), 21.
34. Pressman, "Bookishness."
35. For two theories of media as haunted, see Friedrich Kittler, *Gramophone, Film, Type-writer* (Stanford, CA: Stanford University Press, 1999); and Jeffrey Sconce, *Haunted Media: Electronic Presence from Telegraphy to Television* (Durham, NC: Duke University Press, 2000), as well as Jacques Derrida's theory of hauntology in *Specters of Marx: The State of the Debt, the Work of Mourning, and the New International* (London: Routledge, 2006).

Chapter One: Lost in Transcription

1. Quoted in Lisa Gitelman, *Scripts, Grooves, and Writing Machines: Representing Technology in the Edison Era* (Stanford, CA: Stanford UP, 1999), 204.
2. Gitelman, *Scripts*, 204.
3. Bonnie Mak, *How the Page Matters* (Toronto: University of Toronto Press, 2012), 7.
4. For the original version of Smith's aphorism, see Alice Orr, *No More Rejections: 50 Secrets to Writing a Manuscript that Sells* (Cincinnati, OH: Writers' Digest, 2004), 7. For a discussion of Kerouac's revisions to *On the Road*, see Gerald Nicosia, *Memory Babe: A Critical Biography of Jack Kerouac* (Berkeley: University of California Press, 1994), 334–87. Gibson himself refutes the mythos around his creative practice; see William Gibson, "Since 1948," *William Gibson—Official Website*, November 6, 2002, https://www.williamgibsonbooks.com/source/source.asp. For a more extensive discussion of the Gibson typewriter mythology, see Scott Bukatman, *Matters of Gravity: Special Effects and Supermen in the 20th Century* (Durham, NC: Duke University Press, 2003), 32–47.
5. Friedrich Kittler, *Gramophone, Film, Typewriter* (Stanford, CA: Stanford University Press, 1999), xxxix, 16.
6. Kittler, *Gramophone*, 16, 243.
7. Kittler, *Gramophone*, 14, 214ff.
8. Kittler, *Gramophone*, 226.
9. Kittler, *Gramophone*, 15.
10. For several foundational examples, see Bukatman, *Matters*; Donna Haraway, "A Cyborg Manifesto: Science, Technology, and Socialist-Feminism in the Late Twentieth Century," in *Simians, Cyborgs, and Women: The Reinvention of Nature* (New York: Routledge, 1991), 149–81; and N. Katherine Hayles, *How We Became Posthuman: Virtual*

Bodies in Cybernetics, Literature, and Informatics (Chicago: University of Chicago Press, 1999).

11. Richard N. Current, *The Typewriter and the Men Who Made It* (Urbana: University of Illinois Press, 1954), 121.

12. Current, *Typewriter*, 121.

13. *The Typing Explosion*, directed by Cynthia Rose (Mucha Creative, 2003), DVD.

14. Gitelman, *Scripts*, 205–6.

15. Gitelman, *Scripts*, 211–12.

16. Allien Russon and S. J. Wanous, *Philosophy and Psychology of Teaching Typewriting, with Suggested Teaching Procedures* (Nashville, TN: South-western Publishing, 1960), 351.

17. Frederick Lyman Wells, "On the Psychomotor Mechanisms of Typewriting," *American Journal of Psychology* 27, no. 1 (January 1916): 56.

18. Wells, "Typewriting," 59; Russon and Wanous, *Philosophy*, 358.

19. Jane E. Clem, *The Technique of Teaching Typewriting* (New York: Gregg, 1929), 142.

20. Earl Glen Blackstone and Sofrona Lucretia Smith, *Improvement of Instruction in Typewriting* (New York: Prentice-Hall, 1949), 163.

21. Leonard J. West, *Acquisition of Typewriting Skills* (New York: Pitman, 1969), 228.

22. Russon and Wanous, *Philosophy*, 356.

23. Gitelman, *Scripts*, 218.

24. For the fullest theorization of blankness as writing, see Craig Dworkin, *No Medium* (Cambridge, MA: MIT Press, 2013).

25. Matthew Kirschenbaum, *Mechanisms: New Media and the Forensic Imagination* (Cambridge, MA: MIT Press, 2008), 236.

26. Alan Delgado notes that early businesses had a "general office [as] the nerve centre of the establishment." While this space was often disorderly and "not designed for the work it had to undertake," its unsuitability is precisely what made it flexible. Alan Delgado, *The Enormous File: A Social History of the Office* (London: John Murray, 1979), 91.

27. For an example of this work that is particularly attuned to questions of inscription and textuality, see Leah Price and Pamela Thurschwell, "Invisible Hands," introduction to *Literary Secretaries/Secretarial Culture*, ed. Leah Price and Pamela Thurschwell (Burlington, VT: Ashgate, 2005), 1–12.

28. For one discussion of these changes, see Margaret L. Hedstrom, "Beyond Feminisation: Clerical Workers in the United States from the 1920s through the 1960s," in *The White-Blouse Revolution: Female Office Workers since 1870*, ed. Gregory Anderson (Manchester, UK: Manchester University Press, 1988), 143–69.

29. "Use of Office Space," in *Office Management: A Handbook*, ed. Coleman L. Maze (New York: Ronald, 1947), 379–426.

30. Gitelman, *Scripts*, 217–18.

31. I describe this composition as "purported" here because for reasons both intentional and circumstantial, based in factors ranging from convenience to publicity, Warhol, his Factory collaborators, and the Grove Press employees who worked on the book violated and disregarded these constraints in various ways. Mulroney offers a thorough history of the production process along these lines; see below for a fuller engagement with her argument. Lucy Mulroney, "Editing Andy Warhol," *Grey Room* 46 (Winter 2012): 46–71.

32. T. S. Eliot, "The Waste Land," in *"The Waste Land" and Other Writings* (New York: Random House, 2002), 45.

33. For a similar framework, see Rubén Gallo's discussion of mechanographic and mechanogenic writing in Rubén Gallo, *Mexican Modernity: The Avant-Garde and the Technological Revolution* (Cambridge MA: MIT Press, 2005), 97, 114.

34. Brian McHale, *Postmodernist Fiction* (New York: Methuen, 1987), 160, 154.

35. Allen Ginsberg, *Howl and Other Poems* (San Francisco, CA: City Lights, 2006), 3; Norman Lavers, "Some Parafictions: What Are, How Enjoyed, Where Next," *American Poetry Review* 7, no. 2, 45; Marianne DeKoven, *Utopia Limited: The Sixties and the Emergence of the Postmodern* (Durham, NC: Duke UP, 2004), 3.

36. For a discussion of these literary strategies, see McHale, *Postmodernist*, 156–61.

37. Alan Liu, *The Laws of Cool: Knowledge Work and the Culture of Information* (Chicago, IL: University of Chicago Press, 2004), 331.

38. Andy Warhol, *a: a novel* (New York: Grove Press, 1968), 157.

39. Paul Carroll's discussion of *a* is an example of this minority reaction to the novel: "At first, *a* strikes readers as a bore. . . . But gradually . . . it becomes obvious that this is how most people actually sound when they talk with one another . . . the blablabla that surrounds us every day and often far into the night." Paul Carroll, "What's a Warhol?," in *The Critical Response to Andy Warhol*, ed. Alan R. Pratt (Westport, CT: Greenwood, 1997), 44.

40. Anonymous, "*a*," review of *a: a novel*, by Andy Warhol, *New Yorker*, January 4, 1969, 82; Sally Beauman, "*a*: A Novel," *New York Times*, January 12, 1969, 32.

41. Beauman, "*a*: A Novel"; ellipses in source.

42. Mulroney ("Warhol," 48–53) offers a further history of the initial critical reception of the novel, with a valuable focus on the relations between reactions to its formal experimentation and to its homosexual content.

43. Craig Dworkin, "Whereof One Cannot Speak," *Grey Room* 21 (2005): 47. Dworkin's reading echoes Arthur Danto's claim that Warhol's visual art "reveal[s] as merely accidental most of the things his predecessors supposed essential to art." Arthur C. Danto, "Art," *Nation* 248, no. 13 (April 3, 1989): 459.

44. Andy Warhol, *The Philosophy of Andy Warhol (From A to B and Back Again)* (New York: Harcourt Brace Jovanovich, 1975), 287.

45. Mulroney, "Warhol," 60.

46. Given the complexities and irregularities of *a*'s mode of production, it would be virtually impossible to discern the identity of the typist who transcribed any given section of the novel. Thus I use the term "the typists" to refer to the group as a generalized whole, and "the typist" (in the sense of the typist in question) to refer to the individual who transcribed any single moment in the novel. The inseparability of the four bodily subjectivities that this second term must cover is central to the problematic of authorship in the novel, which I discuss in greater depth in the following section.

47. Mulroney, "Warhol," 60.

48. Warhol, *a*, 1.

49. Kittler, *Gramophone*, 16.

50. Kittler, *Gramophone*, 14.

51. Warhol, *a*, 1.

52. Warhol, *a*, 1.

53. Warhol, *a*, 3.

54. Warhol, *a*, 3.
55. John Perreault, "Andy Warhol," in *The Critical Response to Andy Warhol*, ed. Alan R. Pratt (Westport, CT: Greenwood, 1997), 63.
56. Mulroney, "Warhol," 59, 62.
57. Mulroney, "Warhol," 63.
58. Warhol, *a*, 265.
59. Dworkin, "Whereof," 54. Dworkin attributes lines in this passage that are seemingly marked "O" for Ondine to Warhol, and lines seemingly marked "R" for Rink to Ondine. This transposed attribution, whether deliberate or not, echoes the novel's own internal problems of transcription.
60. Warhol, *a*, 32.
61. Warhol, *a*, 173; emphasis in source.
62. Warhol, *a*, 58.
63. Warhol, *Philosophy*, 95.
64. Warhol, *Philosophy*, 93.
65. For useful discussions of the place of Warhol's sexuality within his life and work, see Wayne Koestenbaum, *Andy Warhol* (New York: Viking, 2001); and Jennifer Doyle, Jonathan Flatley, and José Esteban Muñoz, eds., *Pop Out: Queer Warhol* (Durham, NC: Duke UP, 1996).
66. Warhol, *a*, 32.
67. Warhol, *a*, 375, 61. Given the novel's title as well as the more general relations between typewritten text and embodied sexual identity that I attempt to outline here, much might be said about what it means to be *a*sexual in *a*.
68. Caroll M. Gantz, *Design Chronicles: Significant Mass-Produced Designs of the Twentieth Century* (Atglen, PA: Schiffer, 2005), 145. For a history of the Selectric and other IBM models, see Cornelius E. DeLoca and Samuel J. Kalow, *The Romance Division . . . A Different Side of IBM* (New York: Vantage, 1991).
69. While I focus in this coda on the work of the Typing Explosion in order to draw specific resonances between typewritten and digital cultures, Derek Beaulieu's *a, A Novel* provides another important contemporary engagement with the poetics of typewriting and transcription, one that is both directly in dialogue with Warhol's novel and directly literary (albeit experimentally so). A work of conceptual writing, Beaulieu's project is an erasure-based appropriation that removes all text from Warhol's novel, leaving 451 pages of only punctuation marks, typists' insertions (such as the italicized examples I discuss in the previous section), and onomatopoeic words. Whereas the Typing Explosion investigates typewriting itself as a media practice across history—hence my interest in the group here—*a, A Novel* foregrounds the condition of Warhol's original novel as an inscriptive and transcriptive object in ways that also resonate with my thinking in this chapter and across *Archival Fictions*. Derek Beaulieu, *a, A Novel* (Paris: Jean Boîte Éditions, 2017).
70. Darren Wershler-Henry, *The Iron Whim: A Fragmented History of Typewriting* (Ithaca, NY: Cornell University Press, 2005), 18.
71. Jessica Bruder, "The Digital Generation Rediscovers the Magic of Manual Typewriters," *New York Times*, March 30, 2011.
72. Typing Explosion, "Calendar," last modified September 2006, http://typingexplosion.com/html/appointments.html; Typing Explosion, "Press Kit," accessed September 4, 2020, http://typingexplosion.com/presskit/presskit.pdf, 2.

73. Rose, *Typing Explosion*
74. Rose, *Typing Explosion.*
75. Typing Explosion, "Press Kit," 4.
76. Rose, *Typing Explosion.*
77. Rose, *Typing Explosion.*
78. Rose, *Typing Explosion.*
79. Rose, *Typing Explosion.*
80. Current, *Typewriter*, 121.

Chapter Two: Unheard Frequencies

1. Lisa Gitelman, *Always Already New: Media, History, and the Data of Culture* (Cambridge, MA: MIT Press, 2008), 25. For a much fuller history of this process of remediation, see Gitelman's *Scripts, Grooves, and Writing Machines: Representing Technology in the Edison Era* (Stanford, CA: Stanford University Press, 1999), particularly chapters 1 and 2.
2. Douglas Kahn, "Concerning the Line: Music, Noise, and Phonography," in *From Energy to Information: Representation in Science and Technology, Art, and Literature*, ed. Bruce Clarke and Linda Dalyrmple Henderson (Stanford, CA: Stanford University Press, 2002), 179.
3. Kahn, "Line," 182.
4. Robert M. Brain, "Representation on the Line: Graphic Recording Instruments and Scientific Modernism," in Clarke and Dalyrmple, *From Energy to Information*, 156.
5. Gitelman, *Scripts*, 63.
6. Roland Gelatt, *The Fabulous Phonograph: From Edison to Stereo* (New York: Appleton-Century, 1966), 29.
7. Alexander Weheliye, *Phonographies: Grooves in Sonic Afro-Modernity* (Durham, NC: Duke University Press, 2005), 27.
8. For fuller histories of the machine's transformation from its inception as a two-way business technology to its ascendancy as a home entertainment device by the late 1890s, see A. J. Millard, *America on Record: A History of Recorded Sound* (New York, NY: Cambridge University Press, 1995), 37–64; and Gitelman, *Always*, 25–58.
9. Friedrich Kittler, *Gramophone, Film, Typewriter* (Stanford, CA: Stanford University Press, 1999), 33.
10. Brain, "Representation," 168.
11. "The Talking Phonograph," *Scientific American*, December 22, 1877, 384.
12. Kevin Young, *To Repel Ghosts: Five Sides in B Minor* (South Royalton, VT: Zoland Books, 2001), 345.
13. Gitelman, *Always*, 26.
14. Gitelman, *Always*, 18–19.
15. Gitelman, *Always*, 36. In keeping material objecthood at the center of my analysis of the turntable and the record, my approach follows from Adorno's focus on "the contours of [the record's] thingness" in his 1934 essay "The Form of the Phonograph Record": "[I]t is not in the play of the gramophone as a surrogate for music but rather in the phonograph record as a thing that its potential significance—and also its aesthetic significance—resides. Theodor W. Adorno, "The Form of the Phonograph Record," *October* 55 (Winter 1990): 58.
16. Weheliye, *Phonographies*, 32–33.

17. Weheliye, *Phonographies*, 32.
18. Young, *Ghosts*, 345–47, 348.
19. See Bonnie Mak, *How the Page Matters* (Toronto: University of Toronto Press, 2012), 34–46.
20. Gérard Genette, *Paratexts: Thresholds of Interpretation* (New York: Cambridge University Press, 1997), 2, 1.
21. For a comprehensive theoretical and critical exploration of how "the interface of [sound recording and reproduction and twentieth-century black cultural production] provides a singular mode of (black) modernity" (3), see Weheliye, *Phonographies*.
22. Ralph Ellison, *Invisible Man* (New York: Vintage International, 1995), 7–8.
23. Weheliye, *Phonographies*, 70.
24. Henry Louis Gates, Jr., *The Signifying Monkey: A Theory of Afro-American Literary Criticism* (New York: Oxford University Press, 1988), 127ff.
25. "Talking Phonograph," 384; Gates, *Monkey*, 132ff.
26. Gates, *Monkey*, 137.
27. Gates, *Monkey*, 131.
28. Maurice Wallace, "Print, Prosthesis, (Im)Personation: Morrison's *Jazz* and the Limits of Literary History," *American Literary History* 20, no. 4 (December 2008): 797.
29. Weheliye, *Phonographies*, 39.
30. Joseph Conte, *Unending Design: The Forms of Postmodern Poetry* (Ithaca, NY: Cornell University Press, 1992), 3.
31. Conte, *Design*, 43.
32. Young, *Ghosts*, i.
33. Jean-Michel Basquiat, *Now's the Time*, 1985, acrylic and oil stick on plywood, 92½ x 92½ in., Artists Rights Society.
34. Young, *Ghosts*, v.
35. I discuss Parker's work in the Savoy Sessions and Basquiat's and Young's representation of these recordings more directly and in greater depth in the section on *Discography* below.
36. Gitelman, *Always* 26.
37. Quoted in Millard, *Record*, 25.
38. For a full discussion of McHale's application of mise en abyme to postmodernist fiction, see chapter 8, "Chinese-Box Worlds," in Brian McHale, *Postmodernist Fiction* (New York: Methuen, 1987), 112–32.
39. The material-narrative disjuncture of these imaginary phonographs resonates uncannily in its form with Weheliye's description of the visual alterity of blackness: "a *lumen* of blackness, a veritable black hole around which meaning spirals in the cross-reflections of the surrounding mirrors, but which cannot be accessed itself." Weheliye, *Phonographies*, 49.
40. Young, *Ghosts*, 25.
41. Brent Hayes Edwards, "Black Serial Poetics: An Introduction to Ed Roberson," *Callaloo* 33, no. 3 (Summer 2010): 622–23, 626.
42. Peter Stallybrass, "Books and Scrolls: Navigating the Bible," in *Books and Readers in Early Modern England: Material Studies*, ed. Jennifer Andersen and Elizabeth Sauer (Philadelphia: University of Pennsylvania Press, 2001), 46–47.
43. Stallybrass, "Books," 47.

44. Young, *Ghosts*, 5.

45. Young, *Ghosts*, 5.

46. Young, *Ghosts*, 99.

47. Young, *Ghosts*, 349.

48. Young, *Ghosts*, 167, 280.

49. Henry Geldzahler, "Art: From Subways to SoHo, Jean-Michel Basquiat," in *Jean-Michel Basquiat*, ed. Rudy Chiappini (Lugano, Switzerland: Museo d'Arte Moderna della Città di Lugano, 2005), 40, 42.

50. Jeffrey Hoffeld, "Word Hunger: Basquiat and Leonardo," in in *Jean-Michel Basquiat*, ed. Rudy Chiappini (Lugano, Switzerland: Museo d'Arte Moderna della Città di Lugano, 2005), 92.

51. Janine Barchas, *Graphic Design, Print Culture, and the Eighteenth-Century Novel* (Cambridge: Cambridge University Press, 2008), 200.

52. Stallybrass's explanation of digital textuality confirms from the opposite historical direction this vision of the book as a digital textuality avant la lettre: "[C]omputers take to a new level a crucial aspect of the ways in which we often use books—our ability, through bookmarks, to have our fingers in many different places at the same time, and to move rapidly from one to another." Stallybrass, "Books," 42.

53. Basquiat, *Pork*, 1981, acrylic, oil and oilstick on glass and wood with fabric and metal attachments, 83 ¼ x 33 7/8 x 3 in., privately owned.

54. Young explicitly explains this "dating" technique in the text's liner notes: "Titles often correspond to paintings; the dates following titles apply to the work and are included to indicate a sense of the history of the art & artist. (Dates are *not* the dates of my composition)." Young, *Ghosts*, 345; emphasis in source.

55. Quoted in W. J. T. Mitchell, *Picture Theory: Essays on Verbal and Visual Representation* (Chicago: University of Chicago Press, 1995), 152.

56. Willard Spiegelman, *How Poets See the World: The Art of Description in Contemporary Poetry* (New York: Oxford University Press, 2005), 112.

57. *Oxford English Dictionary*, s.v. "discography," accessed May 2, 2016.

58. Basquiat, *Discography (One)*, 1983, acrylic and oil paintstick on canvas, 66 x 60 in., private collection; Basquiat, *Discography (Two)*, 1983, acrylic and oilstick on canvas, 66 1/8 x 60 1/8 in., private collection.

59. Mitchell, *Theory*, 154.

60. Young, *Ghosts*, 158.

61. Young, *Ghosts*, 157, 156.

62. Young, *Ghosts*, 157.

63. Young, *Ghosts*, 156.

64. Young, *Ghosts*, 186.

65. Craig Dworkin, *Reading the Illegible* (Evanston, IL: Northwestern University Press, 2003), 5.

66. Young, *Ghosts*, 187.

67. Kittler, *Gramophone*, 45.

68. Young, *Ghosts*, 342.

69. Franklin Sirmans, "In the Cipher: Basquiat and Hip-Hop Culture," in *Basquiat*, ed. Marc Mayer (Brooklyn, NY: Brooklyn Museum, 2005), 99.

70. "Talking Phonograph," 385.

71. For a discussion of this history, see Patrick Feaster, "Extracting Audio from Pictures," *Media Preservation*, Media Preservation Initiative at Indiana University Bloomington, June 20, 2012, https://mediapreservation.wordpress.com/2012/06/20/extracting -audio-from-pictures/.

72. Feaster, "Extracting Audio from Pictures."

Chapter Three: Archive, Film, Novel

1. For two canonical examples of literary experiments that borrow from cinematic formal methodologies, see the "Wandering Rocks" episode of James Joyce's *Ulysses* (New York: Vintage, 1990) and the "newsreel" sections of John Dos Passos's *U.S.A.* (New York: Library of America, 1996).

2. Lisa Gitelman, *Always Already New: Media, History, and the Data of Culture* (Cambridge, MA: MIT Press, 2008), 1.

3. John Johnston, *Information Multiplicity: American Fiction in the Age of Media Saturation* (Baltimore, MD: Johns Hopkins University Press, 1998), 71.

4. Thomas Pynchon, *Gravity's Rainbow* (New York: Penguin, 2012), 113.

5. Pynchon, *Gravity's Rainbow*, 3.

6. Pynchon, *Gravity's Rainbow*, 745.

7. Pynchon, *Gravity's Rainbow*, 760.

8. Johnston, *Information Multiplicity*, 63, 77.

9. Pynchon, *Gravity's Rainbow*, 760.

10. Walter Benjamin, "The Work of Art in the Age of Mechanical Reproduction," in *Illuminations*, ed. Hannah Arendt (New York: Schocken, 1968), 221.

11. Fredric Jameson, *Postmodernism, or The Cultural Logic of Late Capitalism* (Durham, NC: Duke University Press, 1991), 69.

12. Jameson, *Postmodernism*, 76.

13. Jameson, *Postmodernism*, 95.

14. Anthony Slide notes that nitrate's chemical composition "is very similar to that of guncotton, used in the manufacture of explosives, resulting in its burning 20 times as fast as wood." Anthony Slide, *Nitrate Won't Wait: A History of Film Preservation in the United States* (Jefferson, NC: McFarland, 1992), 1.

15. Slide, *Nitrate*, 5. For a history of these fires, see Roger Smither, ed., *This Film Is Dangerous: A History of Nitrate Film* (Brussels: Fédération International des Archives du Film, 2002), 421–90.

16. André Habib, "Ruin, Archive, and the Time of Cinema: Peter Delpeut's *Lyrical Nitrate*," *SubStance* 35, no. 2 (2006): 125.

17. Paolo Cherchi Usai, *The Death of Cinema: History, Cultural Memory, and the Digital Dark Age* (London: British Film Institute, 2001), 18–19.

18. Cherchi Usai, *Cinema*, 91.

19. Akira Mizuta Lippit, *Atomic Light (Shadow Optics)* (Minneapolis: University of Minnesota Press, 2005), 9.

20. Lippit, *Atomic Light*, 11.

21. Don DeLillo, *Running Dog* (New York: Vintage Contemporaries, 1989), 18.

22. DeLillo, *Running Dog*, 20.

23. DeLillo, *Running Dog*, 18, 98.

24. DeLillo, *Running Dog*, 150.

25. Don DeLillo, "*Running Dog*: Research Materials," container 55.6, Don DeLillo Papers, Harry Ransom Center, University of Texas at Austin.

26. Grace Lichtenstein, "Flash: Movietone Struggling to Save Its Old Newsreels," *New York Times*, December 17, 1977, 52. The phrase "highly perishable nitrate film" is underlined in DeLillo's copy of the article, providing a visible indication of the importance of this material contingency for his conceptualization of the novel. DeLillo, "Research Materials."

27. Lichtenstein, "Flash," 52.

28. Don Silz quoted in Lichtenstein, "Flash," 52.

29. For foundational theories of this technique, see Linda Hutcheon, *A Poetics of Postmodernism: History, Theory, Fiction* (New York: Routledge, 1988); and Jameson, *Postmodernism*.

30. Michel Foucault, *The Archaeology of Knowledge and The Discourse on Language* (New York: Pantheon, 1972), 129.

31. DeLillo, *Running Dog*, 18.

32. DeLillo, *Running Dog*, 19.

33. DeLillo, *Running Dog*, 51, 147.

34. DeLillo, *Running Dog*, 18.

35. Lippit, *Atomic Light*, 12.

36. DeLillo, *Running Dog*, 52; Susan Sontag, "Fascinating Fascism," in *Under the Sign of Saturn* (New York: Vintage, 1981), 104. Later in the novel, Lightborne explicitly underscores the novel's connection to Sontag's essay in a moment of quasi-Heideggerean etymology: "Fascinating, yes. An interesting word. From the Latin fascinus. An amulet shaped like a phallus. A word progressing from the same root as the word 'fascism.'" Here DeLillo not only "synthesizes the novel's themes," as Mark Osteen suggests, but also directly invokes the title of Sontag's essay. DeLillo, *Running Dog*, 151; Mark Osteen, *American Magic and Dread: Don DeLillo's Dialogue with Culture* (Philadelphia: University of Pennsylvania Press, 2000), 106.

37. Sontag, "Fascism," 102.

38. Osteen, *Magic*, 106.

39. Gilles Deleuze, *Cinema 2: The Time-Image* (Minneapolis: University of Minnesota Press, 1989), 270.

40. Deleuze, *Cinema 2*, 264.

41. Deleuze, *Cinema 2*, 268–69.

42. Deleuze, *Cinema 2*, 269; emphasis in original.

43. DeLillo, *Running Dog*, 150; Deleuze, 269.

44. DeLillo himself of course takes up the problem of electronic media along strikingly similar lines in *White Noise*, satirizing the convergent worlds of a fictional collegiate "Hitler studies" department as the apex (or nadir) of depoliticized postmodern culture and the technology and culture of television. Don DeLillo, *White Noise* (New York: Penguin, 1985).

45. Deleuze, *Cinema 2*, 263.

46. Deleuze, *Cinema 2*, xi; see also 41, 105, 112, and 271.

47. Deleuze, *Cinema 2*, 41.

48. Deleuze, *Cinema 2*, 270.

49. Habib, "Ruin," 122.

50. Richard Dienst, "Breaking Down: Godard's Histories," in *New Media, Old Media: A History and Theory Reader*, ed. Wendy Hui Kyong Chun and Thomas Keenan (New York: Routledge, 2006), 127. Godard is a vital influence on the thinking of both Deleuze and DeLillo. For Deleuze's most extensive discussion of Godard, see Deleuze, *Cinema 2*, 156–215. For an analysis of Godard's impact on DeLillo's early work, see Osteen, *Magic*, 8–30.

51. Johnston, *Information Multiplicity*, 174.

52. DeLillo, *Running Dog*, 14.

53. DeLillo, *Running Dog*, 40, 42.

54. DeLillo, *Running Dog*, 59.

55. DeLillo, *Running Dog*, 60.

56. *The Great Dictator*, directed by Charlie Chaplin (United Artists, 1940).

57. Charlie Chaplin, *My Autobiography* (New York: Simon and Schuster, 1960), 392. Moll echoes this sentiment after watching the revival: "Charlie said he never would have made The Great Dictator later on in the war or after the war, knowing by that time what the Nazis were capable of." DeLillo, *Running Dog*, 61.

58. Habib, "Ruin," 120. Habib writes, "Cinema, since the early 1930s, has become part of 'our archive.' If the classical archive's principal task was to group and classify for an ulterior use documents which, together, represent a site of authority and a locus of origin, early film archives emerge as a rescue operation."

59. Jacques Derrida, "Archive and Draft," unpublished interview. Quoted in Matthew Kirschenbaum, "And Thereafter: 'There Isn't One Archive, There Is an Archiving Process with Different States, but Never One Established Archive,'" @mkirschenbaum, Twitter, November 9, 2019, https://twitter.com/mkirschenbaum/status/1193152108 859707395.

60. Don DeLillo, "*Running Dog*: Notebook," container 55.6, Don DeLillo Papers, Harry Ransom Center, University of Texas at Austin.

61. Don DeLillo, "*Running Dog*: Notebook"; DeLillo, *Running Dog*, 60.

62. Don DeLillo, "*Running Dog*: Notebook"; DeLillo, *Running Dog*, 61.

63. Lippit, *Atomic Light*, 120–21.

64. Don DeLillo, "*Running Dog*: Final Draft, 1978," containers 56.7 and 57.1–2, Don DeLillo Papers, Harry Ransom Center, University of Texas at Austin.

65. Deleuze, *Cinema 2*, 243–44.

66. Scott Rettberg, "American Simulacra: Don DeLillo's Fiction in Light of Postmodernism," *Undercurrent* 7 (Spring 1999), https://www.retts.net/documents/americansim ulacra.pdf

67. Patrick O'Donnell, "Engendering Paranoia in Contemporary Narrative," *boundary 2* 19, no. 1 (1992): 194; Tim Engels, "DeLillo and the Political Thriller," in *The Cambridge Companion to Don DeLillo*, ed. John N. Duvall (Cambridge: Cambridge University Press, 2008), 69.

68. DeLillo, *Running Dog*, 224.

69. DeLillo, *Running Dog*, 225.

70. DeLillo, *Running Dog*, 225.

71. DeLillo, *Running Dog*, 226.

72. DeLillo, *Running Dog*, 188.

73. DeLillo, *Running Dog*, 149–50.

74. DeLillo, *Running Dog*, 225.

75. DeLillo, *Running Dog*, 225, 229.

76. DeLillo, *Running Dog*, 234–35.

77. Lippit, *Atomic Light*, 119.

78. DeLillo, *Running Dog*, 234.

79. Osteen, *Magic*, 106.

80. Lippit, *Atomic Light*, 111.

81. Lippit, *Atomic Light*, 111.

82. DeLillo, *Running Dog*, 237, 240.

83. *Downfall*, directed by Oliver Hirschbiegel (Constantin Film, 2004).

84. Ruknowyourmeme, "Sim Heil (English version)," YouTube, August 10, 2006, https://www.youtube.com/watch?v=Gz1_pUMwnE0&.

85. Ryan M. Milner, *The World Made Meme: Public Conversations and Participatory Media* (Cambridge, MA: MIT Press, 2016), 23, 26. On memetic logics more broadly, see Milner as well as Limor Shifman, *Memes in Digital Culture* (Cambridge, MA: MIT Press, 2013).

86. Mark Dery, *I Must Not Think Bad Thoughts: Drive-By Essays on American Dread, American Dreams* (Minneapolis: University of Minnesota Press, 1014), 107.

87. M. G. Siegler, "Hitler Is Very Upset That Constantin Film Is Taking Down Hitler Parodies," *TechCrunch*, April 20, 2010, https://techcrunch.com/2010/04/19/hitler-parody-takedown/.

88. Dery, *Thoughts*, 295n10. See also "History of *Downfall* Parodies." *Hitler Parody Wiki*. January 25, 2016, https://hitlerparody.fandom.com/wiki/History_of_Downfall_parodies.

89. Ruknowyourmeme, "Sim Heil."

90. Matthew Kirschenbaum, *Mechanisms: New Media and the Forensic Imagination* (Cambridge, MA: MIT Press, 2008), 247.

91. Kirschenbaum, *Mechanisms*, 240.

Chapter Four: Digital Materiality on Paper

1. For a history of this rhetoric and the technology related to it, see Tung-Hui Hu, *A Prehistory of the Cloud* (Cambridge, MA: MIT Press, 2015).

2. Wendy Hui Kyong Chun, "The Enduring Ephemeral, or The Future Is a Memory," in *Media Archaeology: Approaches, Applications, and Implications*, ed. Erkki Huhtamo and Jussi Parikka (Berkeley: University of California Press, 2011), 188.

3. Wendy Hui Kyong Chun, *Programmed Visions: Software and Memory* (Cambridge, MA: MIT Press, 2011), 133.

4. Lisa Gitelman, *Always Already New: Media, History, and the Data of Culture* (Cambridge, MA: MIT Press, 2008), 131.

5. Chun, *Programmed*, 95.

6. Chun, *Programmed*, 133.

7. Gitelman, *Always*, 130.

8. Gitelman, *Always*, 178n19.

9. Relatedly, see Gitelman (*Always*, 107) for a discussion of the study of the Web as a bibliographic study, approaching the network as both text and thing.

10. Hari Kunzru, *Transmission* (New York: Simon and Schuster, 2004).

11. Nicole Starosielski, "Underwater Flow," *Flow*, October 16, 2011, https://www.flow-journal.org/2011/10/underwaterflow/.

12. Neal Stephenson, "Mother Earth Mother Board," *Wired*, December 1, 1996, https://www.wired.com/1996/12/ffglass/. In this sense, the hacker tourist is also a hacker historian, noting, "Everything that has occurred in Silicon Valley in the last couple of decades also occurred in the 1850s. Anyone who thinks that wildass high tech venture capitalism is a late20thcentury California phenomenon needs to read about the maniacs who built the first transatlantic cable projects."

13. Stephenson, "Mother Earth."

14. Gitelman, *Always*, 147.

15. Jussi Parikka, *Digital Contagions: A Media Archaeology of Computer Viruses* (New York: Peter Lang, 2007), 294.

16. Parikka, *Contagions*, 295, 285.

17. Kunzru, *Transmission*, 4–5.

18. Parikka, *Contagions*, 56.

19. Free Word, "Hari Kunzru on Writing in a Digital Age," YouTube, July 13, 2012, https://www.youtube.com/watch?v=PJdHelJcbRM.

20. Kunzru, *Transmission*, 22.

21. Kunzru, *Transmission*, 39.

22. Kunzru, *Transmission*, 39.

23. Kunzru, *Transmission*, 44.

24. For a foundational account of posthumanism within literary and media studies, see N. Katherine Hayles, *How We Became Posthuman: Virtual Bodies in Cybernetics, Literature, and Informatics* (Chicago, IL: University of Chicago Press, 1999).

25. Kunzru, *Transmission*, 3.

26. Kunzru, *Transmission*, 120.

27. Kunzru, *Transmission*, 130, 240.

28. Kunzru, *Transmission*, 187.

29. Kunzru, *Transmission*, 4.

30. Kunzru, *Transmission*, 263.

31. In this sense, it offers a parody of the network aesthetics that Patrick Jagoda sees as a defining characteristic of contemporary cultural production: "[T]he problem of global connectedness cannot be understood, in our historical present, independently of the formal features of a network imaginary. . . . Networks exceed rational description or mapping, and it is at this point that we might turn to aesthetics and cultural production for a more robust account." Patrick Jagoda, *Network Aesthetics* (Chicago, IL: University of Chicago Press, 2016), 3.

32. Kunzru, *Transmission*, 265.

33. For an in-depth discussion of *Underworld* and other contemporary network novels, see Jagoda, *Network Aesthetics*, 43–72.

34. Kunzru, *Transmission*, 297.

35. Kunzru, *Transmission*, 253–54.

36. Gitelman, *Always*, 21.

37. Kunzru, *Transmission*, 109.

38. Kunzru, *Transmission*, 106.

39. Kunzru, *Transmission*, 4.

40. Chun, *Programmed Visions*, 181; emphasis in source.

41. Kunzru, *Transmission*, 108; ellipses in source.
42. N. Katherine Hayles, *My Mother Was a Computer: Digital Subjects and Literary Texts* (Chicago, IL: University of Chicago Press, 2005), 53–54.
43. Brad Evans, "*Vogue* and Ephemera: The Little Magazines of the 1890s," *Modernist Journals Project*, accessed September 9, 2020, https://modjourn.org/wp-content/uploads/2019/02/vogueandephemera.pdf.
44. Brad Evans, "*Vogue* and Ephemera: Scenes of Circulation in the Little Magazines of the 1890s," unpublished manuscript, November 26, 2006.
45. Craig Dworkin, *Reading the Illegible* (Evanston, IL: Northwestern University Press, 2003), 4.
46. Alan Liu, *The Laws of Cool: Knowledge Work and the Culture of Information* (Chicago, IL: University of Chicago Press, 2004), 324–25.
47. Liu, *Laws*, 331.
48. Evans, "Scenes of Circulation," 7.
49. Hayles, *Posthuman*, 30; emphasis in source.
50. "Net Art Anthology: *Grobari*," *New Museum*, accessed September 9, 2020, https://anthology.rhizome.org/grobari; wall text, *The Art Happens Here: Net Art's Archival Poetics*, New Museum, New York, January 22, 2019–May 26, 2019.
51. As Dworkin suggests, "To insist on the sculptural possibilities of paper is to insist on its weight and thickness, however slight and negligible—however 'paper thin' it indeed may be." Craig Dworkin, *No Medium* (Cambridge, MA: MIT Press, 2013), 17.
52. Lisa Gitelman, *Paper Knowledge: Toward a Media History of Documents* (Durham, NC: Duke University Press, 2014), 114.
53. Aleksandra Domanović, "*Grobari*," *Private Circulation*, November 2009, accessed at http://archive.rhizome.org/anthology/grobari/private-circulation.pdf.
54. For further consideration of this undead statehood, see Domanović's documentary film, *From .yu to Me*, Rhizome, 2014, https://vimeo.com/95833310. Even outside of Domanović's artistic work, this history of digital statehood is itself mediated in complex, evanescent ways. As Anat Ben-David notes, "[T]he deletion of the .yu domain serves as an extreme case for Web historiography. . . . [T]he mere possibility of remembering a national Web's past is constituted by two structural dependencies on the present: first, the structural ties between nation-states and Internet protocol (IP), and second, the dependence of the Web archive on the live Web." "What Does the Web Remember of Its Deleted Past? An Archival Reconstruction of the Former Yugoslav Top-Level Domain," *New Media & Society* 18, no. 7 (2016): 1104.
55. Gitelman, *Always*, 21.

Chapter Five: Page Shredding

1. Jessica Pressman, "The Aesthetic of Bookishness in Twenty-First-Century Literature," *Michigan Quarterly Review* 48, no. 4 (Fall 2009), http://hdl.handle.net/2027/spo.act 2080.0048.402.
2. For a history of recent fluctuations in the e-book market, see Alexandra Alter, "The Plot Twist: E-Book Sales Slip, and Print Is Far from Dead," *New York Times*, September 22, 2015.
3. Bruce Tognazzini, Apple employee number 66, explains this etymology: "Early computers used printers as their sole output. When programmers at various large traditional computer companies were first give [sic] monitors, they immediately

duplicated the printer interface on their green, glowing screens, giving rise to the term 'glass Teletype.'" Bruce Tognazzini, *TOG on Interface* (Boston, MA: Addison-Wesley Professional, 1992), 131.

4. Michael Bloomberg, *Bloomberg by Bloomberg* (Hoboken, NJ: John Wiley & Sons, 2019), 129–30.

5. David Leinweber, "Knowledge-Based Systems for Financial Applications," *IEEE Expert* 3, no. 3 (September 1988): 24.

6. Leinweber, "Systems," 24.

7. N. Katherine Hayles, *Electronic Literature: New Horizons for the Literary* (Notre Dame: University of Notre Dame Press, 2008), 7. For discussions of the difference between first-generation, or classical, and second-generation electronic literature, see N. Katherine Hayles, *Electronic Literature*, 1–43 and "Print Is Flat, Code Is Deep: The Importance of Media-Specific Analysis," *Poetics Today* 25, no. 1 (April 2004): 86.

8. For two extensive and rich discussions of *Dakota* in relation to modernism, see Jessica Pressman, "The Strategy of Digital Modernism: Young-Hae Chang Heavy Industries's *Dakota*," *MFS: Modern Fiction Studies* 54, no. 2 (Summer 2008): 302–26; and *Digital Modernism: Making It New in New Media* (Oxford: Oxford University Press, 2014).

9. Rebecca Walkowitz, *Born Translated: The Contemporary Novel in an Age of World Literature* (New York: Columbia University Press, 2015).

10. Walkowitz, *Born Translated*, 233.

11. Walkowitz, *Born Translated*, 233, 235.

12. For a thorough discussion of *Dakota*'s cinematic vocabulary, see Pressman, *Digital Modernism*, 78–100.

13. Tom Gunning, "The Transforming Image: The Roots of Animation in Metamorphosis and Motion," in *Pervasive Animation*, ed. Suzanne Buchan (New York: Routledge, 2000), 56.

14. Gunning notes in a parenthetical aside to this assertion, "[T]he implied teleology of both these terms disturbs me and I hope to avoid them." While I use these terms at times in what follows for convenience, I share the historiographic concerns Gunning articulates here; perhaps one way to avoid such teleology is to imagine the "post-" and the "pre-" as in a state of constant recursion and remediation. Gunning, "Transforming Image," 56.

15. Jessica Pressman, Mark C. Marino, and Jeremy Douglass, *Reading "Project": A Collaborative Analysis of William Poundstone's "Project for Tachistoscope {Bottomless Pit}"* (Iowa City: University of Iowa Press, 2015), 19.

16. Pressman, Marino, and Douglass, *Reading "Project,"* 18.

17. As Anastasia Salter and John Murray note, generating these surfaces and layers is a materially and archivally intensive process, yielding "piles of physical pages." Anastasia Salter and John Murray, *Flash: Building the Interactive Web* (Cambridge, MA: MIT Press, 2014), 23.

18. Pressman, Marino, and Douglass, *Reading "Project,"* 18.

19. As I discuss in the following section, even these movements themselves are not literal movements but rather actually substitutions, one iteration of a word instantaneously taking the place of the previous iteration that has disappeared.

20. For a discussion of the relations between copyright, cinematic form, and "[t]he slipperiness associated with the ontological status of the image," see Mary Anne Doane,

The Emergence of Cinematic Time: Modernity, Contingency, the Archive (Cambridge, MA: Harvard University Press, 2002), 156–58, My concern here is less with how the films being copyrighted as photographs articulate this status and more with the slipperiness produced by the paper print itself as a media object.

21. Howard L. Walls, "Motion Picture Incunabula in the Library of Congress," *Journal of the Society of Motion Picture Engineers* 42, no. 3: 155–58.

22. Charles "Buckey" Grimm, "A Paper Print Pre-History," *Film History* 11, no. 2 (1999): 204.

23. Paolo Cherchi Usai, *The Death of Cinema: History, Cultural Memory, and the Digital Dark Age* (London: British Film Institute, 2001), 18.

24. The commonness of paper as a substrate also meant that there was no single or standardized format on which the films submitted to the Library of Congress were printed: Kemp R. Niver notes that some films arrived at the Library of Congress cut by hand from butcher paper. While this is perhaps an extreme instance of material variation, it nonetheless attests to the wide range of difference in available material during this period. Kemp R. Niver, "From Film to Paper to Film: The Story of the Library of Congress Paper-Print Conversion Program," *Quarterly Journal of the Library of Congress* 21, no. 4 (1964): 252.

25. For a thorough history of the flip-book, see Pascal Fouché, "History," *Flipbook.info*, 2021, last accessed January 19, 2021, http://www.flipbook.info/history.php#.

26. This is the generally held history of the form. However, some histories trace its origins back to the Middle Ages; for an example of one such account, see Gunning, "Transforming Image," 62–63. While this account is highly speculative, to the extent that it suggests how the flip-book might predate other nineteenth-century optical toys rather than follow them, it also suggests that at some level—even if only speculatively— the history of the book is at the heart of the history of the moving image.

27. John Barnes Linnett, "Producing Optical Illusions," United Kingdom Patent 925, filed March 18, 1868.

28. Henry Van Hoevenbergh, Optical Toy," United States Patent US258164 A, filed April 7, 1882, and issued May 16, 1882. Van Hoevenbergh's patent is notable not only for its being the first instance of such a technology in the United States but also for its use of the imagery of an oncoming train to demonstrate the technology in his illustrations, a representation that would appear again in Auguste and Louis Lumière's famous film *L'Arrivée d'un train en gare de La Ciotat*, first exhibited in 1896.

29. "Another Scope," *New York Herald*, February 7, 1897, 9D.

30. "The Art of Moving Photography," *Scientific American* 76, no. 16 (April 17, 1897): 248; "The Mutoscope and Machinery in Motion," *Scientific American* 84, no. 13 (March 30, 1901): 196.

31. Lawrence Kardish, *Reel Plastic Magic: A History of Film and Filmmaking* (New York: Little, Brown, 1974), 22.

32. Tom Gunning, "Machines That Give Birth to Images: Douglas Crockwell," in *Lovers of Cinema: The First American Film Avant-Garde, 1919–1945*, ed. Jan-Christopher Horak (Madison: University of Wisconsin Press, 1995), 343.

33. Gunning, "Machines," 343. For a different approach to the relations between movement, sequence, and images, see chapter 1 of Scott McCloud, *Understanding Comics: The Invisible Art* (New York: Harper Perennial, 1994), 2–23.

34. Pressman, *Digital Modernism*, 90, 88.

35. For an overview of the critical conversation on this noninteractivity and its implications, see Walkowitz, *Born Translated*, 226–28.

36. Gary Alexander, "Designing Human Interfaces for Collaborative Learning," in *Collaborative Learning through Computer Conferencing: The Najaden Papers*, ed. Anthony R. Kaye (Berlin: Springer Science and Business Media, 2012), 205.

37. Many of YHCHI's works appear in multiple languages on their website. Walkowitz writes of this multiplicity that "what we can identify as a unique object, or even as a unique language, is not self-evident. . . . The work consists of editions that have to be understood collectively in relation to each other." While a full discussion of the group's linguistic work is outside the scope of this chapter, Walkowitz's claim about language also holds true with regard to technology, in particular the overlapping, complex commensurabilities among versions of the work as manifested within platform, code, surface, and other domains. Each linguistic edition linked from the group's home page contains within itself multiple material, textual versions that collectively constellate a complex, self-contradictory conception of medium specificity and media history. Walkowitz, *Born Translated*, 207.

38. Young-hae Chang Heavy Industries, "Young-Hae Chang Heavy Industries Presents," yhchang.com, accessed September 9, 2020. At a superficial level, a Vimeo or YouTube clip can be paused and scrubbed forward and backward in ways that wholly negate the noninteractivity Chang describes as central to the group's work. Yet this interactivity, such as it is, is dictated and circumscribed by the locked-down nature of these formats; it invites an interaction that ultimately resides in passive viewing rather than any engagement through which the viewer might transform or remake the text. *Dakota* in particular is hosted as a Vimeo file.

39. Adobe Communications Team, "Flash & the Future of Interactive Content," *Adobe Blog*, July 25, 2017, https://blog.adobe.com/en/publish/2017/07/25/adobe-flash-update.html#gs.f70mmp.

40. See, for example, "view-source," Internet Archive, March 31, 2001, https://web.archive.org/web/20010331225946/http://www.yhchang.com:80/DAKOTA.html. This page holds the earliest capture of *Dakota* on the Internet Archive. For a useful discussion of the Internet Archive, see Jill Lepore, "The Cobweb," *New Yorker*, January 19, 2015, https://www.newyorker.com/magazine/2015/01/26/cobweb.

41. "View-source," March 30, 2001.

42. For an example of this recurrent emphasis on speed within *Dakota*, see Pressman's discussion of the work as a study in speed reading, in which, "[u]nable to control the reading pace, the reader can only sit back and try to absorb the stream of text flashing before her eyes." Pressman, *Digital Modernism*, 79.

43. Young-hae Chang Heavy Industries, *Dakota* [flash file], March 31, 2001, archived at https://web.archive.org/web/20010331225946e_/http://www.yhchang.com/DAKOTA.swf.

44. Young-hae Chang Heavy Industries, *Dakota* [flash file].

45. Lev Manovich, quoted in Salter and Murray, *Flash*, 23.

46. Young-hae Chang Heavy Industries, *Dakota* [flash file].

47. Young-hae Chang Heavy Industries, *Dakota* [flash file].

48. *Dont Look Back*, directed by D. A. Pennebaker (Leacock-Pennebaker, 1967).

49. Bob Neuwirth, "Audio Commentary," *Dont Look Back*, DVD, directed by D. A. Pennebaker (New York: Criterion Collection, 2015).

50. Robin Edgerton, "Le Scopitone!," accessed September 11, 2018, https://www.stim.com/Stim-x/9.4/scopitone/scopitone-09.4.html.

51. David Yaffe, *Bob Dylan: Like a Complete Unknown* (New Haven, CT: Yale University Press, 2011), 94.

52. D. A. Pennebaker, "Audio Commentary," *Dont Look Back*, DVD.

53. Al Yankovic, "Bob," *YouTube*, December 20, 2012, https://www.youtube.com/watch?v=JUQDzj6R3p4; INXS, "Mediate," YouTube, December 24, 2012, https://www.youtube.com/watch?v=Pr-Vfnd7Yno. Google also notably chose the "Subterranean Homesick Blues" sequence as the foundation for advertising its "Google Instant" autocomplete search feature; Google, "Google Instant with Bob Dylan," *YouTube*, September 8, 2010, https://www.youtube.com/watch?v=qcmorG8EKXI. For a more complete history of works that invoke this sequence, see Keith Beattie, *D. A. Pennebaker* (Chicago: University of Illinois Press, 2011), 93–95.

54. William Rothman, *Documentary Film Classics* (Cambridge: Cambridge University Press, 1997), 150.

55. Keith Beattie, "It's Not Only Rock and Roll: 'Rockumentary', Direct Cinema, and Performative Display," *Australasian Journal of American Studies* 24, no. 2 (December 2005): 28.

56. Yaffe, *Bob Dylan*, 94.

57. D. A. Pennebaker, "Commentary." For other examples of this pattern, see Ian Bell, *Once Upon a Time: The Lives of Bob Dylan* (New York: Pegasus Books, 2012), 299; Sean Wilentz, *Bob Dylan in America* (New York: Anchor, 2011), 156, and Rothman, *Documentary Film Classics*, 149ff; Dave Saunders similarly refers to them as "prompt cards." Dave Saunders, *Direct Cinema: Observational Documentary and the Politics of the Sixties* (London: Wallflower Press, 2007), 59.

58. Rothman, *Documentary Film Classics*, 151.

59. N. Katherine Hayles, *How We Became Posthuman: Virtual Bodies in Cybernetics, Literature, and Informatics* (Chicago: University of Chicago Press, 1999), 43.

60. Hayles, *Posthuman*, 43.

Conclusion: Valeria Luiselli's Undocumentary Novel

1. Valeria Luiselli, *Lost Children Archive* (New York: Vintage Books, 2019), 6.

2. Luiselli, *Lost Children Archive*, 21, 141.

3. On images and visuality in Sebald's work, see Carol Jacobs, *Sebald's Vision* (New York: Columbia University Press, 2015).

4. Luiselli, *Lost Children Archive*, 358.

5. On narrative worlds-within-worlds and *mise en abyme* in postmodern fiction, see Brian McHale, *Postmodernist Fiction* (New York: Methuen, 1987).

6. Luiselli, *Lost Children Archive*, 86, 138–39.

7. Luiselli, *Lost Children Archive*, 192.

8. Lisa Gitelman, *Paper Knowledge: Toward a Media History of Documents* (Durham, NC: Duke University Press, 2014), 1.

9. Gitelman, *Paper Knowledge*, 6, 5.

10. Gitelman, *Paper Knowledge*, 5.

11. Jacques Derrida, *Paper Machine* (Stanford, CA: Stanford University Press, 2005), 61.

12. Derrida, *Paper Machine*, 61.

13. Derrida, *Paper Machine*, 60.

14. My thinking about the prefix "un-" in undocumented here builds on my conception of "unpublishing" in relation to Katie Paterson's bookwork project *Future Library*: "[B]y unpublication I mean not the absence or deferral of publication but its utter inverse: the printing of texts in order to be secreted, held from view, and circulated in . . . secure space." Paul Benzon, "On Unpublishing: Fugitive Materiality and the Future of the Anthropocene Book," in *Publishing as Artistic Practice*, ed. Annette Gilbert (Berlin: Sternberg Press, 2016), 288.

15. Luiselli, *Lost Children Archive*, 115.

16. Jacques Derrida, *Archive Fever: A Freudian Impression*, trans. Eric Prenowitz (Chicago: University of Chicago Press, 1998), 2.

17. Luiselli, *Lost Children Archive*, 255–56.

18. Akira Mizuta Lippit, *Atomic Light (Shadow Optics)* (Minneapolis: University of Minnesota Press, 2005), 11.

19. Early in the novel, the mother praises the "tension between document and fabrication, between capturing a unique fleeting instant and staging an instant" in the photographs within Sally Mann's *Immediate Family*. Luiselli, *Lost Children Archive*, 42.

20. Luiselli, *Lost Children Archive*, 38, 55. Luiselli's recurrent description recalls the richly blank Polaroid photograph depicted on the cover of Craig Dworkin's *No Medium*. Dworkin describes the phantasmic nature of spirit photography as "an allegory of photography itself," yet Luiselli frames this allegory not in terms of an absent presence (the spirit haunting the image, "the *medium* of the process . . . taken literally," as Dworkin terms it), but rather the opposite, a present absence. Craig Dworkin, *No Medium* (Cambridge, MA: MIT Press, 2013), 104, 103.

21. Luiselli, *Lost Children Archive*, 55.

22. Luiselli, *Lost Children Archive*, 75.

Index

Page references in *italics* refer to figures.

PAUL BENZON is assistant professor in the English Department at Skidmore College, where he also teaches courses in the Media and Film Studies program. His work has appeared in *PMLA*, *Narrative*, *electronic book review*, *Media-N*, and *College Literature*.